Mayas in Postwar Guatemala

CONTEMPORARY AMERICAN INDIAN STUDIES

J. Anthony Paredes, *Series Editor*

Mayas in Postwar Guatemala

Harvest of Violence Revisited

EDITED BY WALTER E. LITTLE AND TIMOTHY J. SMITH

THE UNIVERSITY OF ALABAMA PRESS
Tuscaloosa

Copyright © 2009
The University of Alabama Press
Tuscaloosa, Alabama 35487-0380
All rights reserved
Manufactured in the United States of America

Typeface: ACaslon

∞

The paper on which this book is printed meets the minimum requirements of American
National Standard for Information Sciences-Permanence of Paper for Printed Library
Materials, ANSI Z39.48-1984.

Library of Congress Cataloging-in-Publication Data

Mayas in postwar Guatemala : harvest of violence revisited / edited by Walter E. Little and
Timothy J. Smith.
    p.   cm. — (Contemporary American Indian studies)
  Includes bibliographical references and index.
  ISBN 978-0-8173-1655-6 (cloth : alk. paper) — ISBN 978-0-8173-5536-4 (pbk. : alk.
paper) — ISBN 978-0-8173-8243-8 (electronic : alk. paper) 1. Mayas—Guatemala—Politics
and government. 2. Mayas—Crimes against—Guatemala. 3. Mayas—Guatemala—
Government relations. 4. Guatemala—History—1945–1985. 5. Guatemala—History—
1985– I. Little, Walter E., 1963– II. Smith, Timothy J.
  F1435.3.P7M38 2009
  305.897′420728109049—dc22

                                                                    2008039549

Contents

Illustrations

Mayas in Postwar Guatemala

Introduction

Revisiting *Harvest of Violence* in Postwar Guatemala

Walter E. Little

Guatemala has fascinated popular, mainstream imaginations for years. It is the home of the Mayas, tropical forests, rugged landscapes, and wild animals. These have attracted travel writers, tourists, and television and movie producers for decades. In 1935's *The New Adventures of Tarzan* (also known as *Tarzan in Guatemala*), Tarzan recovered a high-powered explosive that "could threaten world safety" from natives living in a Guatemalan tropical forest. Although Homer Simpson of the television cartoon series *The Simpsons* has yet to visit, he has eaten the "merciless peppers of Quetzlzacatenango! Grown deep in the jungle primeval by the inmates of a Guatemalan insane asylum" in the 1997 episode titled "*El Viaje Misterioso de Nuestro Homer*." Even the 2005–2006 television season of Survivor, subtitled "Guatemala, The Maya Empire," pitted cast members against the wild tropical forest and each other with pre-Columbian Mayan ruins as a backdrop.

The above examples may seem trivial in a volume concerned with how Mayas contend with crime, political violence, and internal community struggles. The popular fascination with Guatemala as a place of exotic people living in an exotic locale goes hand in hand with the other common representation of the country and people—a violent, repressive country, ruled more often than not by the military. This latter representation, of which there are ample examples by journalists, activists, academics, and others, tends to characterize Mayas as victims. We aim to counter these powerful representations—exotic and victim—with the arguments that constitute this volume.

This volume is our ethnographic response to the lack of attention—scholarly and popular—given to how Mayas themselves try to constructively contend with the violence that constitutes a large part of their lives. In the strictest since, we do not *revisit* the *Harvest of Violence* (Carmack 1988), since this is not a reassessment of that project. However, we *revisit* it in the sense that we are concerned with the dearth of information about actual Mayan social reality, not merely the ways that Mayas have been represented and misrepresented. We especially want to draw attention to the difficulties that have faced Mayas and point to how they contend with those difficulties.

Mayan Politics and Guatemalan Political Change

2000s Guatemala is a categorically different place than 1980s Guatemala that Robert M. Carmack and David Stoll (the two *Harvest of Violence* contributors whose chapters are in this volume) witnessed. Subtitled *The Maya Indians and the Guatemalan Crisis, Harvest of Violence* appeared just a few years after Guatemalan Mayas were subjected to the most intense forms of violence since the Spanish Conquest. The work of thirteen scholars, edited by Carmack, has since become a benchmark for assessing what has transpired.

Not all has been downward to perdition since the late 1980s. In December 1996, after more than three decades of insurgency and counter-insurgency, the Guatemalan government and the Guatemalan National Revolutionary Unity (URNG) signed a peace agreement in which the guerrillas laid down their arms and the army accepted new restrictions. The countryside has been demilitarized, hundreds of thousands of refugees have returned to their homes, and Mayas are in firm control of many municipal governments, which used to be run by Ladino minorities (see Hale 2006). New cohorts of Mayan educators, scholars, engineers, doctors, and lawyers have joined the Guatemalan state and other institutions from which they used to be excluded.

The postwar, however, has not been a time of peace. The 1998 murder of the head of the Catholic truth commission, Bishop Juan Gerardi, is only the most dramatic example of continued violence against critics of Guatemala's power structure. Peasant leaders pursuing land claims against plantations are still vulnerable to assassination. Crime has skyrocketed and so have lynchings of suspected criminals by mobs that have lost faith in a weak national police and judiciary. Kidnapping rings, drug trafficking, and youth gangs have fueled a profound sense of insecurity. As a result, many Mayas and other Guatemalans have supported army involvement in crime patrols—even though this violates the Peace Accords—and supported General Efraín Ríos Montt, an ex-dictator accused of responsibility for the worst era of village massacres in the early 1980s. The gravity of the Guatemalan situation rarely leaves the country itself, except in the most dramatic cases, as in the assault, rape, and robbery of Saint Mary's College students in 1998.

While the most favorably situated Mayas are prospering, the majority face some of the worst economic conditions in the hemisphere. Chronic underemployment has been worsened by falling coffee and sugar prices on the world market. Income gaps between the poor and the wealthy are among the worst on the globe. Refugee repatriation, the demobilization of army and guerrilla forces, and a drop in tourism revenue because of a poor global economy and fear of terrorism contribute to Guatemala's dire political and social conditions.

The social and political conditions of Guatemala in the 2000s are the result of the legacies of Spanish colonialism, U.S. foreign policy, and neoliberal economic reforms (see especially Cojtí Cuxil 1997; Hale 2006; C. Smith 1990c). While major historical events (Spanish invasion in 1523, the death of Tekum near Xelaju in 1524, the surrender of Canek in 1697, Catholic missionization in the 1500s and 1600s, Protestant missionization in the 1900s, exploitative labor policies from the colonial period to the present) constitute the backdrop of the 13 chapters comprising this volume, Mayas' smaller everyday acts over this long, harsh period of history have allowed them to survive and guard their particularly distinctive worldview through oral history (Carey 2001, 2006).

Events over the last 50 years, however, have contributed profoundly to Mayas' social practices and political actions in response to contemporary problems. These directly inform and are referenced by the contributors to this volume. In 1945, Juan José Arévalo Bermejo began a six-year term that marked a period of unparalleled political freedom and reform for Guatemalans. He was followed by Jacobo Árbenz Guzmán in 1951, who was ousted by a military coup d'état sponsored by the CIA in 1954, thus ending Guatemala's social experiment. Árbenz drew the wrath of elite Guatemalans, foreign businesspersons (namely, the United Fruit Company), and the U.S. government when he enacted agrarian reforms in 1952. Arévalo's and Árbenz's respective administrations were characterized by Guatemalans in opposition and U.S. politicians as fomenting communistic policies through social reforms. With Árbenz forced into exile, Guatemalans were ruled for the next 30 years by military juntas and generals.

Military rule was marked by extremely repressive economic, political, and social policies, often aimed directly at Mayas but also at poor urban and rural Ladinos. It was in this period that the Catholic Church responded to the intensification of Protestant missionization by enacting changes to religious practice in Mayan communities. This program, Catholic Action, was an attempt to break down Mayan communities and get Mayas to participate more fully in the national economy. It opened many Mayan communities to internal conflict as individuals, especially Catholic Action catechists, who challenged traditional community leaders (Brintnall 1979; Warren 1989). In essence, this church ideology, along with that of Protestant ideologies, served to reinforce the military government's stranglehold on Mayan communities and provide a rationale for their exploitation in the national economy and social and political discrimination at local and national levels.

When civilian president Vinicio Cerezo was elected in 1986, he enacted modest government reforms but was still beholden to the military, which operated with impunity. This period also marks the beginning of visible Mayan cultural activism (see Bastos and Camus 2003; Cojtí Cuxil 1997; Fischer and Brown 1996; Warren 1998). Depending on one's perspective, the roots of Pan-Mayan activism (the Maya Movement) can be traced to the Spanish invasion or to the 1945–54 reform governments and religious change, be it via Catholic Action or Protestant missionization. Over the next several presidential terms, Mayas slowly saw political changes in their favor, with the Peace Accords being signed during Alvaro Arzú's term in 1996. Most reforms pertaining to Mayas opened some spaces for cultural expression, but most failed to address the lack of access to politics and the poverty that plagued Guatemala. Several of the contributors in this volume provide examples of how positive cultural and economic changes are threatened by the neoliberal policies followed by Guatemala's presidents from Marco Vinicio Cerezo Arévalo to Álvaro Colom Caballeros (2008–2012) and rising crime and violence, due to interrelated political and economic policies that have further impoverished the country. Perhaps the most significant change over the last 20 years of civilian rule has been the weakening of the Guatemalan military.

Ethnographic Understanding and Contributor Aims

Like the contributors to the original *Harvest of Violence* volume, we are concerned with how Mayas have had to live and continue to live under such adverse social, economic, and political conditions. In our chapters, we take a critical look at contemporary Mayan life in Guatemala from ethnographically informed positions. All contributors are social-cultural anthropologists with, sometimes, years of experience living and working in collaboration with and alongside Mayas. We explore issues that confront Guatemalans and anthropologists in these tense but politically productive times. Genocide, reconstruction and reconciliation, the Columbus Quincentennial, the peace process, the Maya Movement, truth commission reports, a sharp upsurge in crime and "popular justice," and an intensification of the role of nongovernmental organizations (NGOs) in many of these processes mark the last two decades.

Mayas in Postwar Guatemala: Harvest of Violence *Revisited* grew out of a panel at the 2002 American Anthropological Association's annual meeting. We assessed the successes and failures of the peace process. We also compared the different ways that Mayas perceive violence, past and present. We wanted to know how they debate the challenges they face, struggle for solutions, and redefine themselves, their communities, and their country. Having had lengthy relationships with Mayan communities, we knew that we could get beneath the headlines generated by the latest disasters, to the intelligence and tenacity that has enabled the Mayas to survive so much adversity.

Following in the tradition of the original *Harvest of Violence*, we share a deep love and concern for Guatemala and its inhabitants. By describing the current conditions in which Mayas live, we seek to expose the institutional forces and structural conditions that continue to jeopardize the welfare of Mayas. Taking ethnographic approaches, we offer alternative analyses to those of political scientists, such as Deborah Yashar (2005), who explains that the 36-year war in Guatemala was not an ethnic conflict. Indeed, *I, Rigoberta Menchú* (Burgos-Debray 1984), is more about Left and Right political struggles rather than Ladino-Mayan, intra-Mayan, or intra-Ladino conflicts, which are important points made by Stoll (1993, 1999).

The significance of *Harvest of Violence* is that it countered explanations current in the 1980s that emphasized ethnically neutral political descriptions of the extremely violent period. It called attention to the fact that Mayas were suffering the worst of this violence, which was informed by the long-term ethnographic research of the participants. Working in Mayan languages, as the majority of us do, we also bring to our analyses at least a decade of experience (some contributors have much longer histories) in Guatemalan communities. This long-term engagement with the people, places, and languages unifies the perspectives of the contributors methodologically and informs how we witnessed the often creative and positive ways that Mayas deal with difficult conditions on a daily basis.

Given the activist-oriented scholarship that typifies the contributors' work, it may be surprising that no Mayas are represented in the volume. In short, some Mayan scholars had been invited to participate, but as their commitments in Guatemala intensified, due to their being appointed to key positions in government and in NGOs, they elected to devote their energies elsewhere. They are also perennially besieged by requests for their time by competing institutions and groups that would like to enhance their legitimacy by including Mayas. Furthermore, when Fischer and Brown published *Maya Cultural Activism* in 1996, an emerging group of Mayan scholars struggled to find venues to publish their ideas. Edward Fischer and Robert McKenna Brown's volume was a vehicle for this, but unlike the original *Harvest of Violence*, it included few essays that Guatemala's neoliberal civilian government found threatening.

Today, Mayan intellectuals do not need the assistance of foreign scholars to publish their work. Furthermore, since the 1980s thousands of Mayas have embarked on careers in teaching, scholarship, law, and other professions. They have started hundreds of new organizations (Bastos and Camus 2003, 1993). This means that foreign scholars and Mayan intellectuals are forging new equal working relationships, in which Mayas have the power to say no to foreign scholars as well as require them to work for them. Judith Maxwell's chapter is a clear indication of this, when she worked for Mayas in bilingual education. As she and Walter Little can attest, such inverses of power are not relegated just to cultural spheres. Unable to cash a $20,000 check through official means, the Kaqchikel Maya language program they co-direct looked as if it would not run one year, due to their inability to access course operating funds. A Mayan businessman from Panajachel unflinchingly cashed the check, surprised that so little money could run a six-week class. Saved by this powerful Mayan entrepreneur, we commented to each other that the times have certainly changed.

Ideally, we could begin again, invite Mayas to participate, and submit a new set of essays. This, however, would produce a significantly different but not necessarily better collection of essays. Such a collection is something that Timothy Smith and Little eventually hope to do. Mayan scholars and politicians have given us blessings to proceed with the project. Scholars such as Edgar Esquit, Irma Velásquez Nimatuj, Ajb'ee Jimenez, and others were already involved in time-consuming research of their own. Little interviewed Rigoberto Quemé (the ex-mayor of Quetzaltenango), Pablo Ceto (the URNG leader elected to Congress), and María Carmen Tuy Tococh (the president of Kaqchikel Cholchi' and member of the executive board of the Guatemalan Academy of Mayan Languages). These intellectuals and scholars took time to discuss our findings with us. We all continue to be in dialogue with Mayan intellectuals and members of the communities in which we study. It is important to note that these Mayan leaders, and others like them, are in positions of power and are regularly consulted by development organizations, foreign diplomats, national and international news media, and elected officials in the Guatemalan government. By contrast, our Mayan friends and consultants who populate the pages of this volume are generally not in comparable positions of power. Quite often, they are at risk, and we do not want to contribute to this risk. For this reason, we decided to use pseudonyms to protect their anonymity.

This collection of ethnographic essays is our and the contributors' commitment to call attention to the difficult social, economic, and political conditions that Mayas continue to endure. We go beyond other analyses of postwar Guatemala (Jonas 2000; Sieder 1998; Sanford 2003) to highlight the complexity of Mayan political action and positive ways that they can resolve internal conflict and overcome repression. Our work complements and provides region-wide context for recent comparable scholarship (Foxen 2007; Stølen 2007).

Although different themes of violence frame *Mayas in Postwar Guatemala: Harvest of Violence Revisited* and specific violent events often stimulated the dialogues between us and our Mayan friends and colleagues, we stress the active roles that Mayas take and the ways that they interpret these violent situations. This has four primary effects. First, Mayas are represented as having agency, *not* as powerless victims. They play positive roles in combating crime and improving their daily conditions. They can also be complicit in the violence, for example, lynching fellow townspeople and tourists (see Mendoza and Torres-Rivas 2003; and, in this volume, Barrera Nuñez; Burrell; Little; Stoll). Second, despite the overwhelming poverty, racial and ethnic discrimination, and general criminal violence they suffer in their lives, Mayas organize politically, socially, and economically to lead productive and hopeful lives (see, in this volume, Benson and Fischer; Goldín and Rosenbaum; Smith). Third, Mayas themselves have ideas about and can offer analyses of and solutions for the difficult social, economic, and political conditions in which they live (see, in this volume, Bocek; DeHart; Maxwell). Fourth, Mayas take serious, critical positions on the Peace Accords and the peace process, enacting local action to make change and come to terms with the contradictions of a state that appears to encourage Mayan cultural expression on one hand and fails to address economic and political inequity on the other hand (Hale 2006; see, in this volume, Adams; Philpot-Munson). Most contributors touch on these overlapping themes in their respective chapters.

The 11 case studies in this volume illustrate how ordinary Mayas working in factories, fields, and markets, as they participate in community-level politics, provide critiques of the government, the Maya Movement, and the general state of insecurity and violence that they face on a daily basis. Their critical assessments and efforts to improve their conditions illustrate their resiliency and their solutions to and opinions on Guatemala's ongoing problems. We feel these deserve serious consideration by Guatemalan and U.S. policy makers, international nongovernmental organizations, peace activists, and even academics studying politics, social agency, and the survival of indigenous people.

Organization of the Volume

Thirty-six years of warfare between government and guerrilla forces haunt every chapter in this collection. Although this dark legacy is one of the most significant factors shaping Mayas' responses to crime and political violence today, our contributors share a desire to move beyond it. We focus on pressing new issues such as the impact of international intervention, including neoliberal economic reforms and the ubiquitous nongovernmental organizations. We are also interested in power struggles between different interests in Mayan society. Thus, we are keen to register the critiques that Mayas make, not just of the army, the guerrillas, and the Guatemalan state, but also of the NGOs that come to help them and of each other. Solidarity with Mayas as victims of violence—the premise of the first *Harvest of Violence* and of most scholarship on the war since then—cannot be an excuse for avoiding the conflicts between Mayas, including the violence they sometimes wreak on each other, or our own contradictions as foreign sympathizers.

In general, the contributors treat crime seriously, not just crime as perpetrated against Mayas, as Walter Little and Liliana Goldín and Brenda Rosenbaum illustrate, but also how they are complicit in it, as Jennifer Burrell and Peter Benson and Edward Fischer describe. As José Oscar Barrera Nuñez, Monica DeHart, and Judith Maxwell show, this violence also operates on symbolic and structural levels that have *real* impacts on Mayas. The contributors explain how Mayas get caught up in a complex matrix of events: internal community conflicts over economic and political resources, changing labor conditions in the global economy, and uneven access to basic services like education (see especially Adams; Philpot-Munson; Smith).

Several of the contributors' chapters discuss internal conflicts within Mayan communities. Local Mayan politicians struggle for power (Smith; Bocek). Community members compete over resources and the best ways to attract those resources (DeHart; Philpot-Munson). Others disagree over religious views (Adams). And others argue about the appropriate ways to contend with crime (Burrell; Goldín and Rosenbaum; Little; Benson and Fischer). As Stoll explains, the contributors have largely dropped the morality that has shaped Guatemalan scholarship, where internal conflicts were ignored as a show of solidarity for Mayas. Simply, political struggles, economic competition, and violence in contemporary Guatemala cannot be reduced to Mayas versus the government or Mayan-Ladino ethnic and class conflict.

Although identity politics are not the explicit concerns of the contributors to this volume, they all are careful to contextualize the identities of the Mayan subjects described. Interestingly, the traditional Mayan-Ladino division matters in certain social and political situations, but in many contexts it is not relevant. For instance, for Little and Maxwell this sociopolitical dichotomy is maintained most strongly by the attitudes and actions of the Mayan vendors and intellectuals with whom they each, respectively, work. By comparison, ethnic identity is moot in the case provided by Goldín and Rosenbaum. Here class and gender identities are more salient for the women they discuss, even though those women come from "Mayan" and "Ladino" households and home communities. Many of the chapters fall in between these positions. Ethnic identity matters especially for the cases provided by Barrera Nuñez and DeHart. Characterizing ethnicity in terms of Mayas versus Ladinos, however, is not the most cogent way of considering the social and political relations of the people being described, or even the most productive way to explain the crime and violence that they face on a regular basis. Several of the contributors (Smith;

Adams; Philpot-Munson; Burrell; Bocek; Benson and Fischer; DeHart) describe rural-urban distinctions, and cosmopolitanism also serves to distinguish among Mayas. In other cases, religion proves to be a powerful way of identity orientation (Adams; Bocek; Philpot-Munson).

Both internal conflicts and the ways identity is used by the people described in *Mayas in Postwar Guatemala:* Harvest of Violence *Revisited* help inform the types of critiques that Mayas make. Just as the contributors have not avoided sensitive topics like internal conflict and just as they have taken care in not reproducing stale, stereotypical arguments about Mayan and Ladino differences, they offer a range of critiques emanating out of different communities and social groups. Mayas in Tecpán (Benson and Fischer), Todos Santos (Barrera Nuñez; Burrell), and Totonicapán (DeHart) describe what can be considered Mayan critiques of globalization. Mayan critiques of local politics enter into the previous cases, but especially so for Mayas in Alta Verapaz (Adams), Antigua (Little), Sololá (Smith), and Totonicapán (Bocek). In Sololá (Smith), Mayas critique the Pan-Mayan identity movement itself. In Nebaj (Philpot-Munson), Tierra Blanca, a hamlet of Totonicapán (Bocek), and San Juan Chamelco (Adams), authors critique the peace process and the Guatemalan government. Mayan intellectuals and educators (Maxwell) offer especially powerful critiques of the government and make astute observations of the structural inequalities experienced by Mayas; this was not lost on Mayas living in Guatemala City (Goldín and Rosenbaum), Tecpán (Benson and Fischer), Todos Santos (Burrell), and Totonicapán (DeHart).

These critiques of local- and national-level politics, globalization, gender relations (Goldín and Rosenbaum), and the Mayan identity movement are positive indicators that Mayas are engaged in their respective communities and are trying to move forward. They offer valuable Mayan perspectives for those in nongovernmental agencies, academics, and government and for officials to listen to and heed. They point out the possibilities for these agents to become involved in Mayan communities in ways that build collaborative relationships.

Although the previously described, overlapping economic, political, and social conditions and preoccupations of Mayas frame all the contributions to this volume, the editors have intentionally arranged the chapters to challenge readers to think about Guatemala, but especially Mayas, in new ways. First, Smith's and Stoll's contributions serve to bracket the others by outlining histories of struggle at the local and national level, respectively. Each provides important context to the political and economic conditions described in the other chapters.

The editors also wanted to highlight the complexity of Mayan communi-

Fig 1. Guatemalan political divisions at department level. Map by Justin Lowry.

ties' political decision-making processes by including multiple contributions with overlapping themes. For example, local politics frame Smith's, Benson and Fischer's, and Bocek's examples, but Mayas' responses are not uniform. Burrell's and Barrera Nuñez's respective chapters on Todos Santos highlight just how different, yet complementary, the interpretations of two scholars working in the same town at the same time can be.

At another level, Stoll's analysis—self-reflexive and reflexive of the other case studies—provides an alternative perspective to Carmack's conclusion. Both Carmack and Stoll were participants in *Harvest of Violence*. Their participation adds important analytical depth to *Mayas in Postwar Guatemala:*

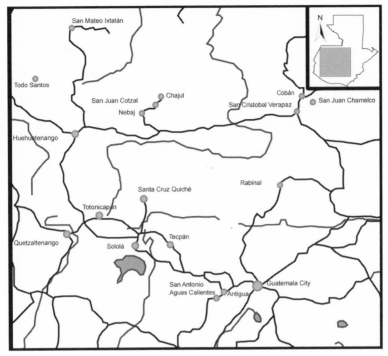

Fig 2. Major Guatemalan roads, cities, and towns. Map by Justin Lowry.

Harvest of Violence *Revisited* and helps us connect intellectually and politically to *Harvest of Violence.* Stoll focuses on tracing scholarship on Mayas since the earlier volume, while Carmack focuses on how the forms of violence afflicting Mayas have changed over that same time. The most profound contrast between the two is the assessment of the revolutionary movement. Stoll appraises it as a failure rejected by the majority of Mayas, while Carmack believes that ultimately Mayas will draw inspiration from it. The contributors, however, are not so bold to offer such predictions, but their cases do point to examples where Mayas themselves are gaining more power and contending with the potential conflicts that arise when holding power.

Julio Chalcú Ben

Kaqchikel Mayan artist Julio Chalcú Ben created the paintings in figures 4–8. They are based on his interpretations of Mayan history and Guatemalan contemporary life. Given that he was brutally tortured by the Guatemalan army on December 16, 1990, his artwork serves as a testament to the strong will and

Fig 3. Mayan language areas referred to in the text. Map by Justin Lowry.

fortitude of thousands of Mayas. He was held for eleven days; firemen discovered him lying by the side of the road 130 kilometers from his home. The Marjorie Kovler Center for the Treatment of Survivors of Torture and the Su Casa Catholic Worker House in the United States treated his severe injuries, which left his right arm paralyzed and also left him unable to speak. However, it took him almost five months before he was able to write his name, allowing his family to learn that he was still alive. When he eventually returned to Guatemala, he was unable to return to his work as a farmer, due to his disabilities as a result of the torture. Rather than give up, he took a custodial position with the Maya Association of Development, a women's weaving cooperative based in Sololá. In his spare time, he taught himself to draw, paint, and write with his left hand. The paintings included in this volume were purchased from the artist by Timothy J. Smith. Chalcú Ben uses the proceeds from such sales and painting itself to continue to recover from the emotional and physical torture he endured.

Fig 4. *Traje pueblo Sololá Guatemala/Trabajando en el campo* (Sololá, Guatemala, clothing/Working in the country) and *Mujer tejiendo un mundo mejor/ Traje pueblo Sololá Guatemala* (Woman weaving a better world/Sololá, Guatemala, clothing). Courtesy of the artist, Julio Chalcú Ben.

Fig 5. *Cantar al señor/Traje pueblo San Antonio Palópo Guatemala* (To sing to the Lord/San Antonio Palopó, Guatemala, clothing) and *Traje pueblo San Antonio Palópo Guatemala* (San Antonio Palopó, Guatemala, clothing). Courtesy of the artist, Julio Chalcú Ben.

Fig 6. *El joven Maya cortando la leña* (A Mayan youth chopping firewood) and *El joven Maya caminando cargando el palo* (A Mayan youth walking, carrying a pole). Courtesy of the artist, Julio Chalcú Ben.

Fig 7. *Traje pueblo Sololá* (Sololá clothing) and *El joven Maya caminando el templo* (A Mayan youth walking to the temple). Courtesy of the artist, Julio Chalcú Ben.

Fig 8. *El abuelo lee la* Prensa Libre (Grandfather reads the *Prensa Libre*) and *Apostol Pedro predicando palabra de Díos* (Apostle Peter preaching the Word of God). Courtesy of the artist, Julio Chalcú Ben.

1

Democracy Is Dissent

Political Confrontations and Indigenous Mobilization in Sololá

Timothy J. Smith

This ethnographic portrait of rural democracy in postwar Guatemala stems from the first complete study of Sololá, in which I offer a critical interpretation of Pan-Mayan activism through a study of a conflict between two predominantly indigenous political groups. The history of a local "anti-party" of Mayan activists, who controlled both the official municipal government and the indigenous (Mayan) municipal government between 1996 and 2000, is detailed. After enjoying a successful campaign to reform local and regional institutions which had discriminated against indigenous populations, their authority was challenged by the local wing of the Guatemalan National Revolutionary Unity's (URNG) political party (a political offshoot of the umbrella guerilla organization that signed the 1996 Peace Accords), which took control of both municipal governments after a bitter, contested election in 2001. The dispute included death threats, an outpouring of media, police response, mass protest, court indictments, legal grievances, and destruction of public buildings. The two-year conflict between local URNG representatives and Pan-Mayanists started in 1999 amidst the national "failure" of the National Referendum on Indigenous Rights and the presidential election (see Warren 2003; Carey 2004).

Similar to strife in many other rural Guatemalan municipalities, this conflict is but one event on a longer thread of local and regional histories. Factional cleavages have intensified over the last four years between indigenous organizations, especially the local affiliate of the URNG political party and Sololá's civic committee, revealing discordant political agendas and ethnic strategies. By focusing on local processes and outcomes, I complicate urban-centric stereotypes of rural politics and illustrate the salience of multiple political identities and differing ideas on what democracy and "participation" mean for the indigenous actors of Sololá. By examining the political conflict that took place in the indigenous stronghold of Sololá during the years 1999–2001, I present

Fig 9. Calming down the masses at second election protest in Sololá, December 2001.
Photo by Timothy J. Smith.

the slippage between Mayan nationalism and the key issues that drive local politics—including the adoption and dismissal of Pan-Mayan agendas, the significance and continuation of Mayan participation in electoral politics, the multiple meanings of democracy, and factionalism in the municipality.

While some critics emphasize conflicts in Mayan communities in order to undermine the Pan-Maya Movement, my purpose in this chapter is the exact opposite. Indigenous politics in postwar Guatemala are as complex and dynamic as those of North America, Europe, or any other region of the world. This is a story that disrupts binaries of culture versus class, the national versus the local, Pan-Mayanism versus Mayan localism, universal modernist narratives and development, and others. It calls for "an ethnography of decline" (Ferguson 1999:1). Rather than write off these events as disappointments in modernity and political shortcomings, we must look at local histories and processes in order to ask not only what happened, but also what comes from failure? What does it mean?

Moreover, the continual introduction of modernizing technologies and talk of "democracy" and Western modernist ideologies in this rural township create situational contexts that shape narratives of social experience that precede agency, political participation, and the collective protests of civil society. Rather than remaining fixed upon the logic of ideas and transmission of systems of knowledge, our studies should involve individuals and their navigation through political structures (Geertz 2000:218). I flesh out these navigations through the different agendas indigenous leaders pursue.

Sololá provides an interesting ethnographic case study of electoral politics and democratic participation at the local level. It challenges perceptions that the defeat of the 1999 referendum was a failure of indigenous democratic participation or political aspirations. Sololá provides rich evidence for strong political aspirations and collective organization that counter notions of Mayas feeling "defeated" after the referendum or being further marginalized in Guatemala's postwar transition to democracy. In fact, the defeat of the constitutional reforms did not diminish Mayan political interests and participation. An analysis focused upon the local and national events around the referendum, the 1999 presidential election, and the 2001 indigenous municipal government elections brings an alternative interpretation of Mayan responses to light. Politics are more complex than any particular moment of voting. The complexity is due, in part, to the idea that Mayan leaders and intellectuals in Guatemala address not only non-Mayan populations, but very different Mayan communities. Studying intra-group competitions between Mayan political factions shows how indigenous competitions between Mayan groups occur as a result of shifts from ethnic conflict to those framed by class, gender, personal interests, and party politics.

The "Jacket" in Sololá (1990–99): Renaissance, Community Activism, and Electoral Politics

The municipality of Sololá, with a population of 37,127 (89 percent indigenous) (INE 1996), is a county-like unit with a municipal and market center that lies in the western highlands of Guatemala overlooking Lake Atitlán. It also serves as the administrative center of the department (state), which bears its name. The indigenous municipal government of Sololá (locally referred to as the *muni indígena*) serves as the administrative meeting place for traditional leaders of the community, mayors, council members, mayor's assistants, and executive commissions. A remnant of the Spanish colonial period in Guatemala (1524–1821), the indigenous municipal government has existed in Sololá for nearly 450 years (Maxwell and Hill 2006; T. J. Smith 2004). It is a quasi-autonomous local organization that is not accorded official recognition by the national government. Timothy J. Smith (2004), Guisela Mayén de Castellanos (1986), Lina Barrios (1998a,b), and the Municipalidad Indígena de Sololá (1998) all provide detailed descriptions of the offices and history of the indigenous municipal government. Sololá is one of the few towns in Guatemala to have an official municipal government and an indigenous municipal government. The latter is not officially recognized by the state.

The indigenous municipal government underwent several significant changes in the 1970s that included an orthodox Catholic reform movement (Catholic Action, see Warren 1989), charismatic Catholic conversions, the devastating 1976 earthquake, and the 36-year counterinsurgency war (which peaked between 1978 and 1982 under the military dictatorships of Romeo Lucas García and Efraín Ríos Montt). During the height of the violence, the indigenous municipal government was threatened by a military presence in the region, the National Police, the arrival of military intelligence agents, a rise in kidnappings and disappearances, and the installation of civil patrols and military reservists. Despite this legacy of violence, on July 14, 2003, Guatemala's Constitutional Court ruled that Ríos Montt was legally eligible to run as the presidential candidate of his party, the FRG (Guatemalan Republican Front), in the 2003 elections irrespective of Article 186 of the 1985 Guatemalan Constitution, which forbids two-term presidencies. He finished in third place, ending his bid for the presidency and potentially stripping him of his immunity from prosecution for human rights abuses and crimes against humanity during his 1982 presidency.

After nearly 20 years of decline, clandestine operation, and marginalization, local indigenous leaders planned a revival of the indigenous municipal government as the armed conflict in Guatemala drew to a close in the mid-1990s. By 1994, Mayan leaders in Sololá split the traditional civil-religious hierarchy of the Indigenous Mayoral Council into two separate organs: a civil council and a religious council. This was a strategic move by Mayan revitalizationists. In different highland communities the splitting of municipal governments occurred for other reasons. Activists cited this strategic move as the need to create a stronger secular government that could oversee and cement relations among the emerging *popular* organizations (the grassroots Left) and Mayan NGOs during a rebuilding process that commenced before the conflict's end in 1996. Some of these organizations included CUC (Campesino Unity Committee, which works for rural affairs), CONIC (National Indigenous and Campesino Coordinator, which focuses on land issues), CONAVIGUA (National Coordinating Committee of Guatemalan Widows, a grassroots organization of widows of the war), Majawil Q'ij (New Dawn), Comité Indígena de Sololá (Sololá Indigenous Committee, responsible for revitalizing indigenous political resurgence), and Usaqil Tinamït (People's Dawn, a Mayan legal defense team). In the spring of 1995, a number of indigenous leaders in Sololá met and discussed the possibility of forming a *comité cívico* (civic committee) to challenge the Christian Democrats' control of the official municipal government for the past nine years. Gaining considerable support in recent years, civic committees are community-based alternatives to traditional political parties. Billed as an "anti-party," the civic committee was created due to continually corrupt national politics, the marginalization of an indigenous voice at all levels of government, and puppet-rulers who answered to concerns outside of the municipality. The new civic committee was dubbed Sololatecos Unidos para Desarrollo (Solotecos United for Development, SUD) and would provide the majority indigenous population with an alternative to the national political parties.

In the fall elections of 1995, local activists celebrated the much anticipated but surprising win of the SUD candidate for official mayor, Pedro Iboy, who had campaigned with a platform that he was free of the favoritism and corruption of national political parties, and who promised to focus more upon the community and local concerns. A local schoolteacher with ties to the ALMG (Guatemalan Academy of Mayan Languages), his election marked the first time in nearly 450 years in which an indigenous candidate was elected mayor to the official municipal government of Sololá; he represented both the indigenous and Ladino citizens of the municipality. It was an unprecedented win and the new SUD committee controlled both municipal governments in Sololá. It also reflected a larger national outcome, in which nearly one hundred indigenous mayors were elected to official municipal governments throughout the country.

After the signing of the Peace Accords in 1996, many indigenous ex-guerillas from Sololá joined the SUD in order to help indigenous Sololatecos, who made up 89 percent of the municipality's population. Between the years of 1996 and 2000, both municipal governments worked hand in hand toward improving town-center and rural infrastructure (including roads, electric lines, drinking water, bus stops, phone lines, and irrigation lines). Leaders from both governments were instrumental in introducing new fertilizers to farming cooperatives. In addition to building a strong working relation between both municipal governments and campaigning for an end to the armed conflict, Iboy's high priorities included a focus on education, indigenous rights, and cultural events. He was instrumental in revitalizing local Mayan culture (through workshops centering around the use of the Kaqchikel Mayan language, ethnic dress, Mayan cosmology, and the practices of Mayan spiritual leaders).

Country People, City People: The Jacket versus the Maize

In the beginning of 1999, ex-guerillas and URNG supporters left the ranks of the SUD anti-party in order to form the core of the Sololá affiliate of the URNG political party, which had received official recognition by the Guatemalan national government in December 1998. The split also entailed a flight of URNG supporters from their positions in the two municipal governments as well as from the SUD ranks. When the URNG members left to strengthen their local party, the SUD criticized them for selling out, pursuing personal interests, joining politics in search of money and power, and abandoning the Mayan population of Sololá. It remains an especially painful moment for SUD members, who explain it as the original cause for the divisions that have marked Sololá's Mayan organizations for the past ten years. To further complicate this staled relationship, the URNG candidate for office was elected under a cloud of suspicion and claims of voter fraud in 1999.

During 2000, relations between the two governments unraveled. Still upset over the outcome of the 1999 election, SUD leadership argued that the elections were fraudulent and that their candidate had been elected. URNG supporters said that the entire conflict stemmed from the civic committee's unwillingness to accept the URNG candidate as the legitimate official mayor. According to a village representative from the *caserío* (hamlet) of Orotorio, the SUD members were "warring a little bit" because they lost. He also told me, however, that a lot of the anti-SUD sentiments came from the indigenous municipal mayor's unwillingness to give financial support to the rural communities: "The only thing is that the official mayor gives little financial support, a little he gives to the *cantónes* [cantons]. Well, at times we must create a road. I've asked for financial help [but] here [in the indigenous municipal government] none is given." His comment resonated with the Sacbochol village representative, a strong URNG supporter who claimed that the official municipal mayor was the true official of the community and that the people had voted for him. He said that once people from the cantón of Tablón had asked the indigenous municipal mayor for financial aid, but he denied it: "He didn't agree with that, he said. 'This is politics. I don't want [it] nor [any other] shit,' he said. That's what the families say over there." The village representative went on to say that the indigenous municipal mayor had not worked for the people like his official counterpart and the two have not been on good terms since they both took office.

While it may be valid for critics to attack the official municipal government for not allocating resources under Iboy's administration, the indigenous municipal government does not have money. It is a volunteer organization and the only hope for earning a living or receiving compensation comes from the other side of the street, according to a previous indigenous vice-mayor. He explains:

> First, the indigenous municipal government gives more respect to the official municipal government [than it receives] because the truth is that the indigenous municipal government doesn't administer funding.

Second, the indigenous municipal government . . . works voluntarily; they don't charge one cent. . . . You give advice; you give something direct that is free. You evaluate documents, you explain books, and you make a citation, also for free. . . . Well, the people have a vision of the indigenous municipal government, that it works for free, where the people here, the indigenous people, [have] no possibility of them paying and they have nothing to give.

While he did agree that there was a division between the two governments, he couldn't say whether it was the fault of the official municipal mayor or the URNG leadership. On the other hand, a previous indigenous civil mayor said directly that the URNG was to blame because they didn't respect the indigenous municipal government. He voiced his thoughts on the financial differences between the two sides:

We had meetings about the necessities of the people. For that, we did more; we went out together. A little was done, but a time came when those of the URNG left. It became necessary for them; I don't know, for personal interests. . . . Well, what I myself see more of is that in the civic committee there isn't one rich man who works toward increasing his own wealth; they work directly with the indigenous people, the Sololatecos.

Although the SUD civic committee had accomplished much on behalf of the indigenous population of Sololá, its members still came under fire for economic shortcomings. Most of the criticism revolved around inefficiency and lack of concern for the people's immediate concerns and material desires. URNG members criticized the SUD leadership for being self-interested and corrupt, a "house of prostitutes," and wanting to retain control over the *indígenas*—in short, keeping them from due economic and political development. They pointed to Iboy's inefficiency in securing funds for roads and bridges and in creating jobs, and criticized him for spending too much time with abstract ideologies that have no tangible manifestation in a municipality where 83.4 percent of the population live in poverty (FUNCEDE 2000). The Iboy administration spent 14,687,477 quetzals in the town, compared to 10,170,738 quetzals in the rural areas. In the urban sector, a majority of this money was invested in water, infrastructure (mainly renovating the city hall, park, and clock tower), and plants. In the rural area, however, money was spent on electricity, water, and education. The village representatives complain that Iboy spent too much money on schools and basketball courts and not enough on drainage systems, water for irrigation, agriculture, and land.

During his first seven months in office in 2000, the new URNG official municipal mayor allocated more money to supplement salaries for committee workers in the rural areas, to the IGSS social security fund, repairing of streets, paying for electricity in the caseríos, and supervision for community projects. He gave more money to the rural areas and invested in local projects because the URNG draws most of its support from the outlying cantónes and caseríos. Many of the most influential party members come from outside the city center of Sololá, and that is where a large amount of their budget has gone. The SUD, in turn, has a leadership whose members hail mostly from the urban center and from the *aldea* (village) of San Jorge, relatively prosperous compared to the other three aldeas. Critics claim that this explains why Iboy's administration contributed more to the city of Sololá and to San Jorge. URNG supporters have placed more emphasis on what they consider to be concrete moves toward development and economic betterment, addressing "real issues" for an indigenous population that has, in their mind, been exploited in Guatemala's history as a result of its poverty, lack of political influence, and inability to confront the state through a system that has continued to marginalize *campesinos ignorables* (ignorant rural people).

Meanwhile, SUD members continue to be outspoken critics of the URNG in Sololá. URNG officials, although indigenous, are denounced as political puppets and "apostles" who have *ajawa'* (lords) outside of the community. Criticized as a "traditional political party," the URNG is viewed by SUD members as being a group made up of members who care more about the economy and politics outside of Sololá than about discrimination, women's issues, cultural revitalization, and the status of the peace process within the community. An indigenous leader who represented the indigenous municipal government at the official municipal government went into a long diatribe about the URNG and politicians, arguing that once people get involved in politics, they forget about the people and the struggle:

> The people will not protest anymore; they are stuck because now they are within the URNG politics, from which there are politicians. It has to be the force of the people; [the struggle] must be made. But, it's not made because I know well enough that they have entered politics receiving something. For us, not them, our desire has to be toward fulfilling something, and it must be done in communities most affected [by the armed conflict].
>
> Furthermore, however, we are thinking like other elites; we say to [the people], as part of the URNG says to us, that it's their responsibility to be with us. Like I said, they enter into politics and [that's it]. And, like I am saying, I see that this is not a time of protest because we are in a political time.

This idea that protest, action, and participation are not political is a major argument—that democracy in postwar indigenous Guatemala might be about the right to act and participate, rather than about fulfilling any preset agenda or ideological platform.

Many of the SUD members complain that the URNG has been spreading lies about them and criticizing their leadership in the rural areas. According to another SUD supporter, the URNG immediately started a smear campaign upon taking power in early 2000:

> The URNG leadership did this, to speak clearly. Because of what they did, because of what they did, I was sad, and they gave me sadness when the next day (following the election) we saw the result of the election, the elections. On their behalf, the URNG arrived to the various communities with a negative criticism, but they didn't have to say those negative criticisms because they won, although with black propaganda they won.

She is not alone in outing the URNG affiliate's disrespect for the SUD and the indigenous municipal government. It is not simply a matter of political differences. According to a member of the indigenous municipal government's council,

> Their work is no good because there is a division between the two, between the two [governments]. This we have seen when we enter [to speak] with the *señor alcalde* [official municipal mayor]. He doesn't attend to us well, and when we enter [to speak] with him, in Spanish he speaks with us. But when we don't know Spanish, we can't explain to him what we want to say. The situation is actually a little difficult.

The difficulty here is that the official municipal mayor is indigenous and his native language is Kaqchikel. They claim that when they approach him, he only speaks Spanish with them, out of disrespect. Like Iboy's administration before him, the majority of the 2000–2004 municipal mayor's administration was indigenous. When I spent time at the official municipal government, Kaqchikel was always the language of choice in the office. It would appear that, if true, the above complaints are strong. One of the stronger criticisms, however, had more to do with the overall efficiency of both municipal governments working together for the people of the municipality. Critics wish that the two would work out their differences, so that things would go more smoothly for both sides:

> There is no other way for them to communicate with themselves about what work is being done. Their work is done alone [and] on their own

accord. Only this is causing one to work more because [she or he] has to bring the administration to the communities, to the aldeas, to the caseríos. Meanwhile, the other one only goes to a few people. That's one of the biggest difficulties that we have had, continuing the division that exists between the two.

One perception that both groups share is that, if this conflict continues, it will divide the town even more. A young woman who worked at the official municipal government had this to say: "They divided themselves up [and] the problems for us have been questions of power . . . a struggle of 'who is better.' It's hard because, at the very least, they split themselves up, they divided themselves up. Like divide and conquer, it favors the Ladino groups." Her opinion about Ladino groups possibly taking advantage of the situation is similar to the ideas expressed by other URNG and SUD leaders whom I interviewed.

A local Pan-Mayan activist believes that the unity of Sololá has already been broken and fears a more negative climate to come:

I think that in Sololá . . . it has been broken, the unity of the people. It has been broken because of political matters, political partisanship, because again there are half the objectives, half the promises. [They are] already not with the community if not with a party again. The people can no longer do what the community wants. Because of this there is a problem. Oh, it's hard; it's hard because they can't do what the people want. [When you do] what the party wants, it's hard.

Other sectors of both government and nongovernment organizations have also been caught up in the factionalism and its call for allies. SUD members accuse the URNG leadership of being collaborators with AECI (Agencia Española de Cooperación Internacional) in Sololá (whose members, in turn, are viewed as outsiders with a "neocolonial" mindset) and controlling the Office of the PDH (Ombudsman of Human Rights). Meanwhile, URNG supporters claim that MINUGUA (the UN Mission for the Verification of Human Rights in Guatemala) and CALDH (Center for Legal Action in Human Rights) are aligned with SUD. These organizations are starting to fracture along lines of loyalty, and indigenous activists fear being viewed by their groups as choosing the URNG or SUD in their participation in otherwise neutral events.

Democracy Is Dissent

On December 16, 2001, nearly two thousand Sololateco Mayas gathered at a local basketball court in the heart of Sololá in order to exercise their right to vote for a new mayoral corporation in the indigenous municipal government for the upcoming 2002–2004 administration. Although elections for the corporation have taken place every two years since 1993, what distinguished this particular event was that it marked a second election in two weeks. The first election, on December 2, had been declared a fraud. To correct the outcome, voters took a break from the modest Sunday market and traveled to the municipal center from their home hamlets on a normal day of rest. The first election for the Indigenous Mayoral Council was held at the Universidad del Valle-Altiplano campus, but it was considered by many Sololá Mayas to have been manipulated by the SUD civic committee in order to retain control over the indigenous municipal government.

If one peels away the layers of heated debates, protests, and public defiance of the first election outcome and the authority of the indigenous municipal government, it appears that it was the local representatives of the URNG political party who were responsible for challenging the SUD members' decision to change the original election date (moved up from December 16 to December 2) and voting location. For two weeks, the indigenous civil mayor and vice president of the SUD committee defended these changes, arguing that more people would participate on a Sunday and that the election costs at the university were significantly lower than those of the public locales. However, the URNG representatives, including officials from both the indigenous municipal government and the official municipal government, instead denounced the SUD leadership and, invoking *democracia en la sociedad civil* (democracy in civil society), accused them of having tried to steal the people's right to vote and wanting to retain control of the indigenous municipal government. The first election was not democratic because the *aj siwan aj tinamït* (people, literally, "those of the ravine, those of the town") had not been present. Such couplets are commonly used in public discourse, at town hall meetings, and during *cofradía* (confraternity of the Catholic Church) ceremonies. It refers to the entire indigenous population—the people—of Sololá, those who live in the countryside (ravine) and municipal center (town).

Emphasizing democracy as involving the act of participation, URNG sympathizers argued that *mucho menos chi ronojel* (hardly anybody, "much less than all") had been granted that right. Death threats, mass protests, destruction of public buildings, court indictments, and a media frenzy boiled over for two weeks before the URNG finally gained control of the indigenous municipal government's headquarters on January 1, 2002.

Over the course of the conflict described in this chapter, local subjectivities for voters shifted from that of Sololatecos organized by a bond to their community (localism)—which the comité cívico grabbed onto—to a group of disadvantaged people who had their right to vote taken from them and, ultimately, their voice taken from them, which opened the door for the URNG to step in after the disputed 2001 election. The meanings attached to political activities and claims of representation are extremely important for organizing collective opinion and, where needed, manufacturing dissent. Furthermore, my portrayal of this conflict has emphasized that the Sololatecos' version of democracy has more to do with the act of participation than with any particular election outcome. This right to vote was valued more than consensus. While SUD marketed the idea of "We speak as one people. We *are* Sololá and *for* Sololá," the URNG leadership capitalized on their fraudulent election and marketed their own platform: "We will give you that opportunity to speak, because that's democracy." Whereas the SUD focused on who was speaking for whom, the URNG focused upon the right to speak. It may, however, have included something beyond just the "right" to speak. I would argue that Sololatecos were eager to speak as a way of talking about themselves. The act of voting gave individuals a voice and presented to the public a particular subjectivity of citizenship and inclusion. They are the poor masses in Jacques Rancière's *Names of History,* who are "eager" to write and to be heard by the historian, scholar, and reader (1994:18). This also holds true for indigenous groups in Guatemala, which have been historically marginalized or manipulated in elections. This eagerness, of both individuals and groups, is exemplified in Sololá's recent voting history, with a steady increase over the past ten years.

While SUD activists viewed the second election of 2001 as fraudulent and really believed that voters were being manipulated by the URNG members (whether this was true or not), they misinterpreted the situation as illegitimate in the eyes of the people, and this was their greatest mistake. To be sure, many of the people with whom I spoke, both in the urban and rural sectors, both rich and poor, were upset with the slow pace of development and the building of public works. They were grateful to the SUD and the Pan-Mayanists for all that they had done for the indigenous population of Sololá. However, no amount of activism or indigenous agendas could balance the circumstances surrounding the second election and how they were perceived to have altered an outcome. For all Chiroy (the leader of the SUD) knew, the SUD might have been reelected, but their fatal mistake was not giving the people the chance to make that decision.

The revalorization of democracy has helped to increase decentralization and open up spaces for participation (Kymlicka 2001; Hopenhayn 2001). This has given more operating power to social movements, where various groups may attempt to best express the opinions and needs of the populations which they claim to represent. Political actors must maintain control of the discourse of democracy in order to hold onto their leadership positions and continue to justify their legitimacy. This must be done while at the same time representing the people and adjusting to their concerns. Indigenous movements in Guatemala may be on the rise, but they will continue to face the challenges of representing the people. Part of overcoming electoral difficulties in Sololá means focusing upon decentralization (retaining sympathies toward localism) and promoting democracy. SUD was originally given the people's mandate for its commitment to the local level and rejection of national parties. In the beginning, SUD members worked for them to show that they did represent the indigenous population because *they were* the indigenous population. And it is true that this was only further strengthened by their relative success in organizing the people in the electoral process.

In a democratic society, however, politicians must still be authorized and legitimated in the eyes of the people by continuing to represent them and attend to their concerns after being elected. Most important is the need to protect citizens' right to voice their opinion, whether in dissent or not. Because of this, leaders within a democracy must be able to reposition themselves accordingly and understand their constituents' version of democracy, if they are going to promote that version as one of their legitimizing qualifications. It is here where political discourse becomes ever the more precarious, when democracy and legitimacy are contested. The survival and possibility of what is said, created, and propagated is dictated by a mandate given by target group members—where the Pan-Mayanist SUD leadership was influenced by the people of Sololá. Concerning larger processes in Guatemala, this corroborates Kay Warren's belief that an idea stemming from a program of standardized Mayan culture "will impress families when it reaffirms generalized translocal values and will be treated as just another form of esoteric knowledge—another academic discipline—when it strays from recognized forms" (1998:202).

The SUD originally won on a platform that included localism and, arguably, Pan-Mayanism, but the people later wanted to see development and economic change (a shift in their own geo-historically contingent subjectivities). They lost their support when the URNG leadership in the official municipal government began to produce, funded projects, and visually showed that they were capable of addressing the general desires and needs of the population. Above all, the people of Sololá wanted two things: to see a continuation of their freedom to participate (which held more weight than the outcome) and to see change. It was one thing when the SUD couldn't produce the funds and development projects of the URNG, but it was another when it interfered with the people's right to vote. The minute that democracy as participation lost, the SUD lost its legitimacy.

When SUD lost its legitimacy in the first election of 2001, whether it was a shady takeover by the URNG or not, it opened up a space for others to enter via "democracy." SUD members kept saying that "they were Sololá" and that they cared more about Sololá than national parties, but they were accused of not representing the people (regardless of the nature of their activism or platform) and not promoting the people's version of democracy, of participation over outcome. Like the planning state of old and the political groups before them, SUD thus lost legitimacy. The URNG group was able to fill this political space because their second election was viewed as democratic and was ultimately recognized by the people because they were at least given the opportunity to participate.

The range of current political voices in Sololá is a result of the conflict between the civic committee and the URNG, both having affiliations with the regional, national, and international aid organizations that entered this town after the end of the Guatemalan armed conflict. The political conflict between the two Mayan factions in Sololá led to waves of violence, protests, and the destruction of communal and indigenous buildings, much of this stemming from the differing ideas of "Mayaness" and "Sololateconess" that have been promoted and used by these groups in order to fulfill their own political agendas. Given the intra-group competition between Mayan political factions and their continual jockeying for power, as well as their talk of democratic reforms under the rubric of indigenous government, it is important to emphasize how such conflicts shifted from ethnic issues (Maya versus Ladino) to those framed by class, gender, personal interests, and party politics. Although it appears that there is a strong sense of group identity that stems from community attachment, the platforms and activities of both competing groups were continually being negotiated and revised in order to attract popular support, and these repositionings cut across traditional boundaries. However, the fluctuation of party support from the local population suggests that neither group has successfully tapped into the community vision of the trans-local relations of their concerns to national issues. Until that happens, it remains to be seen whether or not voters will continue to dissent through the democratic process.

2
Reviving Our Spirits

Revelation, *Re-encuentro,* and *Retroceso* in Post–Peace Accords Verapaz

Abigail E. Adams

On December 19, 2002, hundreds of people accompanied the body of Antonio Pop Caal in a procession to the cemetery of Coban, Alta Verapaz. His funeral, a traditionalist Mayan ceremony, began with the procession, accompanied by Mayan musicians playing *sones* on the *chirrimia,* violin, and *tun.* People carried offerings of candles, money, *copalpom,* and other incenses. Mayan-produced clothing predominated as did the Q'eqchi' language. A variety of Mayan ritual specialists carried out the rites. Prayers and dances honored the Verapaz region's emblematic earth beings, the Tzuultaq'a, which in Q'eqchi' Maya means "mountain–valley."

Quite a range of people gathered, including young and old, Maya-language speakers, non-indigenous and other *kaxlan* (foreigners), Catholics, Protestants, the rural poor and urban well-to-do, the monolingual and multilingual, the educated and unlettered. Pop Caal's funeral gathered public officials, ex-PAC (*ex-patrullas de auto-defensa civil*) members, and former guerrillas. It included those who had worshipped together before the war and those only recently introduced to non-Christian Mayan worship.

The range of Pop Caal's mourners testified to the impact of his life. Pop Caal (June 1941–October 2002) was a Mayan intellectual, lawyer, and spiritual guide whose work during the 1970s and 1980s opened the door to the vibrant Mayan cultural and spiritual revitalization in the Verapaz and elsewhere (A. Adams 2003; Pop 2003). The revitalization of traditionalist Mayan worship was disrupted when the 1980s wave of sharp violence overwhelmed the Verapaz region. During the years of a de facto state of siege, religious freedom suffered along with other civil liberties for members of all religious groups (Evans 1991; Garrard-Burnett 1998; Stoll 1988, 1993). Pop Caal's funeral, although somber, was a celebration of the renewed vigor of the Mayan spiritual recovery, emerging in the post-peace process context of religious pluralism.

Pop Caal's death was what anthropologists since Robert Hertz have called a "bad death" (1960). He was kidnapped October 2002 in full daylight from a busy Coban street. His body was recovered months later, in December. Although three Mayan men were apprehended, his family suspects that the intellectual authors remain at large.

Pop Caal's many mourners were not strangers to violent death; the Verapaz was a major battlefield during over 36 years of Guatemala's civil war and counterinsurgency. Over one-fifth of communities destroyed were in Alta Verapaz, according to Catholic diocesan records (R. Wilson 1995:218–219). Neither the initiation of the peace process in the late 1980s, nor the December 1996 signing of its Peace Accords led to the freedom from violence sufficient to establish personal or community security (see, in this volume, Burrell; Stoll; Benson and Fischer). Pop Caal's murder created one more irreplaceable loss.

Compounding the circumstances of "bad death," Pop Caal died after an ugly split within the group of spiritual seekers with whom he had the longest history. These were the Q'eqchi' Mayan men and women, including Pop Caal, who mobilized during the 1960s Catholic re-catechism of the Verapaz. These pioneers initiated a *re-encuentro* (a spiritual re-encounter) with the Mayan faith practices that were repressed by Catholic and Protestant foreign missionaries. The group had recently ruptured over radically divided interpretations of the practice and public face of their spirituality. They did not settle their differences before Pop Caal's murder.

I learned about the urban leaders' re-encuentro while researching a rural spirit possession cult in nearby San Juan Chamelco. Members of this cult began their faith recovery in 1992. The cult features elder Q'eqchi' women entering trances and channeling messages from the region's Tzuultaq'a, the mountain-valley beings. The urban Q'eqchi' re-encuentro members knew about the rural cult and had joined their vigils. Members of the different worship groups met initially during pilgrimages to the region's various Tzuultaq'a cave shrines. They all attended the funeral for Pop Caal.

The differences between the two groups—differences of class, education, and political participation—are striking. The rural Mayas are monolingual, poor, and illiterate, while the urban leaders are relatively well educated; many are middle-class education professionals. The re-encuentro members are vocal activists in national policy circles. The rural cult members, however, weathered the war years in communities where all adult men served in the PACs. They were the first in the Verapaz to join the ex-PAC movement, demanding compensation from the government for their forced labor.

Members of both groups regard their practices as a contribution to the region's post-counterinsurgency healing. But in the decade since the Peace Accords, Mayan spirituality faces deep ambivalence within the nation. Ambivalence about religious practice, in and of itself, is nothing new. Human spirituality is universally a source of social ambiguity and power, attraction and awe.

The tension heightened with the West's late-19th-century entry into secular modernity (Harding 2001; Marsden 1980) and full commitment to the dichotomy between progress and spirituality. Guatemala's 19th-century Liberals firmly subscribed to this dichotomy. When post-Positivist Western approaches to spirituality, opposing science and religion (modern progress and religious practice), are conjugated with Western approaches to indigenous peoples, the stakes rise exponentially for the indigenous faithful.

In Guatemala, the Mayas must contend with stereotypes that they are "more spiritual" than Westerners. Indian spirituality, a long-standing subject of fascination for Westerners and anthropologists, is projected as exotic and transcendent, the West's mystical Other. This stereotype is deployed by the state in creating national identity and, profitably, in tourism. For example, the government requested that its Mayan officials stage a ceremony when U.S. president George W. Bush visited in March 2007.

The stereotype can handicap Mayas, however, in claiming citizenship, when the stereotype emerges as part of Guatemala's "Indian problem." This is the 19th-century (and perennially circulating) ideology that Guatemala's failures as a modern state, society, and economy are the direct responsibility of the allegedly mysterious and regressive closed Indian countryside.

In Guatemala, as in the West, spirituality brings up two questions. First, the rationality of its practitioners and, by extension, their status as full members of modernity (and, therefore, modern states); and, second, the legitimacy of their practices: Are they faking it or is it real? If it is "real," then the actors are authentic but faced with dilemma number one. If they are faking it, they lose their legitimacy as "authentic" and, therefore, lose political capital.

In this chapter, I argue that the rift between the members of the re-encuentro group formed in part over these concerns, between members promoting practices that could be embraced as more universal and rational and other members deeply interested in a mystical spirituality. I describe how Mayan spirituality is both political resource and burden for those Mayas who seek to expand their citizenship in post–Peace Accords Guatemala.

A Rural Mayan Spirituality Recovery Movement

The story for the purposes of this chapter begins with the Catholic re-evangelization of the Verapaz. The Dominicans were expelled after 1870 during Justo Rufino Barrios' Liberal reforms. The region was in the midst of development largely by German coffee entrepreneurs, who created a prosperous enclave out of a colonial economic backwater.

The expatriate Germans established no new churches or congregations of their own; they did not import their own pastors and they did not missionize their forced laborers, the Q'eqchi' Mayas of the region. The U.S.-introduced evangelical Church of the Nazarene established a permanent presence by the first decade of the 20th century but did not work with rural Q'eqchi' until mid-century (A. Adams 1999; T. L. Smith 1962).

The re-entry of Catholics began later in the Verapaz than in other regions of Guatemala. In 1935, the diocese of the Verapaz was restored under the care of the Salesian Order, but until the 1960s there were only five foreign priests who attended the entire Verapaz region (Calder 1970:27). In the 1960s, Benedictine missionaries arrived from South Dakota, as well as other foreign priests assigned to diocesan duties. By 1967, all the Catholic personnel in Alta Verapaz were foreign, and today foreigners are still the majority (R. Wilson 1995:163).

The Catholics confronted a religious landscape dominated by the Nazarenes—and by Mayan traditionalist do-it-yourselfers who were well installed in the folk Catholicism infrastructure. The missionaries responded with a vigorous catechism program that recruited much of the upcoming generation of indigenous men. They launched a campaign to eradicate worship of the mountain-valley spirits, the Tzuultaq'a, complete with catechist course pamphlets, *Xtenamitex li Dios,* stating, "It is necessary that we [Q'eqchi's] reject fully the ways of our ancestors so that our lives bear fruit" (R. Wilson 1995:190).

According to all reports, the campaign was effective. Mayan traditionalists repressed their practices under the unaccepting eye of the Catholic Church, which in so many other ways fought for the rights and survival of Mayan peoples. The U.S. Protestant missionaries had introduced the practice of religious repression in the earlier part of the 20th century, informed by an evangelical perspective that took Mayan practices as demonic. Migration added another factor. As people left the highlands for the frontier lowlands further north, they also left the recognized Tzuultaq'a sites and cycles of worship.

In 1992, news spread across highland Verapaz that the Tzuultaq'a were speaking again. Several rural women had entered trances, in communication with the mountain-valley spirits, during the spring of that year, which was the 500th anniversary of European contact. Many Q'eqchi' heralded the trances as good omens, the return of the beings and of an important tradition.

I first encountered the spirit possessions in 1993 at an all-night agrarian vigil in a rural community. James Brady, an archaeologist, and I were researching the Q'eqchi' Mayas' contemporary ritual use of caves (Adams and Brady 2004). We were invited to the vigil held at a rural elder's home, about a 45-minute walk from the town of San Juan Chamelco. That evening, a woman elder was possessed by several Tzuultaq'a.

The spirit possession occurred during an agrarian ritual for Q'eqchi' Mayas. These rituals are held for clearing, planting, weeding, and harvesting as well as for extraordinary occasions. To prepare, the communities choose a date, gather at a home which is beautifully decorated with spectacular rustic altars, and invite musicians. Everyone has a role; children are the dancers who enact the songs requested by the mountain spirits; men and women have their separate duties in cooking, praying, and making offerings.

This has all been well documented. What have not been documented are the spirit mediums. The earth spirits visit the vigil through the mediums and give detailed instructions for the pilgrimages to their cave homes. Typically, the possession occurs around midnight, with someone entering a *lubuk* (trance) and then speaking in the voices of various spirits. An interpreter calls out the messages.

I was taken aback when I first witnessed their worship, for various reasons, one of which is that spirit possession tends to startle Western ethnographers. More to the point, nothing I had read, or have now read, in the considerable literature on the Q'eqchi' Mayas would have led me to expect spirit possession (I have yet to read the untranslated German-language sources). The Tzuultaq'a and agrarian rituals are focal in most of the ethnography of the Verapaz and Q'eqchi', but there is no mention of a possession cult organized around channeling these beings.

My literature search contrasted sharply with interviews with Q'eqchi' spirit mediums, elders, and cultural leaders. In San Juan Chamelco and elsewhere, people knew of the trances and described these as a tradition. In San Juan Chamelco, several mediums are recognized, young girls, women with young families, elder women. Several communities are involved. These are farming communities located near the town; despite their proximity to the bilingual town, these are largely monolingual communities.

During the summer of 2000, I met with the first spirit medium I had witnessed, Tomasa Butz, 59 years old then, Q'eqchi' speaker, invalid, grandmother, weaver. Her gift was revealed to her in her thirties, when she was walking to market. She was able to hear the Tzuultaq'a when they spoke on the roads. The first time, she went home ill and lay stricken, blind and deaf, for several days. Gradually, she began to accommodate the gift and participate in the agrarian rituals. Her experience of the events, she says, is remembering an encounter with some manifestation of the Tzuultaq'a on a road but having no memory of the words that she spoke. She and her husband assured me that it has been an ongoing practice, organized by ritual elders ever since they, their parents, and their grandparents were small. Yet it was clear that both they and the other spirit mediums were leading a spiritual revival movement. They trained the young dancers, sought out the musicians, and even sent young seminarians to read the Q'eqchi' ethnographies written by foreigners.

I have now worked with this group for 15 years and introduced many others from the region to their worship. They always include me and other newcomers to their worship. They honor our requests for information; they carry our offerings to the Tzuultaq'a. They, in turn, are invited as spiritual elders to the region's various patron saint festivals and to public events of the re-encuentro movement.

The *Re-Encuentro* in the Verapaz

The urban re-encuentro activists trace their movement to a group of catechists trained largely by the Benedictines who founded Coban's Centro San Benito. These were members of the Mayan generation well documented in Guatemalan literature marked by the Catholic missionary impact (see Falla 1978; Brintnall 1979; Warren 1989). Young people were most open to the new movement, and they clashed with the traditionalist elders who had run the *cofradía* (confraternity of the Catholic Church) system during the decades-long dearth of priests. The priests stood behind the young catechists, determined to abolish drinking, dancing, and idol worship (see Burrell, this volume).

These men (and a few women) rode the post–World War Two development opportunity wave of formal education and credentialing. For Antonio Pop Caal, the story continued with study in European universities arranged by the missionary priests, who hoped he would take vows and become the first ordained Q'eqchi' Mayan Catholic priest. But when Pop Caal returned from Spain in 1969, he left Christianity as his faith and began study with a Western Guatemala Mayan spiritual guide.

Meanwhile, a concurrent movement to recover Mayan identity developed in the Verapaz with a group of catechists working at the Centro San Benito. Many had been born in the countryside to parents who abruptly quit their "pagan" practices during the Catholic re-evangelization. For example, Andres Cuz Mucu and Esteban Pop Caal were the rural protégés of Belgium priest Esteban Haeserijn in San Juan Chamelco, who was working on a Q'eqchi' dictionary (Haeserijn 1979). Haeserijn encouraged the young Q'eqchi' to recover their spiritual practices. In providing this encouragement, the priest was definitively going against the grain of the rest of the Catholic priests, who were proactive on poverty and cultural identity issues but inflexible in doctrinal matters concerning "false idols" such as the Tzuultaq'a. Haeserijn held that the Q'eqchi' use of the term *yiosil* (godliness) to describe elements of their world also demonstrated their respect for God.

In 1976, an elder relative of one of the catechists, Eduardo Pacay, dreamed about a sacred site on Coban's outskirts. The group located the place, based on the information from the dream, and gave it the name spoken in the dream, Chajxucub'. The group of seekers centered their worship on Chajxucub'. They worked with an *ajq'ij* (ritual practitioner) from San Andres Xecul in western Guatemala. They built a little house and altar on the site, and their teacher placed a special Mayan cross there. Chajxucub' gained regional renown; on May 24–25, 1978, Panzos people visited the group in Coban, went to Chajxucub', and held a ceremony at a local home. They then "returned to their deaths" (the Panzos massacre), according to Cuz Mucu.

The acute phase of the 1970s and 1980s violence scattered the group of seekers. The options for Mayan leaders after 1980 were clear, in the words of one re-encuentro member: join the insurgency, go into exile—or remain in your community and run the risk of being killed. Some of the group joined the insurgency, some left, and some died. Vitalino Calel, from San Cristobal Verapaz and a re-encuentro member, was among those who remained and was killed.

At the waning of the violence, the surviving members of the group gathered again, cautiously. Around the country as the peace talks opened, others were expanding the heavily constricted arenas of worship, including traditionalist practices. The peace negotiations directly addressed Mayan spirituality in *El Acuerdo sobre identidad y derechos de los pueblos indigenas* (Accord on identity and the rights of indigenous peoples) (Saqb'ichil/COPMAGUA 1996). From this, the Commission on Sacred Sites was established in the late 1990s. The commission was charged with identifying Mayan sacred sites and developing procedures for protecting these. Eduardo Pacay was one of the Verapaz delegates to the commission.

As earth-centered worship renewed, so did conflict and pre-existing tensions. During the 1997 convocation of the Commission on Sacred Sites and other venues, people described their experiences carrying out Mayan worship. These reports included ongoing religious repression, such as the destruction of mountaintop altars by evangelicals, the looting of tombs and archaeological sites for the international market in antiquities, the blocking of diviners' access to traditional ceremonial centers by property owners, the hostility of Catholic Action and charismatic groups toward practitioners of Mayan spirituality, and even the disdain of the Ladino-dominated Left (see also Maxwell, this volume, on schoolteacher training). There were also reports of communities (including Verapaz communities) promoting the reconciliation of Catholic catechists and Mayan spiritual guides (Warren 1998:57–58).

Schisms also formed within the Mayan spirituality movement. In the Verapaz, a split was apparent as the re-encuentro reconvened. The sacred site of Chajxucub' served as the focus for the re-encuentro group's eruption into open conflict by the late 1990s. Antonio Pop Caal built a chapel in 1986 and moved the Mayan cross to his *ermita* (shrine) in 1986. The group accommodated that fait accompli by placing another Mayan cross at the original altar and nominally forming a cofradía for the new chapel.

Pop Caal began constructing a scale model of Tikal (an ancient Mayan city) for the education of the numerous visitors to Chajxucub'. Pacay, recognized by the Commission on Sacred Sites as an official spiritual guide for Chajxucub', petitioned for formal recognition of the site and raised concerns about desecration of the site. At one meeting, with Pop Caal listening, Pacay reported that the *cerro* (mountain) had spoken to him in a dream and said to stop Pop Caal from moving the stones.

Pop Caal and his supporters continued construction on the model Tikal. Those opposed petitioned the Ministry of Culture and Sports to recognize Chajxucub' as "patrimonio cultural y natural de la nación" [cultural and natural patrimony of the nation]. Ministry officials forbade Pop Caal in May 2001 to "touch another stone of this patrimony." Amidst the argument that ensued, the ministry officials stuck by their ruling, but also suggested that the group members reach an agreement and reapply. Further attempts to arrange a meeting or come to agreement failed.

The Rift over "Revelation"

Hard feelings ran high over the scandal of Chajxucub'. As with the larger Mayan cultural movement, it is no news that many Mayas involved in the spiritual recovery movement experience intolerance from other Mayas and differences among themselves. Other quarrels between the two factions concerned the exact timing of the *uayeb*, the five "crazy" days of unnaming in the Mayan *hab'* (solar calendar). But first, it is important to highlight how much both groups share in their common history and the status they enjoy in the region. Many are respected educators, businesspeople, rising epigraphers, government agency officials, and Maya Movement bureaucrats (see Maxwell, this volume). Each faction has some three generations of activists invested in moving these explorations forward.

Leaders in both factions identified "revelation" as the issue that divides them. "Revelation" refers to acts of receiving information from supernatural sources. One group, which includes Pacay, subscribes to the possibility of revelations. Its members are well known and respected in the region as the *sacerdotes* Mayas. They are called by the ill of urban Coban to pray and diagnose. They are the officially sanctioned guides for the increasing numbers of visitors who arrive at Chajxucub'. They are apprenticing with rural religious specialists and with Western Mayas to learn the "signs" they feel are all around, but which only a select few can read. These include "reading" blood (pulsing), fire, or the day-names of peoples' birth. Reading fire and reading day-names are not traditional in the Q'eqchi' Mayan area.

One member of the revelation tendency, for example, is a DIGEBI (Dirección General de Educación Bilingüe-Pluricultural) director, decorated with Guatemala's highest award for teachers, the Francisco Marroquin. We began our acquaintance with sharing each other's day-name. He described the difficulties he faced connecting his family life, his life as a state-recognized professional, and his spiritual calling. He talked about the various divination techniques he was pursuing and, leaning toward me, related how, at last, he could feel the answers in his body.

The other group, affiliated with Antonio Pop Caal's educational efforts, is uncomfortable with the idea of esoteric mysticism, of privileged knowledge. The members of this group seek the practices of their ancestors through the social sciences mode of oral histories and heritage pilgrimages. So, while the little model of Tikal deteriorated on Chajxucub', its thwarted builders initiated another educational mission. They pursued their re-encuentro by conducting interviews with rural elders. "We were all wrong before, when we would go to the rural communities and 'teach' them in workshops," exclaimed one leader, Esteban Pop Caal, Antonio Pop Caal's brother and, in his own right, a renowned Verapaz teacher and bilingual education pioneer. "We should have been listening!" Decades earlier, he said, he was among those charismatic catechists who actively and vociferously campaigned against those very traditions of the elders. Today, he is featured with his wife, Armenia Ac Caal, in the Smithsonian's National Museum of the American Indian (NMAI). He served as one of the community curators for the museum's exhibition, Our Universes: Traditional Knowledge Shapes Our World, which depicts indigenous cosmologies around the Americas. His group's work recovering the practices of the Q'eqchi' elders is thus available to every visitor to the museum. The spirit possession practices of the rural San Juan Chamelco cult are not featured at the NMAI.

When I talked with members of the different re-encuentro factions about the rural possession cult in Chamelco, their responses were consistent with their split over the issue of revelation. The education-oriented oral historians were skeptical about the autochthonicity of the possession cult. They trusted that the mediums and cult members were "sincere," "politically disinterested," "authentic." Yet they were also adamant that the trances were not lo nuestro (ours). Esteban Pop Caal suspected the influence of 19th-century Spiritist movements imported to northern Guatemala by European plantation owners, and of U.S. Pentecostalism. His hunch proved very useful to my research, as I later unraveled decades of contact between earlier generations of cult members and interested outsiders. The sacerdotes Mayas group members, on the other hand, were fascinated and joined me on a number of occasions to visit with the Chamelco worship group.

A Problem for These "Indians"

The tension between revelation and the rational approach to spirituality is long-standing in the region. In the Verapaz, rural and urban Q'eqchi' have developed similar language to describe the distinction between "hot" and "formal" churches; the former describes congregations with expressive, sign-seeking, ecstatic, and supernatural practices, while the latter describes churches that follow protocols and reason, such as the Catholic Church and the U.S.-introduced Church of the Nazarene.

Today in the Verapaz the differences over revelation take place in the transnational context of Guatemala's nation-building, the Maya Movement, the legacy of foreign missionizing (Catholic and Protestant), progressive activism, and armed insurgency—and the current work to end the political exclusion of Mayas as citizens within the multi-ethnic nation of Guatemala.

The consequences for Mayan spiritual revelations, historically, have been hard, as the massacres following the 19th-century Mexican cases of the Yucatec War of the Castes and the Chiapas War of Santa Rosa demonstrate. In 1886 Alta Verapaz, "news" of indigenous prophecy in San Juan Chamelco was used to justify armed state intervention. The regional newspapers reported that one "Juan de la Cruz," or the prophet of Xucaneb, began a revival movement. When freakish weather ending in frost damaged the coffee plantations that year, de la Cruz announced that the Tzuultaq'a had declared, "The day is not far away when the true believers will recover free possession of their lands." A force of some one hundred Remington rifles was organized to take de la Cruz prisoner; he died in prison a few years later (Stone 1990). Although even the Ladino version of the events mentions no indigenous call for violence in the prophecy, the prophet paid for his call with his life.

The 20th-century Guatemalan state targeted religious practitioners again in the 1980s as part of its genocidal counterinsurgency. That century, however, saw the beginning of Guatemalan state performances using Mayan otherworldly operations; and the mystical and magical was also marketed in the country for the burgeoning tourist industry. In April 1988, President Vinicio Cerezo, the first civilian elected leader since the 1970s, invited Mayan *cofrades* (lay religious leaders) to a large festive meeting in the capital. The Guatemalan military adopted the Shrine of Esquipulas as its "tribal" spiritual home and promoted pilgrimages. In the Verapaz, it displayed the slogan "Home of the Tzuultaq'a" over the entranceway to its military base. Today, in the 21st century, the state is pointedly promoting the Verapaz as a destination for tourism; it is billed as *el Corazon verde* (the green heart) of Guatemala, complete with its earth-worshipping Indians to make the ecotourism experience more satisfying.

The re-encuentro leaders, having matured in the national domains of education, bureaucracy, and insurgency, are well aware that their spirituality is subject to the Guatemalan state's mercurial flipping between punishing and rewarding Mayan revelation—or spirituality in general. Nevertheless, in 2001 the flipping caught the Tikal builders off guard. Andres Cuz Mucu, the linguist who helped found the Academia de Lenguas Mayas de Guatemala and obtain its status as an autonomous organization backed by a legislative decree, vented his disgust about the Ministry of Culture and Sport's intervention: "It's exactly the opposite of what the Peace Accords say, which is that the sites need to be of the local people." In this statement sounds the sting of betrayal by the Guatemalan nation builders. Here they are, the "good Indians," promoting the universalizing qualities of rationalism, formal education, history, science, and moral guidance, which will create a narrative thread that is particularly Q'eqchi', another strand to weave into a rich united national history.

But here, unfortunately, they are making the same dangerous claim to descent and national participation through history as the quite active Verapaz movements for land. These movements base their legitimacy, in part, on spiritual claims to the land as well as a case that indigenous claims to land transcend the 19th-century titling backed by Liberal "constitutions," which stole citizenship from indigenous peoples (see Tiney 2000). Their demands resonate with the fears that were ably mobilized in countering the 1999 democratic referendum to act on the Peace Accords. The referendum included the recognition of sacred sites, which was spun nationally as "The Indians will take your land." The national referendum was defeated.

A few years later, the state awarded Chajxucub' to those Verapaz Indians, thus promoting revelation, mysticism, and inarticulate expression of primitive spirits through raced bodies. These were now "useful Indians," in the same sense that the perhaps invented and newly canonized Nahua Juan Diego was useful to Mexico and from whom so many sought signs of miracles.

The other of the three groups featured in this chapter, the Chamelco spirit possession members, also made successful demands on the state. Their communities were the first to join the "ex-PAC" movement in 1999, when it was deployed in an earlier presidential campaign of Otto Perez Molina. "PAC" refers to the so-called voluntary but utterly obligatory militias, *patrullas de autodefensa civil* (civil defense patrols), that were organized in every community during the 1982–83 regime of Efraín Ríos Montt. The PACS were finally demobilized as part of the peace process in the mid-1990s. In San Juan Chamelco, men were forced to *tornar* (take night-watch duty) in the PACs several times a week, through 1993.

The ex-PAC movement first caught international attention in 2002 by seizing the Classic Maya site of Tikal, Guatemala's emblematic accomplishment and the inspiration for the scale model that Pop Caal began on Chajxucub'. International outcry arose over the ex-PACs when the state responded to their demands and paid out compensation—far before any of the victims of the violence saw any of the compensation required by the Peace Accords. In fact, former members of the PACs are blamed with instigating the vigilante violence known as the *linchamientos* (MINUGUA 2002).

In Chamelco, however, those who joined the ex-PAC movement viewed themselves as democratic petitioners and peaceful demonstrators lobbying for their civil rights to receive reparations for what can only be described as forced labor, the antithesis of modernity. In Chamelco, their oblivion regarding the ugly national reputation of the PACs is supported by the fact that San Juan Chamelco suffered few cases of extra-judicial murders during the 1980s or to date, not one record of vigilante lynching. The Chamelco ex-PAC members made no mention of a special spirituality in their lobbying, unlike those in the Verapaz land reform movement. Nor did they mention any support for the dictator Ríos Montt's 2003 presidential campaign. Ríos Montt, charged with directing the Guatemalan military's worst phase of genocide during the early 1980s, was said to have secured his political base in his alleged control over the minds of Mayan peoples. In this version of the Indian problem, Guatemala's towns and capital blamed election outcomes—and their nation's political and partisan underdevelopment—on the *indios*.

One evening in 2003, with the Chamelco possession cult members, walking under a cloud-shrouded full moon to leave offerings with the Tzuultaq'a, I found everyone conversant in the broken promises and corruption of Ríos Montt's FRG (Guatemalan Republican Front). We created a tableau confirming every exotic stereotype about the mystical Mayas and the anthropologists who "uncover" their secrets. But we were engaged in a lively, well-informed political discussion. The results of my (very) informal 50-person survey were confirmed in a national survey that was released the very next morning: Ríos Montt had barely garnered 3.3 percent support of those polled. San Juan Chamelco was one of the communities surveyed.

These rural devout carry out their political and spiritual activities with the transparency and compartmentalization of good citizens enjoying freedom of expression and worship. And, perhaps an indication of further progress in closing the rift concerning revelation that runs across the various movements, that evening they also carried offerings and prayers to the Tzuultaq'a from the grieving family of Antonio Pop Caal.

3

Peace under Fire

Understanding Evangelical Resistance to the Peace Process in a Postwar Guatemalan Town

J. Jailey Philpot-Munson

Over ten years after the signing of the Peace Accords, Guatemala might appear to be out of the danger zone. The country, at first glance, has slowly but successfully negotiated manifold obstacles to democratic transition after 36 years of state-sponsored violence and civil conflict. To be sure, things have improved. Once covert and mercilessly targeted by military violence, human rights groups now proliferate and operate openly in Guatemala, both at the local and national levels. The state, with the help of intergovernmental agencies from around the world, has resettled most of the internal and external refugees. The technically and emotionally difficult process of exhuming hundreds of clandestine cemeteries throughout the country is well under way. And two separate truth commission reports, released in 1998 and 1999, both openly accuse the Guatemalan military of committing gross human rights violations during the war—a charge unthinkable only a few years prior. An encouraging picture, perhaps, but incomplete.

Despite these improvements, the shadow of Guatemala's past continues to hang like a diaphanous pall over the country. Instances of political crime have been on the rise over the past nine years. Human rights organizations throughout the country have had their archives stolen or destroyed, while their representatives regularly receive ominous death threats. Numerous plaintiffs, witnesses, lawyers, and judges involved in court cases regarding past atrocities linked to the military have been forced into exile after repeated threats or attempts on their lives—and for good reason. Dozens of representatives of human rights groups and people linked to polemical legal proceedings, as well as labor organizers and journalists, have been murdered since the signing of the Peace Accords. Such incidents have been enough to demonstrate—as Nery Rodenas, the director of the human rights office of the Guatemalan Archdiocese (ODHA), determined—that "dark forces remain in Guatemala which still enjoy immunity and privilege" (González 2000).

Fig 10. The evangelical message in Guatemala finds unique media in Nebaj. Photo by J. Jailey Philpot-Munson.

Remarkably, Rigoberta Menchú's 2006 *denuncia* (accusation) in Spain has failed to gain anything more than marginal support in Guatemala. Quite to the contrary, one of the ex-dictators whom she and most who are familiar with Guatemalan history consider to be a major contributor to the genocide of the rural indigenous population, Efraín Ríos Montt, was elected president of Congress by a landslide in November 1999.

Known for his dictatorial stance on crime and corruption, Ríos Montt's popularity is often attributed to widespread panic over alarmingly high levels of crime. Generalized crime, even in remote areas of the highlands, is at an all-time high since military downsizing left many ex-combatants jobless: gangs regularly assault vehicles, sack homes and offices, kidnap or murder unsuspecting victims, and create a climate of fear after dark. With a faltering economy and inflation already making subsistence increasingly difficult, such crime has caused public outrage and advanced popular support for the neo-*caudillismo* (adoration of a strong, egocentric leader) of political parties like Ríos Montt's Guatemalan Republican Front (FRG). Yet fear of generalized crime isn't the only reason Ríos Montt has die-hard supporters from overwhelmingly indigenous areas that sustained devastating levels of political violence during his tenure as president. In fact, he has attained what can only be called "mythic status" amongst a large percentage of the population he once sought to eradicate.

This chapter presents a discussion of some of the underlying dynamics behind this paradox. To accomplish this, I examine the historical trajectory and postwar social impact of Pentecostalism within Nebaj, a highland Guatemalan town nearly decimated by the state-sponsored violence of the early 1980s.

Nebaj: Politics of the Local

Located in a narrow valley of the western Cuchumatanes mountain range, Nebaj, at an elevation of 1,616 meters, is the first of the three Ixil towns one encounters on the long bus ride up from the departmental capital of El Quiché, Santa Cruz del Quiché. Out of the three municipalities in the Ixil region— Santa María Nebaj, San Juan Cotzal, and San Gaspar Chajul—Nebaj is the largest by far, with an estimated population of 47,000 (CIIDH-GAM 1996: 50). Like the rest of the departmental population, which is reported to be only 13 percent non-indigenous (UNHDR 1998:220), approximately 88 percent of the population of Nebaj is of Mayan descent, with two-thirds belonging to the Ixil language group, according to a recent census (CIIDH-GAM 1996:50).

In the late 1970s and early 1980s heightened guerrilla activity in the Guatemalan highlands instigated a sweeping military response, colloquially referred to as *la violencia*. During this time the military—under the leadership of Romeo Lucas García and then Ríos Montt—employed a "scorched earth policy" and increased extrajudicial execution of noncombatants in order to dismantle the guerrilla insurgency's presumed indigenous base of support ("Apreciacíon de Asuntos Civiles" 1982). Due to the growing presence of the Guerrilla Army of the Poor (EGP) in the department of El Quiché, the Ixil area was the region hardest hit by counterinsurgency efforts. One hundred and eleven of the estimated 420 army massacres documented by the Catholic Church's independent truth commission, the Recuperation of Historical Memory (REMHI), occurred within the three Ixil municipalities alone (REMHI 1998:35–38).

The effects of the violence, as might be expected, have had a major impact on the social organization of Nebaj. Starting in early 1984, villages destroyed by the army were replaced by heavily patrolled "model villages." Constructed by the Guatemalan Army Corps of Engineers, these villages were sanitized of "godless communism" by twice daily "re-education meetings" led by army officers ("Apreciación de Asuntos Civiles" 1982; "Polos de Desarrollo" 1984). Pentecostal missionaries from the United States, at the bequest of newly converted evangelical Ríos Montt, provided food, medicine, and "spiritual guidance" (Stoll 1990:201–202). Both during and after the worst violence, the atmosphere that pervaded Nebaj was one of intense mistrust and fear, contributing to the further atomization of the war-torn.

Though mistrust is still rampant in Nebaj, the current atmosphere is unmistakably tinged with renewal. Placards for national and international nongovernmental organizations (NGOs) line Nebaj's streets, and the infamous death squad vans have been replaced by white trucks adorned with United Nations (UN) and European Union flags. It seems evident, however, that rebuilding a sense of community in Nebaj will require more than demobilizing the guerrillas and downsizing the military. As mentioned above, Nebajenses still take sides. While some continue to support the insurgency's goal of land reform, many residents of Nebaj insist that it is the fault of the guerrillas that the army targeted the indigenous population and, therefore, refuse to lend their support to any endeavor that could be construed as "leftist." Even many who once belonged to the guerrilla ranks feel that the EGP betrayed the Ixil people by promising them protection from the army, protection that they could not possibly deliver. Moreover, because males who did not fulfill their "voluntary" civil patrol duties were considered subversive by the military and frequently "disappeared," it was not unusual for Ixil men to be forced into armed conflict with family members who had joined the EGP. Taking all of this into account, the process of mending Nebaj's social fabric promises to be long, indeed. Yet a growing number of Nebajenses view this task to be less arduous than others.

Born Again

Long relegated to the margins of Guatemala's religious landscape, novel forms of Protestant belief and practice have gained in both prevalence and influence in recent years. Regionally synonymous with *evangelical*, the term *Pentecostal* is here used to refer to the more charismatic Protestant congregations formed within the past 25 years, usually under the auspices of now-absent North American missionaries. Sometimes further subdivided into Pentecostal and neo-Pentecostal (cf. E. Wilson 1997; B. Smith 1998), to indicate degree of organization and independence from mission associations, both diverge sharply from historical Protestant congregations (i.e., Presbyterian, Lutheran, Methodist, etc.) in their theology—and their politics. While they were scarcely more than 2 percent of the population in the early 1970s, recent surveys show that as many as 30 to 35 percent of Guatemalans now belong to one or more Pentecostal congregations (Stoll 1994:100). This dramatic shift within the religious landscape took place, in large part, between 1976 and 1983—a period during which Guatemalans witnessed a devastating earthquake and the worst violence of the civil war. Due to guerrilla movement through the area during this time, Nebaj was all but razed by the Guatemalan army. Concurrently, it became the site of unprecedented levels of Pentecostal conversion.

Neo-Weberian interpretations (see Annis 1987; Martin 1990; Sherman

1997) have been more successful than Marxian approaches (see Diamond 1989; Huntington and Domínguez 1984; Westropp 1983) at examining the self-understanding of Guatemalan Protestants, though offering scant description of whether or how such understanding deviates from rational-choice theory as an analytic framework. My goal here is not to dispute the validity of data filtered through lenses of either "this-worldly" or "other-worldly" models. Others have already devoted excellent volumes to elucidating the pros and cons of each approach (see Cleary and Stewart-Gambino 1997; Miller 1994; B. Smith 1998). Rather, my goal is to argue the case for a closer look.

Once one comprehends the complexity of Pentecostalism in Latin America—its variations, contingencies, and contradictions—it becomes immediately apparent that no one paradigm explains anything very well. To be sure, generalizations are difficult to make even within the same country. But there is another problem besides over-generalization caused by understanding Pentecostalism in Guatemala too quickly: namely, losing sight of what it means and has meant to those who comprise the evangelical ranks. This is especially problematic when these new moral communities are largely indigenous and blur the categorical boundaries between religion and politics in ways that affect the postwar reconciliation efforts.

The influence of religion over local interpretations of justice and reconciliation in Nebaj involves many evangelicals in activities that directly or indirectly work against the peace process. While Nebajense Catholics largely support the recommendations of the Peace Accords and CEH (the UN Commission for Historical Clarification), evangelicals tend to be more critical. They have been clear in their advocacy of continued military presence in Nebaj, have spread rumors that the proliferation of concepts such as indigenous and human rights will "bring the wrath of God," have opposed seeking justice for war crimes, and have even obstructed the efforts of forensic anthropologists trying to locate and exhume mass graves in Nebaj and throughout the Ixil area.

Laying Blame

The most fundamental difference is how evangelicals tell history. Representatives from human rights NGOs base their understanding of what occurred in Nebaj during the civil war on the two truth commissions produced after the signing of the Peace Accords in 1996. Besides cataloging and publicizing the massacres and other atrocities that took place during the war, the REMHI and UN reports also calculated the percentage of military and guerrilla responsibility for the violence. Both truth commissions stated that the military and its clandestine cohorts were responsible for approximately 90 percent of the massacres, extra-judicial executions, disappearances, and other human rights abuses that occurred during the conflict. Guerrilla groups were determined to have been responsible for approximately 3 percent.

Nebajense *evangélicos* (evangelicals) tell a different story. Their version of history has them caught in the middle of a conflict in which they did not wish to participate (cf. Stoll 1993). Regardless of past affiliations, they claim now that the EGP was a foreign movement that had no popular support in the Ixil area until it made villages vulnerable to army attacks. Nearly all the Pentecostals I interviewed in Nebaj felt the percentage of responsibility was closer to 50–50 than 90–10. They complained frequently that workers from the UN Mission for the Verification of Human Rights in Guatemala (MINUGUA) and other human rights groups were not there: "Didn't see the war. . . . They only came to order everyone in Guatemala around. . . . If they were here during the war they would realize the truth. But . . . they came from outside. What do they know about us?" (Ixil schoolteacher, Pentecostal).

These beliefs about the contested nature of historical memory influence the manner in which evangelicals interpret nearly all other aspects of the peace process—particularly, prevailing trends pertaining to justice for war crimes and the exhumation of clandestine cemeteries.

Love or Justice?

One of the most controversial aspects of the UN Commission for Historical Clarification (CEH) is that it accused the Guatemalan military not only of war crimes, but also of genocide, which nullified all Guatemala's National Reconciliation Law and made war crimes punishable not only in Guatemala, but also in other countries. From an outsider's perspective, it seems a marvelous feat: a brutal apparatus of death finally exposed, no longer protected by institutionalized impunity. Indeed, it is what most of us working in Guatemala have hoped for: broken silence, shattered impunity. But not everyone was so ecstatic about the possibility of watching the country go through dozens of trials in the years to come, reliving the past while searching for an elusive justice.

Evangelicals in Nebaj unabashedly preach forgiveness for war crimes, even when they themselves were victims of army brutality: incongruity incarnate. Miguel (all names have been changed to protect the anonymity of those interviewed), an itinerant Ixil preacher who was orphaned during the war, explains his feelings this way: "When I see people, sad and afflicted because of the war, saying: 'Aah, let's capture the soldiers, those that killed the people!' it saddens me because I can see that they don't have the love of God. He who has killed, if he has asked for forgiveness, God will forgive."

Oftentimes these explanations involve references to "divine healing," a widely held evangelical belief that the Holy Spirit can cure any malady, physical or emotional. Miguel elaborates:

When I see people who harbor so much hatred, I like to pray for them. I tell God, "Lord, give them the heart you gave me. You changed my heart. Give them that heart. Make this change." There are so many people who are still suffering. Every day you can see their faces full of bitterness . . . because the root of anguish is still in their hearts.

Using the individualism so inherent to "born again" Christian doctrine, Miguel and other evangelical pastors in Nebaj employ Pentecostalism to reconstruct a new moral community, explaining their goals in terms of social healing: "Our mission is to reach these people one soul at a time . . . because when Guatemala belongs to Jesus Christ, I think that everyone will find peace in their hearts. That is our mission as evangelicals, to improve Guatemala, not with guns, but with love."

Naturally, there are biblical passages to back the parallel sort of peace evangelicals in Nebaj advocate. For example, the moral criticism of the struggle for justice is based on New Testament teachings of forgiveness: "God's justice isn't man's justice . . . so I don't look for the men who killed my sons because God knows who they are. . . . We have to let God decide their fate, because he is the all-powerful. 'Judge not lest ye be judged'" (evangelical widow and Bible study leader). But, as with most exegetical endeavors, strong moral codes and feelings bound to history influence the way Nebajense evangelicals read the Bible as well as the actions of vocal figures within the peace movement.

When asked their opinion of Rigoberta Menchú and her international lawsuit against Ríos Montt and other ex-military officers, evangelicals generally indicated that she was thought to be "poisoned by hate" and that her legal actions were likely to provoke another war. Consequently, her most common nicknames amongst evangelicals in Nebaj were "La Nobel de Guerra" (the Nobel War Prizewinner) and "Malinche" (synonymous with "traitor," as Malinche was Hernando Cortez's interpreter and consort). Interestingly, considering the theme of forgiveness, one evangelical Ixil schoolteacher even felt Menchú's crimes were capital in nature: "Menchú is putting many people at risk, so she is a traitor, and a traitor deserves to be put to death."

Pentecostal Nebajenses believe that forgiveness is the only way to promote peace in postwar Guatemala. Justice by legal means is widely considered to be dangerous and an imposition of foreigners who do not have Guatemala's best interest at heart. They believe God, and only God, should mete out justice. An ex-guerrilla who leads a weekly Bible study in the outskirts of Nebaj explained, "If Ríos Montt is really guilty, if he had something to do with all those massacres, he will suffer the consequences. In my opinion it's better to leave it all in God's hands."

God's "divine plan" and omniscience, interpreted through the Pentecostal lens in Nebaj, were so widely accepted as incontrovertible that, when asked why they thought Nebaj was the target of so much violence and suffering, a significant number of Ixil evangélicos responded that they deserved to be punished for their paganism:

> [In the Bible] there was a king named Amaziah. God gave him power to defeat his enemies. But when he defeated his enemies, he began to worship their gods, and then God's wrath came against him. . . . God didn't want him to suffer a war. But he . . . started to burn incense, and within a few days war came against him . . . because God sent it. . . . We once burned incense and worshipped pagan gods, so God brought the war to save our souls.

All in all, evangelical Nebajenses prefer to leave the difficult task of punishing those responsible for mass death to a God they trust will do the right thing—perhaps because they view the majority of human endeavors to be sinful and selfish. For this reason, in addition to the almost palpable anxiety about poking fingers in old wounds (cf. Nelson 1999), they do not feel represented by a peace process led by human rights workers, foreign *or* national, who believe there can be no peace without justice.

Digging Up the Past

One of the most difficult tasks of the peace process has been the systematic exhumation of massacre sites in every department of the country. In accordance with the recommendations of both the Peace Accords and CEH, forensic anthropologists from all over the world have been working for over a decade, meticulously unearthing, cataloging, and identifying remains so that relatives of the victims may give them a proper burial. The exhumation of clandestine cemeteries is a slow, grueling, and emotionally taxing process, which is perhaps why little more than one-half of the over 400 massacre sites have been exhumed to date. Though the location of thousands of Guatemalans who disappeared would seem overwhelmingly desirable, it is also highly controversial, and some of the delays forensic teams must deal with are the result of local— primarily evangelical—opposition (cf. Sanford 2003:118–120).

Many evangelicals in Nebaj expressed outright opposition to the exhumation of clandestine cemeteries. In a household survey I conducted in February 2001, approximately 82 percent of evangelicals, as opposed to 12 percent of Catholics, felt clandestine cemeteries should not be exhumed. Again, it was especially interesting to find that many evangelicals who had lost one or more family members during the war felt that the bones "should remain where they are." The most energetic preacher I met in Nebaj, whose father was killed by the army when he was six, had this to say:

> I see now all these institutions coming from other countries, . . . coming to pull up bones. That is horrible! It is waking the hatred again in the people. . . . It already happened! What are they doing?! I thank God that the majority is evangelical now; otherwise people would start to fight with the army again. But the Guatemalans have the love of God now and don't pay attention to those people. Digging up bones, . . . what would you do if they told you: "That is your father. Look, here is his bone"? And if you aren't evangelical: "And who killed him?!" "It was the army." . . . The hatred would start all over again. If the gospel wasn't here in Guatemala, there'd be more war, more violence. Period.

In fact, 68 percent of the evangelicals opposed to the exhumations claimed that at least one immediate family member had disappeared or been killed during the conflict, and all voiced concerns about reawakening hostility within the community. An Ixil textile vendor whose husband, uncle, and three sons were abducted by the civil patrol in 1982 and never seen again said: "It's not good to relive cruel moments, and there just doesn't seem to be much justification for such things. I don't know whose idea it was because it reawakens resentments. If we base ourselves in a sense of peace, those things are erased, and we've got a clean slate." A carpenter whose son disappeared in 1983 said: "Their spirits have already gone to be with God . . . [and] we shouldn't have anything more to do with the dead." A schoolteacher who never saw her brother or two uncles after "men wearing combat boots" took them from the family home in 1982 said:

> I think it's too painful for people . . . even if Jesus is by their side. Exhuming the dead would cause a lot of suffering, and maybe a lot of resentment. Nothing good comes of these, because those feelings could make us hate and kill each another again. . . . Why dig up the bones if they're already dead! It's in the past.

What seems most clear is that evangelicals are fearful that another war could begin if the past occupies too much of the present.

A Parallel Peace Process

Evangelicals' fear of the power of the past, the accumulated force of old resentments, contributes to their suspicion and criticism of national and international human rights organizations in Nebaj. Rather than viewing "human rights" as a non-partisan force with humanitarian goals, evangelicals in Nebaj tend to classify the international human rights movement as ideologically leftist, sometimes going so far as to call it a "tool of the guerrillas" to deceive the Ixiles into fighting the army again. This example of how conflicting interpretations of the past have a direct impact on both Guatemala's present and future has even led some Pentecostal Nebajenses to label the CEH and REMHI reports as "communist" documents.

The worst of these ideological critiques came in the form of limited speculations about the Antichrist's relationship to intergovernmental organizations (IGOs) working in town. While nearly 60 percent of evangelical Nebajenses were critical of IGOs in general, 9 percent went so far as to equate the work of MINUGUA and the European Union with that of the Antichrist. For the most part, these opinions were based on two things: the banners of each organization and biblical passages. First, MINUGUA's banner has a globe encircled by two olive branches that were thought to represent the horns of the devil. The EU's flag in 2000 had 12 stars in a circle, thought to signify the union of nations that occurs in the book of Revelations. Second, a few evangelical Nebajenses who suspected MINUGUA and the EU of ulterior motives cited I Thessalonians 5:3: "For when they shall say, Peace and safety, then sudden destruction cometh upon them." Such opinions were likely influenced by the frequent visits of a dynamic Guatemalan pastor now living in Houston, who favored fire and brimstone sermons peppered with frightening anti-foreigner conspiracy theories. Nonetheless, these ideas have gained a life of their own within more than one Pentecostal congregation in Nebaj.

Ideological opposition notwithstanding, the biggest challenge facing MINUGUA and other human rights organizations in Nebaj is the lack of public awareness of human rights as a concept. Fifty-four percent of all indigenous respondents, both Catholic and Protestant, could not define "human rights," except to say that they thought it might be an office on the other side of town. Breaking language and cultural—let alone political—barriers has been difficult for MINUGUA representatives and even Guatemalan human rights workers from the capital, who speak little or no Ixil.

For the most part, those evangélicos who do understand the work of human rights IGOs and NGOs operating in their community consider the goals of these organizations to be altruistic but an insufficient foundation for long-term peace. The comments of a popular pastor in town exemplify this last point of divergence: "The peace that they want to promote won't work because if a man doesn't have peace in his heart, he can't have peace with his neighbor. . . . MINUGUA tries to ensure that human rights are respected here, but . . . ex-soldiers and ex-guerrillas and many others have wounds that MINUGUA can't heal."

It is important to emphasize that evangelical resistance to the internationally recognized peace process does not translate into resistance against the "idea of peace" itself. Instead, what seems to be apparent is that evangelicals in Nebaj are re-signifying the concept of "peace" in order to make it fit their subjective experience of the conflict, choosing a "Prince of Peace" over the Peace Accords as the medium of conflict resolution. That is to say, although the dominant discourse of the pro-peace movement demands remembering the past—justice for war crimes, exhumation of mass graves, teaching school-children about the war, etc.—evangelicals espouse forgetting. They wish to neither remember nor relive the past. They maintain that it is not worth the risk to their emotional well-being or the well-being of their community. Pentecostals, as Everett Wilson asserts, "living in perpetual crisis, through religious motivation and cohesion [often employ] . . . religious associations as a means of exerting control over their own lives" (1997:139)—control, it would seem, they feel the peace process was slowly and unjustifiably usurping.

In many ways Pentecostalism has helped Nebajenses overcome debilitating emotional states ranging from anxiety to rage and sorrow to terror. It has helped them to discard unrelenting desires for revenge that, in a country as violent and institutionally corrupt as Guatemala, would likely lead to long-term frustration. Instead of hatred, they espouse forgiveness. Rather than anguish, they embody what they call the "joy of the Holy Spirit." Although there are several missionaries still living and working in Nebaj, their political influence is slight. Ixiles and Ladinos alike appear to have made the Pentecostal faith meaningful in ways that reflect their culture, their biographies, and the history of their *pueblo* (community)—sometimes struggling against missionary instruction to do so.

Regardless of the facts and categorical imperatives important to those of us who did not survive epistemology-shattering events, for Nebajenses to be "born again" is to leave behind the fear, hatred, anxiety, and profound sadness caused by the war and work toward rebuilding bonds of trust in their community. Evangelicals throughout Guatemala have successfully created a new sense of community in a context characterized by postwar social fragmentation. Although there is no denying that they still employ and, thus, exacerbate ideological divisions engendered by the conflict to evaluate events and institutions in Guatemala, I contend that they do so as a strategy to comprehend and regain some semblance of control over the world in which they live. In sum, I argue that the moral community created by an appropriated form of charismatic Christianity in Nebaj constitutes a grassroots movement dedicated to healing individuals and others of the trauma of the war, while consistently (and imaginatively) resisting a peace process considered unrepresentative of their collective subjectivity.

A New Approach to Promoting Peace

Richard Wilson once wrote, "If human rights reports strip events free of actors' consciousnesses and social contexts, then part of anthropologists' brief is to restore the richness of subjectivities, and chart the complex field of social relations, [and] contradictory values . . . that human rights accounts often exclude" (1997:15; cf. Schirmer 1997:181). I believe studying the collision of global (i.e., institutionalized) and local interpretations of human rights now evident in Nebaj and elsewhere in Guatemala is a necessary step in comprehending the hostility many Guatemalans exhibit toward national and international groups working to "recuperate the past."

In Nebaj, an unwillingness on the part of some NGOs and IGOs to entertain a dialogue with local evangelicals appears to have effectively alienated a large proportion of Nebajenses—thereby significantly diminishing the efficacy of Peace Accord implementation in that area. I am hopeful that further research will help to create a space wherein academics and non-academics presently working in Guatemala might sustain a conversation regarding the local consumption of increasingly transnational concepts such as "human rights." By locating specific cultural and religious factors that either impede or facilitate the efforts of the international human rights community to rehabilitate Guatemala's human rights record and political practices, we can strive to promote the formulation of more self-critical NGO and IGO programs in regions that sustained decimating levels of political violence. Without such insights, the capacity of international cooperative efforts to eliminate militaristic tradition in Guatemala and replace it with something more closely resembling "liberal democracy" will remain beset by problems generated by local nonparticipation and opposition. Indeed, some might argue, the end product of such efforts can scarcely be called "democratic" if no attempts are made to address the concerns a growing percentage of Guatemalans have regarding reconstructive human rights work and the peace process overall.

4
Living and Selling in the "New Violence" of Guatemala

Walter E. Little

Following the 1996 Peace Accords, Mayan vendors began to complain of a "new violence," commonly considered random criminal acts. By naming street crime—theft, drug deals, assaults, and gang activity—a new violence, they made connections to *la violencia* (the intensification of the Guatemalan military's counterinsurgency campaign in the late 1970s and early 1980s). Like many Guatemalans, la violencia affected them, but Antigua was a haven from the death squads and armed conflict that plagued the highlands. The vendors and I had in common the fact that we had come to Antigua to work where la violencia was less present. Following the Peace Accords, they were increasingly the victims of crime—usually theft, but also assault. Although peace and prosperity were part of neoliberalism's promises, they felt betrayed by social conditions that now made them feel unsafe.

Vendors' criticisms and thoughts on the postwar violence suggest a theory of political and economic activism to show that, even within touristic spaces, community exists as a place from which Mayas organize for common goals. Ethnographic data is used to discuss postmodern theses that contemporary violence is de-personalized, distanced, de-politicized, inscribed in the subject of the Other, and located elsewhere. By contrast, the violence and crime experienced by Mayan handicraft vendors is made personal, immediate, and political.

According to cultural theorists—anthropologists and others (Appadurai 1998; MacCannell 1992; Taussig 1992)—uncertainty, ambiguity, randomness, isolation, and generalized violence characterize life today, in part, due to the collapse of the great metanarratives of modernity that helped us make sense of our globalized world. Arjun Appadurai argues that the increase in ethnic genocide resulted from "the speed and intensity with which both material and ideological elements now circulate across national boundaries [to create] a new order of uncertainty in social life" (1998:228). He contends that how we classify our group, ourselves, and other groups and selves has become difficult in

Fig 11. Mayan street vendors defend one of their peers from Tourism Police intimidation in Antigua, July 2005. Photo by Walter E. Little.

this world of rapidly circulating commodities, people, and ideas that characterizes globalization. Violence is impersonal. As Dean MacCannell explains, "this is not just traditional class-based violence, but new and almost unimaginable postmodern forms. . . . What is more impressive than this violence is its everyday denial" (1992:204). The normalization of violence in the postmodern world is what Michael Taussig addresses when he asks us "to understand our reality as a chronic state of emergency, as a Nervous System" (1992:11).

Taussig argues that we need to be aware of this state of emergency where terror is the norm—terror as the problem of the Other, terror as always elsewhere. His warning to not participate in the "war of silencing" follows most closely the views of Mayan vendors, who are not confounded by globalization and do not deny the violence in their lives. In this case study, I show how one group personalizes violence and does not participate in this "silencing."

Contexts of Postwar Violence

My ethnographic research in Guatemala began in 1992 in the last years of the 36-year conflict and has continued annually with handicraft vendors and other Mayas. As December 1996 approached, Mayan vendors were optimistic. They planned to expand their businesses and recounted how la violencia affected them. Those from San Juan de Comalapa and Tecpán described hiding from soldiers in the countryside and in their homes for fear of being raped, tortured, or killed. They explained why they could not claim the bodies of murdered family members, decomposing in the plazas of their towns, out of fear of being labeled a subversive. Even for vendors from San Antonio Aguas Calientes and Santa Catarina Palopó, who come from towns that suffered relatively low amounts of political violence (see Annis 1988; Hinshaw 1988), la violencia penetrated their everyday social conscience, just as it did their compatriots from regions that had endured much higher levels of violence (Carmack 1988; CEH 1999; Montejo 1999; Stoll 1993). The Peace Accords symbolized potential to vendors, making it possible for them to tell of their suffering and loss while giving them confidence to plan for the future.

Vendors who sell in Antigua come from more than 28 municipalities from diverse parts of the country. They speak Kaqchikel, K'iche', Ixil, Tz'utujiil, and Mam. Although they all share the vendor-craftsperson occupation, what motivated them to go to this tourism-oriented handicraft market varies. Kaqchikel vendors from Sacatepéquez towns (San Antonio Aguas Calientes, Santa Catarina Barahona, Santa Maria de Jésus, and others) consider selling in Antigua a decades-old tradition. Few families from these towns are not connected to handicraft manufacturing and selling. For vendors from the departments of Sololá, Chimaltenango, Quiché, Huehuetenango, and Totonicapán, Antigua was a relatively safe place where politically motivated killings and state forms of terror were difficult to enact, in part, because of the foreign tourist presence. For Mayas with the skills and sufficient capital to make and sell handicrafts, it was easier for them to go to Antigua than to leave the country.

During the most violent period of the 1980s, vendors from places that were under siege entrenched themselves in Antigua life, participating in its economic, political, and educational systems. Travel for adults was dangerous. Huehuetenango and Quiché families explained that those who were not threatened by government forces would seize unused property. One Ixil family recounted that they left their home in the care of their elderly parents, one of which was blind. Once a month, they tried to send a daughter and a young son to check on them and help care for the property. Other vendors listened to the news and gossip networks that operated in the utilitarian market, whose vendors continued to courageously travel despite the violence. For the most part, Sacatepéquez vendors traveled freely between Antigua and their hometowns, taking advantage of local schools and tourism money but quietly returning home each day.

In the 1990s, all vendors regularly traveled between their hometowns and the tourism market in Antigua, as commuters, not as internal refugees who feared death on the road or at home. The social and economic links between Antigua and their hometowns intensified. Parents and children became part of two distinct communities and participated in the political, economic, and social events of each. Vendors used their connections to help others from their hometowns gain entry into the marketplace or market more diverse products by taking advantage of hometown artisans. They also enrolled their children in schools and participated in religious services.

While vendors spoke jubilantly about the coming period of peace, they also began to speak of a new violence that was intensifying throughout the country. They read about it in newspapers, *La Prensa Libre* and *Siglo XXI,* sometimes experienced it themselves, or listened to friends' and family members' accounts. Violent crime—murder and assault—increased, as did armed robbery and kidnapping. Criminal organizations and gangs operated with impunity, controlling various regions of the country, where they freely robbed people in transit, trafficked drugs and other contraband, and killed, raped, or maimed those who sometimes unwittingly entered their domain. Crime became a dominant topic in the news media and in people's conversations. No longer were tourists and Mayas treating major tourism centers, such as Antigua, as neutral zones. The 1990s were not, as Stoll (1993) notes for the 1980s, a period when tourists commonly felt that they were immune to the political violence that plagued Guatemala.

Although crime directed at tourists and handicraft vendors has increased over the last 16 years, during much of Guatemala's history Mayas have been victims. In his ethnohistory of Momostenango, Carmack (1995) explains that merchants have been the targets of thieves since the Spanish colonial period. Christopher Lutz (1994) notes that in Spanish colonial Antigua the robbery of Mayan vendors was common. In the 1800s, the traveler-diplomat John Lloyd Stephens (1993) described the peril of traveling through Guatemala. Not until Jorge Ubico's presidency, 1931–44, was crime significantly curtailed. Kaqchikel Mayas today reflect positively on the lower levels of political and criminal violence during Ubico's dictatorship, despite the economic hardship and generally discriminatory policies toward Mayas (Carey 2001). Indeed, there is nostalgia about Ubico among Mayan vendors, precisely because, as they remember it, state-backed violence and crime was low. In their opinion, crime increases are the result of postwar democratic policies that are too weak. Similarly, Mayas viewed the democracy of the post-Ubico period (the presidencies of Juan José Arévalo Bermejo and Jacobo Árbenz Guzmán) as weak on crime.

Polarized forms of political violence and terror, directed at labor union members, clergy, Mayan spiritual leaders, and agricultural reformers (see Carmack 1988; Green 1999; Manz 1988; Levenson-Estrada 1994), shifted to random, seemingly nonpolitical violence that did not discriminate among political, economic, or sociopathic forms of crime. Human rights groups such as Amnesty International and international economic agencies such as Inter-American Bank (Buvinic et al., 1999) and World Bank (Moser and Shrader 1999) report crime statistics. Annually, the United Nations in Guatemala issues the "Informe de Desarrollo Humano," which provides statistics on social and economic indicators. For Mayan handicraft vendors, such statistics are inconsequential because they cynically believe that crime figures are diminished so as to not scare away foreign businesspersons, tourists, and economic aid.

That the Guatemalan peace process and postwar years have been particularly painful for Guatemalans has been illustrated by the research of anthropologists (Green 1999; Warren 1998), political scientists (Salvesen 2002), and sociologists (Jonas 2000), but criminal violence is not at the center of these respective analyses. By contrast, a Washington Office on Latin America report (Peacock and Beltrán 2003) draws a connection between the rise in crime and the self-interests of powerful Guatemalans opposed to the Peace Accord reforms.

The Penetration of the "New Violence"

For handicraft vendors, the difference between la violencia of the 1980s and the new violence that began in the 1990s is how the latter affects their everyday lives in multiple immediate and personal ways. Tourism centers like Antigua were neutral zones usually immune to state violence. Vendors have a difficult time avoiding the new violence. The extent to which this violence has penetrated the vendors' lives is illustrated in their increasing preoccupations with personal safety and crime. By the close of the 1990s, many vendors had been robbed and some were physically assaulted. They talked about crime and ways to make themselves and tourists safer. What they have not done, in contrast to the postmodern subjects discussed by Appadurai, MacCannell, and Taussig, is deny its existence or resort to violence themselves.

It is important, however, to emphasize that while vendors and other Guatemalans are telling about the atrocities of la violencia, they have a far more difficult time talking about crime in the 1990s and 2000s. This may relate to the immediacy of the experience, but an equally plausible explanation is that the new crimes and the perpetrators are ambiguous. They are not content to accept that the violent crime they experience is merely due to the economy. The connection of crime to broader social, economic, and political issues is a feeling that they have, rather than something they can point to and name.

Although vendors know the victims, the perpetrators are far more slippery for them to name. Numerous theories circulate by the vendors who read the daily newspapers, watch television, and listen to the radio to make sense of the increase of crime that puts them in economic and physical risk. They suggest that it is the influence of organized criminals from El Salvador, drug lords from Colombia who use Guatemala as a staging ground for shipping cocaine to the United States and Europe, old animosities between Mayas and Ladinos, and decommissioned soldiers and guerrillas who have no employment. Certainly, these contribute to the crime that the vendors experience, but what makes them most afraid is that some of the perpetrators of violent crime are members of their own communities. To highlight the difficulties of talking about the crimes, but the desire to do so, and to illustrate the problems of naming the perpetrators, the following conversation I had over several months with a Kaqchikel vendor from San Antonio Aguas Calientes is informative.

In April 1997, I spoke with Herlinda and her daughter Ana, who was watching for customers in the Companía de Jésus handicrafts marketplace (closed February 2003). Herlinda was weaving a *s'ut,* a cloth for carrying babies and groceries. She spoke at length on crime and related that two tourists were robbed close to the market in daylight. She explained, "This never used to happen. Sure, Guatemala has been a violent country and there are a lot of problems, but there were never very many thieves." According to her, most thieves come from Guatemala City and El Salvador, but Antigua and San Antonio have thieves too. She said, "They'll come into the market and steal from vendors."

In general, robberies were rarely reported in the press, but robberies of vendors were never covered in the media, nor were the authorities responsive to vendors who attempted to file theft reports. Only the most sensational crimes against tourists are reported, as the following examples illustrate. In the July 19, 1997, edition of *La Prensa Libre* four tourism police officers were arrested for abuse of power. On August 24, 1997, the same paper published the first of several reports that Antigua was a cocaine and marijuana sales and distribution center. On June 14, 1998, a Chilean, who was part of an organized tour, was shot to death in La Merced Church, a main attraction, in broad daylight. Such violent crimes have been periodically reported, but the predominant image of Antigua is that it is a quiet town, not a city struggling with theft, gangs, assault, rape, and other crimes. A January 16, 2004, Warden Message from the United States Embassy clearly delineates this duality of danger and safety:

Antigua has long been the site of petty theft and pick pocketing seen in many other tourist areas, but the robberies reported to the U.S. Embassy have been, for the most part, non-violent. Recently, however, armed individuals have robbed a hostel, a restaurant, and a private home. These crimes may be an anomaly in Antigua, but should be considered during any visits.

These crimes went unreported in the Guatemalan media. Vendors, however, do not get the U.S. embassy's attention, much less that of the Guatemalan media, when they are the victims of crime.

As Herlinda talked she became agitated—sometimes the words flowed out of her mouth and sometimes they came haltingly. One evening while Herlinda was running errands and talking to middlepersons, her daughters were in charge of taking the family's textiles from the marketplace and putting them into overnight storage. The young women, both around 18 years of age, had traveled that path more times than they could remember, were known by all the families and merchants on the route, and had, literally, helped their mother in the handicrafts market their entire lives. Despite this, a pickup truck pulled along side of them on one of Antigua's busy streets. In the twilight, the thieves took the time to steal the most expensive items, leaving the young women with inexpensive, easily replaced items. They lost several high-quality *huipiles* (hand-woven blouses).

Other Mayan families have been similarly robbed. The robbery of another San Antonio Aguas Calientes family demonstrates the openness and brazenness of some thieves. The family used to sell in front of La Merced Catholic Church. One afternoon two pickup trucks with armed men pulled next to their display and took all their merchandise. They, like Herlinda and others, tried to file a police report, but the officers did not take their statement.

Herlinda described the younger daughter's emotions: "She [Ana] cried about those huipiles, but there was nothing we could do." Ana explained that she did not know who the thieves were but that "they weren't *indígena*." "Maybe they were poor Ladinos or Salvadoreños," she posited. Herlinda suggested, "They could have been policemen. The police don't want to do anything to help us." Such persons were reasonable guesses, since they have had conflicts with each. Ladino residents, with the backing of numerous mayoral administrations and the aid of the police, have tried to expel or restrict Mayan handicraft vendors for years (Little 2004a, 2004b). Salvadorans were more problematic for vendors. Salvadoran tourists, although they do not have the purchasing power of U.S., European, and Japanese tourists, provide a good source of revenue throughout the year because Antigua is close enough for them to take weekend trips. They spend most of their money in restaurants and hotels, but vendors sell low-cost items such as change purses, key chains, and small hand-woven decorations to them. The media dramatize that the Pacific coast highways and those leading to El Salvador are controlled by Salvadoran organized crime. Enough vendors have been robbed taking merchandise to Puerto Cortez on the Pacific coast for them to draw conclusions based on their readings of the media to attribute criminal activity to Salvadorans.

Over the next few months, conversations with vendors always included crime: Who were the thieves? Why did the police not aid them? How do they avoid robberies? Who can they trust? And why do people become criminals? These concerns were topics during the Companía de Jésus vendor association meetings and the collective gatherings of street vendors over the same period of months. In meetings they discussed strategies to identify thieves in the marketplace and to protect themselves and their customers. In one marketplace, the vendors pooled their resources to hire private security guards. Marketplace and street vendors would loudly announce to their peers and customers when known or suspected thieves were present. Periodically, all types of vendors marched on the municipal building to demand that the local government control crime.

Not long after the robbery of the huipiles, Herlinda decided that I should record her and her family's thoughts on the robbery and the new violence in Guatemala. After numerous attempts to record their testimony, I realized how difficult it was for them, Herlinda especially, to discuss the crime. Whenever we met, she asked if I had my tape recorder. However, as we suffered numerous interruptions in the marketplace and in her home, I realized that we would never make the recording. My suspicions were confirmed during our last agreed-upon tape-recording session. She suggested that we meet at the Café Condesa, a restaurant located on the Central Plaza. She felt that it would be a quiet, safe location for us to make the recording. She brought her mother and one of her daughters. She started and stopped her story, eventually letting it drift into a discussion about agricultural work, which her mother then dominated.

During Guatemala's Independence Day observances (September 15, 1997) Herlinda and other San Antonio vendors invited me to participate. Over lunch, she told me about four Ladinas who work together to scam tourists and vendors. She said, "They take advantage of tourists and anybody that they can, but mainly tourists. They stole 3,000 quetzales worth of *traje* [traditional clothing] from Silvia and Ana." I asked if they had been caught, but she said that they had not. "We just warn all tourists to stay away from them and to watch their money."

These women are known con artists. They try to use sex to con male tourists out of money, but the amounts they take or swindle from tourists is small. Most tourists ignore them or are suspicious of women who make themselves sexually available. It is doubtful that such well-known local con artists took her family's merchandise, especially since her daughters know the women and did not name them after the robbery, but it consoled them to have identified some culprits who are considered by locals to be social deviants.

Although these women did not take the merchandise, they and other known criminals are made public. They are made known and, hence, monitored; the vendors are heeding, in effect, Taussig's call to resist the silencing of violence. Rather than resort to lynching persons identified as criminals, they contend that publicly naming criminals protects them from crime. Talk of crime and criminals comprises the gossip networks of the handicraft market, of Catholic and Protestant congregations, and of other social spheres. Persons commonly identified as thieves have fewer opportunities to steal in the communities in which they are known. They even address known thieves as *ladrón* (Spanish) or *eleq'om* (Kaqchikel). Although not all persons perpetrating crimes are known, vendors attempt to name someone and personalize crime. Through the process of naming, known criminals are neutralized and vendors gain a sense of control over crime.

Critiquing the Peace Process and Government

Elisabeth Burgos explains, "The postwar is the continuation of the war by other means" (2001:61). She focuses on the difficult ways that both "winners" and "losers" in Guatemala's civil war have adjusted to the new political climate where all have to live together. As leaders readjust their political ideas, the ways in which violence operates also changes. Although Guatemala's internal war was horrendous, the new violence about which vendors worry penetrates their social and economic spheres in ways that la violencia never did.

According to Alessandro Preti (2002), the violence continues because the vested interests of political leaders and entrepreneurs contrast with those of soldiers, workers, and the poor. Preti contends "that the objective is not always to win the war but to increase the benefits for the belligerents," which can lead enemies to cooperate in the perpetuation of violence (2002:102). Linda Green explains that this legacy of violence from the war and its continuation in other forms is embedded into the life of rural Guatemala, and fear is "a way of life" (1999:172). But as George Lovell (2000) notes, violence will persist as long as well-recognized inequalities related to land and labor exist and the orchestrators of political violence are not dealt with punitively. This is the "Nervous System" (Taussig 1992), where terror is so incorporated in everyday life that it is unbelievable or so commonplace that it is ignored.

Mayan handicraft vendors do not have vested interests in perpetuating violence. They believe this violence should not be ignored. It needs to be identified and made believable. As the example in the previous section illustrates, part of this process is through naming perpetrators and talking, however difficult it may be, about crime. The following example casts light on another part of this process. Postwar violence and crime affect vendors economically, directly when robbed or injured and indirectly when foreign tourists choose not to visit Guatemala because of safety concerns. Vendors have decided to politicize this violence. All crime is also related to politics and can be approached politically. This is a delicate matter because vendors' political relations with the mayor of Antigua and with past administrations, as well as with police forces, have been tenuous at the very best (Little 2004a, 2004b).

In part, there is a contradictory tension between the vendors and the municipality because many vendors prefer selling in an informal market, free from regulation. At the same time, all vendors want the state's protection from criminals. In the intervening years since the robbery of Herlinda's daughters, vendors have continued to be the victims of theft and assault. Vendor organizations have lobbied the municipal, departmental, and state governments to reduce crime and to, specifically, protect them as law-abiding citizens. By using collective strategies, vendors called crime to city officials' attention by petitioning for protection, by filing complaints in mass at city hall, and by inviting the mayor and other politicians to discuss strategies on how to contend with increases in crime. When these failed, they produced flyers warning tourists and vendors of thieves' techniques and advising them about places that were dangerous.

The most common collective strategy that vendors employed was to show genuine concern for their customers' welfare by giving them safety tips as they spoke individually with them. They attempted to convince tourists that handicraft vendors watch out for their safety as well as provide cultural, political, and tourism information. Gaining tourists' confidence has done more for vendors than just sell merchandise. It has made tourists sympathetic to the vendors' political causes, which have included the right to sell in Antigua, access to city services (light, water, and trash removal), and the reduction of crime.

Because crime has not diminished and the local government has not acted in the interest of vendors, crime has become an even more politically charged issue. In fact, vendors have suffered from police crackdowns, where vendors have been arrested and accused of stealing money and merchandise, selling drugs, and assaulting people. One man, who sells with his wife in a small space they rent from a hotel, was arrested for theft and incarcerated for two weeks before the authorities admitted he was not the culprit. The merchandise that was seized when he was arrested and the legal fees and fines that he, his wife, and extended family paid were never returned.

Although vendors have taken matters into their own hands, naming and identifying criminals and dangerous locations, they have become increasingly frustrated with the government. A year after the signing of the Peace Accords, vendors were openly critical of the government and the peace process. For example, Anibal (a male vendor from Momostenango) talked about the

Peace Accords, INGUAT (the Guatemalan Tourism Commission), and violence. Observing that crime continues to increase and vendors throughout the country do not receive protection or aid from the police, he commented, "The signing of the Peace Accords signifies less tourism and more delinquency." He linked this to INGUAT, which has helped promote major hotels and tour companies. Even today, these same large tourism businesses receive police and military protection to provide security for tourists. Smaller operators are left without protection or official endorsement; vendors claim this makes tourists suspicious and afraid of markets, hotels, and restaurants that do not make INGUAT's list of recommended places. According to him, "We do not exist for INGUAT, and INGUAT does not exist for us."

Although vendors feel that crime is out of control and that the government is responsible for it and for fixing it, they do not think that replying with violence is a solution. They are against the lynching (see Carlos Mendoza and Edelberto Torres Rivas's 2003 analysis of lynching in Guatemala) that is commonly reported by the media, claiming that violence only serves to cause more problems, as did the civil defense patrols. A vendor explained, "We are blamed for the offenses of the patrols, but the government made them. Now, if we lynch criminals, we will pay for our actions."

Since the signing of the Peace Accords vendors ask: "How can there be peace when we cannot make a living without fear?" They complain: "The government is for the rich, for the rich Ladinos, that is, who get protected from crime. Indígenas don't matter." Tomás, an itinerant belt vendor from Chichicastenango, put it succinctly: "The peace treaty is just *paz de labios no paz de corazón*" [peace from the mouth, not peace from the heart]. He does not think much is going to change, especially for people like him. He does not see how it can, since they are not part of the whole peace process. I asked if the violence and delinquency would eventually stop or at least lessen. He does not think so, because he read that the police were getting machine guns to fight organized criminal gangs. Tomás does not think more guns will do anything but cause more problems. "The poor who committed theft, committed theft because they were hungry," he said, "they need land; they need work. But the government doesn't do anything to change this; it just gets more guns." However, some thieves are not poor. "They do these things—rape and murder—because they aren't really *seres humanos* [human beings]. Just get rid of them."

Tomás's discourse and that of other vendors who use the same rhetoric reflect common attitudes held by Mayas that are based on a long history of political and economic practices used to exempt them from full citizenship and even basic rights—they literally are not full humans (See Carmack 1988, C. Smith 1990c).

Political and Economic Organizing in the Postwar Violence

The previous discussion and examples illustrate how Mayan handicraft vendors do not behave like the ambiguous postmodern subjects that MacCannell (1992) and Appadurai (1998) describe. They neither deny nor distance themselves from the violence that surrounds them, nor do they resort to violence in retaliation for that which they have suffered. Furthermore, top-down solutions to the ongoing violence, as suggested by Preti (2002:116), call for structural changes that address the extreme inequalities, such as eradicating poverty, increasing democratic participation, redistributing land and wealth through tax reform, and constructing a multicultural society that recognizes indigenous rights. Such solutions will not work without the participation of Mayas and an understanding of Mayan concepts of violence and justice. These issues are far more complicated than I have outlined here. Making such structural changes also stands to fail from the perspective of Ladino business and political leaders. As Lovell (2000) notes, those in power ignore or disregard these structural inequalities.

Mayas have responded to the extreme conditions of la violencia in the 1980s and changes related to the globalization of the economy and politics in ways that were not anticipated by postmodern scholars. Warren's (1998) research on Mayan activism and politics illustrates how the Pan-Mayan cultural movement arose in response to political violence. Mayan leaders rejected violence as a solution to Guatemala's inequalities, along with the rejection of both government and guerrilla politics. Not only did they choose neutrality, they entered the public political sphere with an agenda to radically change Ladino conceptions of Mayan people, build new coalitions based on Mayan cultural values, and strengthen political constituencies to democratically make structural changes. June Nash's 2001 research shows how Chiapan Mayas similarly use global culture, economy, and politics to position themselves against the Mexican government in order to contest national economic and social policies and call worldwide attention to the gross inequalities that plague them. Even more profound are the ways that Mayan women have reorganized their economic and political lives, making connections to international women's organizations and foreign entrepreneurs to change not only their material and political conditions vis-à-vis the Mexican government, but also their respective communities in Chiapas.

Such anthropological research indicates how Mayan forms of political organizing are more complex than simple alliances built on class, culture, gender, or any other singular identity. This is not the same as Ernesto Laclau and Chantal Mouffe's 1985 thesis that other types of identities have taken precedence over class. This can neutralize political subjects because they are too divided by diverse identity interests to form effective coalitions. Instead, Nash and Warren do not erase class or reduce the ways Mayas organize to class or cultural explanations.

Mayan handicraft vendors, in their naming criminals and personalizing crime, organize politically in distinct ways that combine cultural and class-oriented identities. The primary way that this occurs is by repositioning themselves in accordance with what type of political or economic organization they are trying to enlist, modify, or contest. Tourists are presented with cultural-based identities that may draw on stereotyped portrayals of Indians to gain their confidence and warn them about crime. The local government is presented with class identities that downplay culture in order to argue they are valuable participants in the Guatemalan economy.

Rather than fragment into diverse interest groups, which would reduce their political power, vendors are unified in three ways that allow them to use the organizational strategies described above. First, they are unified as vendors through their common experiences of making a living. This constitutes the material conditions of their lives. Second, they are unified by the ways that tourists are fascinated and attracted to them and by the ways government officials and Ladino entrepreneurs are repelled and bothered by their continuing presence in Antigua. Third, they are unified by the common desire and practice of reconstituting their local communities and cultural beliefs. Although this last point may appear to divide the vendors, it does not. This is because, while each town and linguistic group represented by vendors selling in Antigua pursues its unique course and valorizes distinct cultural values or practices, they agree that one's community is instrumental in restoring balance and order.

One vendor explained to me, echoing the sentiments of others:

> There is not much delinquency in indigenous communities. There is internal justice. Indigenous children learn how to work—to cut firewood, to weave, to plant maize, to take care of their homes and families. For those who do not work or do wrong, there is punishment. They are excluded but not forgotten. Their friends and their families know their wrongdoings. They know that by doing what is right they get what they need and want, and they remain a part of the family and the community.

Certainly, this is an ideal perspective, but it is by holding onto such ideals that Mayan handicraft vendors confront the violence of postwar Guatemala to economically and politically position themselves to be safe and earn their livelihoods.

5

Everyday Violence of Exclusion

Women in Precarious Neighborhoods of Guatemala City

Liliana Goldín and Brenda Rosenbaum

Amelia's life epitomizes that of many women living in precarious neighborhoods in Guatemala City and all of Latin America. Her childhood was one of deprivation. Her family lived in a small, rented room, where "they turned the electricity on at 6 p.m. and off by 11 p.m., and there was just a trickle of water coming out of the faucet." She remembers loving school but having to quit after sixth grade because her eyesight was failing. Though her parents had taken her for a free consultation, they never bought her the glasses that she needed to continue in school. Her father was a good provider, she says. He worked hard but was an alcoholic and often did not return home for days at a time. Finally, one day, he left with another woman. That's when the rest of the family heard of the invasion of land in La Esperanza and decided to move there.

> It was 1983 and I was very sad. . . . Everything seemed the same to me. I didn't care. That year my boyfriend had been killed . . . leaving a party; a man shot him. I was with him and saw the man who shot him, but there was nothing I could do about it. . . . That was very difficult for me, and so I decided to move to La Esperanza with my mother and siblings. We made a hut with pieces of wood and sheet metal. . . . I met the father of my children here . . . [and] he was a good friend; he even came to the cemetery with me to bring flowers to my dead boyfriend, and he didn't drink at the time, nor had any vices, and he worked. But then he changed completely. We didn't get married or live together. I became pregnant, but at that time he had already started drinking. I had my first child and was alone with the baby. . . . What hurt me the most was that he wasn't interested in the baby. . . . I worked, I had a salary, and he used to live just a block away, but neither he, nor anyone in his family ever came to visit my baby. It made me so sad . . . and then a few months later I got pregnant again. I also spent this pregnancy by myself. My daughter was al-

ready three months old when we started living together. But often I think it's better to live alone. . . . I left him once.

Amelia's partner would abuse her constantly; he would not work nor contribute to the household and the care of the children. He would get drunk and leave for weeks at a time and then when he returned he would demand her support. After a prolonged absence Amelia asked him to leave for good. She was then expecting her third child. But in spite of such difficulties, Amelia also told us that she had learned much at workshops organized by UPAVIM (Unidas Para Vivir Mejor [United for a better life]), a cooperative in La Esperanza that we describe below:

> I've been lucky to have had the opportunity to attend many workshops. I haven't let him dominate me that much. Because men always say when you leave the home, who knows where you're going. . . . But I don't ask his permission. . . . I just let him know that I'm leaving. I really have benefited from the training I've received here.

Amelia is a well-liked and respected member of UPAVIM, and she has held important positions there. Unfortunately, in the last few years she has faced even more violence in her life, as the father of her children one day simply disappeared—and she doesn't know if he is still alive somewhere, committed suicide, or was murdered. Her 15-year-old son has been repeatedly threatened by the gangs that operate in La Esperanza; and her worst nightmares came true recently when her young teenage daughter and niece were raped in broad daylight by several gang members.

An increase in violence has been documented in all of Latin America since the 1980s, paralleling the effects of the economic crisis, recession, and the execution of neoliberal policies oriented toward the reduction of the size of the state. These latter measures resulted in widespread unemployment, underemployment, an increase in the informalization of the economy, marked pauperization of women and children, and an overall increase in poverty. Analysis of globalization processes in the last 20 years of the 20th century suggest an overall decline in progress in several social and economic indicators associated with income, life expectancy, infant and adult mortality, literacy, and education when compared with the previous 20 years (Weisbrot et al. 2001). While violence affects the entire society, women and children tend to be the most affected as they are usually the most vulnerable sector of society. In this chapter, we analyze the social and economic violence in post-conflict Guatemala in two precarious neighborhoods of Guatemala City. We compare women's experiences with violence and their strategies for coping with it. In an important

Fig 12. La Esperanza from the roof of UPAVIM (Unidas Para Vivir Mejor) in Guatemala City. Photo by Liliana Goldín.

study conducted in Guatemala, among several recommendations for reducing violence in poor areas, Caroline Moser and Cathy McIlwaine encouraged the creation of membership-based community organizations that can provide services to parents and "reconstruct the texture of local communities" that have lost trust and cohesion (2001:10). In our study we show that some women's participation in a membership-based organization strengthens their social, economic, and human capital needed to face some forms of violence, but that this alone is not enough to address other forms of violence. We suggest practical measures that may alleviate this situation in the context of community-based organizations and thus expand on the more global recommendations of Moser and McIlwaine. There is general agreement that there are essential institutional and structural problems associated with poverty that need to be addressed to reduce violence, but those processes are slow and take major state and private efforts. In the meantime, smaller and practical strategies may help alleviate the very serious bouts of violence to which women and children in poor neighborhoods are exposed.

Perspectives on Violence

In order to understand the "conglomerate of violence," we draw from two approaches documented in the literature: the notion of "asset vulnerability"

(Moser 1998), which refers to structural deficiencies due to exclusion from main sources of well-being such as education, health, and good jobs, and the "poverty of resources" model that stands in contrast to a "resources of poverty" model (González de la Rocha 2001). The resources of poverty model emphasizes the complementarity in labor options of household members as a means of confronting poverty. The idea is suggested that very poor people would manage to pool resources to make ends meet. The poverty of resources model, by contrast, acknowledges the changes that urban households have experienced in the context of structural adjustment measures. It recognizes that changes in the economy have deprived many, especially single mothers, of different labor options. Possibilities for survival have been eroded, and this is complicated by the vulnerability and isolation of women and their children exposed to various forms of violence. Moser identified a "gendered continuum of conflict and violence" expressed in political, economic, and social terms (2001:30). We describe here the concerns and complaints about violence mostly focused on social and economic matters and grounded in structural deficiencies of exclusion and inequality (see Moser and McIlwaine 2001). Our emphasis also derives from the findings of Moser (2001) that 50 percent of the reported cases of violence involved social violence, followed by 46 percent of the cases that involved violence for economic reasons.

We try to make sense of the situations encountered by the women with whom we talked in a framework of poverty of resources and in the midst of frequent incidents of gendered violence, as in domestic violence and gang rape. While the murder of women is high and often not resolved, women in our sample had, thankfully, not experienced this directly through the loss of friends or family members; thus we do not include their views on this subject. The affected households have little capital with which to work. This includes social capital, in the form of social networks and support from family members or others; economic capital, expressed in reasonably paid jobs; and symbolic capital, expressed in prestige and authority to extract services, favors, and resources. These households are limited by substantial constraints, not the least being the need for single women to stay near their children and the lack of support networks derived from failing to sustain reciprocity links (Moser 1996). These poor women sometimes have a relative who can help or who can "take" their children. We heard heart-wrenching accounts of this, some of which are described below. The women have the determination and will to "manage" otherwise impossible situations (such as young children taking care of even younger siblings). At times, they have a spouse who may or may not contribute consistently to the household fund. For example, one woman said that her husband did not want her to work because he was "jealous" of her possibly seeing other men. When he found out that she was working a few hours a day, he "stopped giving [her] money" to support the children. Several other women told us stories consistent with this, as they felt their husbands were either idle or not driven to look for jobs and contributed only sporadically to the home. While 89 percent of the women in our sample indicated that their husbands or partners did some work, about 40 percent said that it was their (the women's) responsibility to provide for food, clothing, education, and medical care of the family. Only 36 percent said that their spouses covered most expenses. Men are involved in informal jobs, such as gardening and working in small manufacturing workshops or as assistants to bus drivers. The most common occupations are *maquilas* (workers in export manufacturing) (12 percent) and either plumbers or construction workers (14 percent). All women interviewed felt it was their own responsibility to provide for their children, even at the expense of other sacrifices such as limited supervision. One UPAVIM woman mentioned that, of the 60 members of the cooperative, maybe two or three had "good" husbands, that is, men who treat their wives and children kindly and are responsible providers. Why are domestic violence and male irresponsibility so pervasive? Though we did not pursue this interesting question in our research, we find some suggestions in our data. Both girls and boys are subjected to high levels of violence growing up, and they learn their future roles within that environment. Several women told us that they thought family violence was normal and didn't know that family life could be any different. Furthermore, from the time they are very young, boys are steeped in the ideology of machismo, the glorification of manhood and virility. First, they see it in action in their own homes, as their fathers usually have other women, whether they abandon their families or not. Then, they become further socialized into it within their peer groups, especially during adolescence when they challenge each other to "conquer" women sexually and to drink. Girls, in contrast, learn early on to take responsibility; they are expected to perform domestic chores, care for their younger siblings, and be attentive to the needs of family members. Machismo has deep historical roots in Guatemala. In the context of desperate poverty and lack of access to educational opportunities that might enable people to look at things differently, the vicious circle of domestic violence, alcoholism, and irresponsibility, on the one hand, and women's powerlessness, on the other, is perpetuated. According to an assessment by the U.S. Department of State, Guatemala is a human rights morass (Guatemala Human Rights Commission 2004). The judiciary is inefficient and corrupt; there are constant and increasing cases of discrimination and violence against women, abuse of children, discrimination of persons with disabilities and indigenous peoples, and threat to labor rights, including widespread use of child labor. In the first eight months of 2004, 317 women had been murdered (García 2004:5; Lara 2004:12). In addition to an increase in informality, growth in low-wage export manufacturing, a decrease of employment in agriculture, and an expansion of the private over the public sector, there is no question that the current level of violence is connected, in part, to the 36-year armed conflict. Machismo, racism, and other expressions of authoritarianism are reinforced in an oppressive political system. The atmosphere during these four decades, where violence was the habitual pattern of response, lingers on. Every time a woman complains of violence perpetrated against her, she runs the risk of more violence. Institutions do not yet have the ability to act swiftly and protect women from possible reprisals.

There is little doubt that public policy needs to focus on strengthening the infrastructure of communities where poverty is concentrated. In our chapter we examine the access to social and economic capital and the constraints of living in areas with limited services and controls. Some women in the two communities have joined the membership-based nongovernmental organization UPAVIM, which seems to provide a source of trust and support and a source of labor and child care for many women. By comparing the way women in the two communities structure their access to various forms of capital and cope with the many shortcomings and direct risks encountered in their communities, we assess the impact of the association on the strategies available for managing the violence of everyday.

Precarious Neighborhoods in Guatemala City:
La Esperanza and Villa Lobos II

Consistent with the composite of violence and poverty, and as some of our examples show, children who grow up in precarious neighborhoods in the midst of violence tend to reproduce these patterns when they grow up. The same hopelessness and violence at home are seen by inhabitants of precarious neighborhoods as the major causes driving young people to drugs and delinquency in the form of gangs (AVANCSO 2000:56; see also Thompson 2004; Burrell, this volume; and Benson and Fischer, this volume). Gang violence is one of the worst plagues afflicting Guatemala at this time. There are 90 *maras* (gangs) in Guatemala City (AVANCSO 2000:50), and they are responsible for 80 percent of gun-related deaths.

For six months in 2001, we conducted research in La Esperanza and Villa Lobos II, two *colonias* (marginal neighborhoods) that originated as squatter settlements bordering zones 11 and 12, south of the Guatemala City center. Brenda Rosenbaum has been visiting La Esperanza and doing participant observation and interviews with members of the UPAVIM cooperative since the mid-1990s. With the trust of many women in the cooperative, we were able to have many conversations with several women on the topic of violence. We designed a survey to be administered in the two colonias. The survey instrument is solely based on the issues and problems raised by the women with whom we talked and salient to the communities. In addition, we included numerous questions on labor and economic well-being with the intent of addressing the impact of the cooperative on women's lives. Two university students, a man and a woman, carried out the survey and visited the neighborhoods together during daylight hours, for safety.

Land invasions began there in 1959 and continued until recently. Many of the invasions led to the occupation of land in hills and at the border of ravines. La Esperanza is an established settlement about 16 to 20 years old and has UPAVIM, a voluntary, nongovernmental organization (NGO) for women, and a couple of government organizations involved in housing, water projects, and women's reproductive health. Due to the extended history of the settlement, La Esperanza has basic services such as running water, drainages, paved streets, and transportation, which are lacking in many of the most recently settled colonias. It suffers from high rates of crime and the presence of youth gangs. Accounts of people who had someone they loved hurt or killed during a robbery or on the streets or raped by several gang members are common. Fear and insecurity are prevalent.

The second settlement studied, Villa Lobos II, is located approximately 2,500 meters from La Esperanza and was occupied in the last six to ten years. Services are limited, with access to water limited to a few hours per day. Electricity is shared by groups of about 20 households, streets are unpaved, and there are no drainages. For example, while 46 percent of people in La Esperanza use a latrine rather than toilets, 74 percent of people in Villa Lobos II use a latrine. Income ranges in both communities are between 1,000 and 3,000 quetzales per month or approximately US$125 to US$370. Villa Lobos II has received little attention from government and nongovernment organizations, and many women are unemployed and identify themselves as "housewives." While 41 percent of women in La Esperanza identify their main occupation as housewife, 57 percent of women in Villa Lobos II identify themselves as such. The population in Villa Lobos is younger (mean age is 33, as compared to mean age of 40 in La Esperanza, with more variability in the latter). La Esperanza inhabitants have a slightly higher level of schooling.

With exception of these two variables (age of women, who tend to be younger in Villa Lobos II, and the overall income, which is slightly higher in Villa Lobos II), there are few differences between the two colonias. More women in La Esperanza report health problems than those in Villa Lobos II, particularly heart problems. This could be due to the age differential. There are slight income differences that may be a consequence of the combined impact of youth; the presence of more married women, that is, more women who can stay home with their children because there is a man who helps support the family; and those who work doing so in better paid jobs. Trends in our data also suggest some religious differences, but these were not statistically significant, with 54 percent of people in La Esperanza reporting to be evangelical and 43 percent identifying as evangelical in Villa Lobos II. We compared indigenous Mayan women in the sample to non-Mayan women, and we found that ethnicity was not associated with degrees of exposure to violence. They share their situation in the city as migrants, mostly detached from family and community networks. Violence of poverty and exclusion touched most of these marginal, poor, urban households, regardless of ethnicity.

We interviewed 200 women, 100 in each colonia, and asked them about themselves and their families, with a focus on labor strategies, labor histories, and support networks. We also conducted 30 in-depth interviews with adult members of 12 households in both communities, both men and women. Here we provide representative examples from the open-ended interviews. We selected accounts that describe various instances of violence, including economic, social, and domestic.

The Association Unidas Para Vivir Mejor, UPAVIM

In the early 1990s a U.S. nurse arrived at La Esperanza with the intention of creating a well-child program. With some mother volunteers, she began a program to measure and weigh infants every month. The goal was to combat infant mortality and malnutrition and to detect problems early so as to give the children a better chance of developing well. However, the impact of extreme poverty and the dramatic lack of resources prevented better outcomes. As a result, she changed the focus of her efforts. She developed a program to enable women to obtain an income. The women began by gluing "worry dolls" onto barrettes and headbands purchased in the local market. With the help of the founder's friends in the United States, they began exporting these products. Thus, UPAVIM was born. Their goal was to work together to lift themselves out of extreme poverty and change their lives and the situation of the entire community.

The crafts program, which supports the services that UPAVIM offers, has been very successful (Rosenbaum 2000:96 ff.; see also Littrell and Dickson 1999:202 ff.). The women sew or put together many different types of products. In 2003, their sales were around $500,000. First, the women depended mostly on networks of family and friends of the U.S. founder, but slowly their products (and their hopeful story) captured the imagination of many and made their way into stores, catalogs, and fairs, mainly in the United States but some also in Europe and Japan.

Early on, the philosophy of the project had a clear social emphasis. Thus, they set up services, largely subsidized by the crafts program, for members of UPAVIM and the community of La Esperanza at large. They established a day-care center that allowed UPAVIM members to bring their children along when they came to work. The day-care center grew into an elementary school with a Montessori focus. Additionally, a medical and dental clinic, a lab, and a pharmacy were also created. UPAVIM also organizes eye-opening talks about women's rights and self-esteem, reproductive health, breast-feeding, child rearing, and other topics of interest to women.

In Their Own Words: Violence of Poverty and Overall Exclusion

Cycles of Violence

The following accounts describe the levels of daily violence and the ways in which it perpetuates itself in the communities. Alcohol abuse is often one of the main causes for abuse.

> When we came to live here my mother was six or seven months pregnant. When my father, who drank too much, arrived home he would beat her. We developed hatred for him, because he drank so much and beat her up so much, and we begged him not to do it. And one day he went to work and he had beaten her in the afternoon. She told us that she had a stomachache. We were so worried! The ambulance took her; she was bleeding a lot. (María, UPAVIM member)

This account was very long. María's mother eventually recovered after losing the baby, but the remaining children spent many days alone, scared and with little food. When María was seven, she was responsible for feeding her younger siblings. When she was twelve, her own mother became abusive toward her:

> She used to grab my hair, and as she shouted that I needed to wash clothes she would smash my head against the cement sink. She would then hit me with the first thing she'd find. I never told her, though, that it would have been better if she had died that day. I still loved her, though.

Describing the overall cycle of violence she was subjected to, she added:

> There was a time when I developed rancor toward her. Just like my father treated her badly, she also became angry and full of hatred. She could not take revenge toward him, so she would retaliate against us. And one day when we were folding laundry she said to me, "Look! This blouse is

dirty," and she threw it at me; and when I kneeled to pick it up she picked up a stick and she broke my nose.

When María, now 20 years old, met her boyfriend at age 16, again she endured punishment and repression, but she valued her boyfriend's love and tenderness, which she had never experienced before: "Nunca tuve una caricia" [I had never been caressed]. After becoming pregnant, she married her boyfriend, but at the time of our meeting he had been killed on the streets of La Esperanza. She wishes she would also die. She works at UPAVIM, where her child attends day care.

The following is another sad example of abuse, insecure and serial marriages, multiple pregnancies and loss of children, and the complex distresses of poverty. Billy's mother divorced his father because he abused her. His mother was the only one to work and bring food, but when he was five years old she became sick and Billy had to move in with his older sister. They were very poor and sometimes they "would not eat all day and sometimes longer." His sister was married to a young man who abused her. Billy says, "I would never want to be a child again." At the age of nine he would go with other brothers to wash cars and then to work with a man who made sheets and bed covers. He worked from 6:00 a.m. to 10:00 p.m. and received 45 quetzales per week (about six dollars). When he was ten he went to live with his mother again, but then it was harder than ever because his older brothers would beat him, and his sister was to the point that one day she tried to kill herself to avoid another beating. His stepfather drank excessively, and they continued to be extremely poor. They often went hungry: "We would share a hard-boiled egg between four of us."

These horrible years improved by the time Billy turned 16. He then met friends who helped him by providing advice and who assisted him in finding his first "normal" job at a Wendy's fast-food restaurant and, later, at Taco Bell. Billy is afraid of getting married and reproducing the same patterns of abuse and neglect of which he was a victim:

> I am afraid of getting married. I don't know how I would be. I am very unsure of myself. I am not a person with strong beliefs, and I don't know how to say this. . . . I don't think I'll treat her badly or that I would beat her. . . . But when I see my brothers fight and mistreat their wives.

His fears are emblematic of the ways in which domestic violence affects several generations.

The story of Billy's mother is even more disturbing, but not unusual. She had several partners whom she left because they treated her badly. She had several children and lost some as well. She left some with her mother because she could not take care of them:

> I gave my mother the children [four children] because I could not take care of them. Then I had another one and then another one, and then I got pregnant with a baby that died, and another one who also died. And then I was pregnant and hoping for a girl, but God first let me have her and then he took her away. Next, I was pregnant with twins and they also died, and finally I had her and had to spend the whole pregnancy in the hospital.

She recounts the problems she had with each of her partners, who had various jobs as janitors. She also told us how she left one when he became abusive: "I could not stand him. If I could, I would have become a poisonous snake and I would have killed him, because not even [by] killing him could I forgive what he did to me." She took on numerous jobs, including washing clothes and being a construction worker's helper. Then, she said she had an accident and her breast became infected. When she went to the hospital she was told she needed surgery, but she refused to have the surgery because she had no one to watch her small children: "What will they eat if I have surgery?" She covered her breast with cloth, and one day she cut open her breast with a knife "to remove the infection." She was soon overcome by fever. The next thing she recalled was finding herself in the care of the nuns of Mother Teresa. Her children had been placed in an orphanage, and she had been gone for almost one year. Later, she got her children back and took numerous menial jobs as a laborer, a cook, and a vendor. She had worked so hard that her "body got tired and an ulcer blew up inside" of her. During this time her children stayed with her oldest daughter, just as Billy had told us earlier. After many health problems, she joined a neighborhood committee and ended up working for UPAVIM: "My life has had highs and lows. When I fall, I get up again; I fall down and I get up. I built the house in small steps. I hope my children will appreciate what I have done for them."

Violence of Maternal Anguish and Lack of Spousal Support

Nothing is worse for a mother than not being able to provide for her children. Accounts are common of women who complain that their husbands are often out of work, only look for certain types of jobs, and otherwise expect their wives to provide for their children. Women often say that making sure the children get to school or are dressed is their responsibility. The man's contribution, if any, may be to pay for some of the food. Rosa (21 years old) said:

I always worked. He stopped working several months, and I told him that I would rather be alone than continue the way we were. I can use the money to support my daughter rather than supporting him. Also, he was jealous of anybody around me and complained if I returned late from work.

Rosa finally left him. However, his family refuses to give her back her baby daughter. Her mother-in-law tells her that it is best for the baby to be with them, as she works full time in the maquila or *maquiladora* (a factory or assembly plant). Rosa struggles with great ambivalence. She wants to have her baby back, but she also knows she has little time to care for her. As she asks the police to help her recover the child, she wonders if that would be best for the baby.

Another mother is a maquiladora worker in Villa Lobos II. She is 38 years old and has lived in seven different colonias; she has been in Villa Lobos now for eight months. She says:

> I am not an exemplary mother. I just don't have the time. . . . I have to leave them unsupervised most of the time, but I would like to be able to spend more time with them. At least I provide them with food. If I limit the hours I work, I would have limited food to give them. Maybe here is where I am failing. I put more effort in the job than in them. They are my life. They need me more. But I feel I give them everything I can.

In the following case, we see the same scenario from the perspective of a grandmother taking care of her grandson, whose mother works in the maquila:

> I have had my 12-year-old grandson full time since he was one month old. His mother was alone. She was actually married, but her husband drank too much and she left him. But she had to work and could not take care of her son. So she left him with me. She sells tortillas in La Esperanza.

Violence of Sexual Inequities and Patriarchy: Domestic Violence

Marina's life illustrates the vulnerability of women living in precarious areas such as La Esperanza. Her life changed drastically when her mother died. Marina was 15 or 16 years old at the time and her mother had always been her support, paying for her studies and having great dreams for her daughter. But when her mother died, Marina no longer had any support in the family. Her father and older brothers would bring friends home and they would all get drunk. Marina, the only woman in the house, was afraid that they would rape her. This was the main reason she left with her children's father when he asked her to go with him. Unfortunately, her situation did not improve. They lived with his mother. Some time later, Marina had twin girls. Her mother-in-law ran a bar in the house, and there were men around drinking all the time. She again feared for herself and now also for her babies. Her husband also would drink, and so did his mother. When drunk, they often would start fighting with Marina and then kick her out of the house with her children. She had nowhere to go. Then someone told her about UPAVIM. Marina became a member immediately. She would take her twins to the day care and work sewing handbags. Though her income was limited, she was happy that there was a place where she could work while her children were taken care of. She liked not having to depend on her husband's income.

After two years, Marina had another daughter, Katy. She was born with a serious heart defect, a problem that required immediate attention, but there was no help available in Guatemala. Upon learning about the baby's situation, UPAVIM's advisor contacted international programs to see if she could get the life-saving surgery for Katy. It took some time to find a place, a doctor, and a means of transportation. Finally, Marina and her baby left for New York to get the surgery. The baby was already nine months old. But the doctors determined that the baby would die on the operating table. It was too late to save her life. While she was in the United States, Marina's twins stayed with their father. He would call her long distance from UPAVIM and demand that she return because the twins had become sick with asthma. He would harass her on the phone, saying that she was just having a good time with other men and that she would pay the consequences upon her return. Her friends at UPAVIM urged her to stay in the United States and try to save her baby's life. They took care of the twins at UPAVIM during the day and went to their home in the evenings to give them their medications.

When I was there [in the United States] jealousy was killing him. And you should have seen what kind of reception I got upon my return! He was fighting with me; he told me horrible things, and that I was worthless . . . [and] that I had lovers . . . [and] all I could do was cry. He had been drinking a lot. I came back and I needed support and he treated me like that. . . . Sometimes when I'm not paying attention, he will throw me a punch and I get hurt. I have to try to dodge his blows; it's all I can do. Lately he thinks I have something to do with his younger brother. I can't be happy anywhere I am because he is jealous of everyone—even my father and my brother. . . . Here at UPAVIM we have to run errands, but he won't let me. . . . When he is sober I tell him how he's treated me when he was drunk and he apologizes. But he says he can't control it, that this is who he is, and that he is just very jealous.

Marina now has five children and her life continues to be difficult. She earns some money sewing at UPAVIM, but hardly enough to support five children. She owns her land and now has leverage vis-à-vis her husband—he can no longer oust her in the middle of the night. She says she feels that UPAVIM is her home, her children are in good hands at the association's school, and she has friends there that give her support.

Many of the women we interviewed spoke of similar difficult conditions. Evelina says:

> After eight years of marriage I became pregnant. I was working at a factory then, and his family said that this child wasn't my husband's. When my daughter was born, he arrived at the hospital and began to unwrap her. The nurse asked him, "What are you doing, sir?" "I'm looking to see if this baby is my daughter." . . . Then he started screaming that he wasn't the father, and I was so sad.

She told us that for many years she has feared that her husband would rape their oldest daughter. He still insists that he is not her father, claiming that this girl is too dark and that there is no way he could have fathered her. With support from the other women at UPAVIM, Evelina went to the Office for Human Rights and accused her husband of drunkenness and domestic violence abuses. The police came and took him to jail for a while, but he returned.

Carmela was able to get rid of her husband for good by insisting he leave with the new woman he was seeing. She even helped him gather his things together and gave him her blessing to leave with the woman. He had been abusing her, and later their eight children, ever since they started living together. When she became a member of UPAVIM and went out to meetings and work, he would beat her up and threaten to kill her and the children. Carmela said:

> I used to think, "This is my fate, and there's nothing I can do." I had not awakened; I lived in ignorance. I let my husband beat me up, take my money, and go around with other women. I thought that's the way it was; a woman and a man together lived like that. . . . Every time I became pregnant, he would beat me up and threaten me, force me to take pills and herbs to abort my baby. [Rosenbaum 2000:100–101]

Attending talks on women's rights and self-esteem at UPAVIM made her realize that she was a valuable human being who did not deserve this abuse.

A Strong Organization within a Weak State

Participation in a membership-based organization has helped women in some areas. The association gives women some control over their difficult situations through consciousness-raising about their rights and an atmosphere where they are encouraged to fight abuse and appreciate themselves. And they can count on a regular income and good child-care facilities. Women not associated with the organization tend to work outside their homes, often in the maquilas, and express frustration and anguish at having to leave their children. The association seems to have given women a sense of community often missing among women not associated with it. The latter often said they felt that they were alone with their problems and that there was nowhere to go for help. As illustrated in several of our examples, UPAVIM women felt an implicit commitment toward the membership. Cooperative members serve as support pillars for each other. The provision of child care and the strength women gained (through education and increased self-esteem) to break away from cycles of abuse seem to be among the great successes of the organization. But the organization can do very little against the violence associated with alcohol addiction and the group violence of boys and men under the disguise of manhood, machismo, and street gangs.

Inhabitants of the settlements, researchers, and women's rights advocates propose several measures to reduce the incidence of violence. In the AVANCSO (2000:69) study of three precarious settlements, people in the communities suggested repressive measures as a way to confront the violence of maras—such as demanding the presence of the police and soldiers in their communities and even, in the absence of these, taking justice into their own hands. However, people also stressed the fact that families in these neighborhoods face enormous challenges and that the breakdown of the family can be held responsible for most of the problems in these communities. They proposed the creation of programs by the government and churches to strengthen families, improve communication between parents and children, and discourage the use of alcohol and drugs. Having a harmonious family life and offering young people training and jobs would diminish their attraction to maras.

Moser and McIlwaine's study on community perceptions about violence concludes with the following list of steps to reduce violence: (1) Rebuild trust in the police and the judicial system; (2) attack the problem of alcohol abuse; (3) reduce society's tolerance for family violence; (4) limit the spread of drug consumption; (5) transform maras from perverse organizations into productive ones; and (6) develop sustainable community membership-based organizations (2001:152). Based on our interviews, and on a less costly and more practical level, we would add the development of "don't walk alone" programs, which may help girls and women to get to their jobs and classes in the evenings, and training in neighborhood watch strategies, which may prevent the gang actions so common every day at dusk. Some form of volunteer services for evening transportation for adolescents and adult women may also address important concerns.

Women's and children's rights advocates in Guatemala emphasize the need for a concerted effort, a national campaign to effect changes in the ideology of machismo that propitiates and tolerates forms of violence against women and children. The state must develop the institutional capacity to respond to domestic violence, first, by defining all the different forms of physical and psychological abuse against women and children, by keeping rigorous statistics on it, and by designing programs to make it visible and fight against it. Programs to support families at risk and to rehabilitate women and children who are victims of domestic violence also are needed (Jurado 2000:13).

UPAVIM has countered vulnerability on several fronts, including jobs, child care, health, and education. UPAVIM has had an impact in the area of women's empowerment. Through the years, UPAVIM members have become keenly aware of the culture of machismo and the realities of discrimination against women in Guatemala. Many spoke about arguing with their husbands, not asking them anymore for permission to do what they need to do, or standing up and defending their rights. Many have learned about the legal proceedings to confront domestic abuse at home or to get child support. UPAVIM is a place where women support one another in finding the information and the solidarity they need to deal with their problems.

UPAVIM members also have become empowered through the process of working together in a self-governing cooperative. Though UPAVIM does not participate in political activities per se, the groundwork for their future participation has been laid by their experiences in democracy. UPAVIM has reached out to work with the surrounding population, thus creating important networks that reach far and wide, including other parts of the world.

Despite the positive benefits, there are limitations to the work any such organization can carry out. There is no question that a strategy to combat violence at both the family and community levels must take into account all of the structural and cultural factors mentioned above. It is limited in its scope as an NGO operating only in a specific colonia. It cannot substitute for the necessary governmental attention to the serious problems in these communities. The people's insistence on a strong policing of crime and violence and on the enforcement of existing laws in the fight against gang violence—or, alternatively, their threat to take the law into their own hands—is thus understandable. However, in the absence of governmental intervention, NGOs like UPAVIM can have an impact in transforming the conditions of vulnerability of the inhabitants of these settlements. While UPAVIM could become a model for an organization that tackles aspects of vulnerability of women in precarious neighborhoods, the scope of the problem is such that there is little hope of achieving major changes at the broader level without the full involvement and commitment of the state.

6
Bilingual Bicultural Education
Best Intentions across a Cultural Divide
Judith M. Maxwell

Tijonel: Achike rub'i' re jun chiköp re'?	Teacher: What is the animal called?
Tijoxel: Tz'i'!	Student: Dog!
Tijonel: Ja', ke re'. La k'o jun pa awuj?	Teacher: Yes, that's right. Do you have one on your card?
Tijoxel: Ja'. Xich'akon!	Student: Yes. Bingo!

Yes, Kaqchikel Bingo has come to Guatemalan classrooms. This is a breakthrough on several levels: using an indigenous language in the classroom by teachers and students, using didactic materials in a Mayan language, and moving bilingual education from a transitional to a life-complement model.

The Good News (beyond Bingo)

As the government of Guatemala was signing the Acuerdo sobre Identidad y Derechos de los Pueblos Indígenas (Accord on Identity and the Rights of Indigenous Peoples [Saqb'ichil/COPMAGUA 1996]), the Ministry of Education was making PRONEBI (Programa Nacional de Educación Bilingüe-Bicultural [National Bilingual-Bicultural Education]) into DIGEBI (Dirección General de Educación Bilingüe-Pluricultural [General Directorate of Intercultural Bilingual Education]). This made bilingual education a permanent part of the Ministry of Education, rather than a temporary or stopgap program. Earlier bilingual education philosophies which envisioned the apparatus for teaching in indigenous languages as transitional, withering away in the full light of a totally (possibly monolingual) Spanish-speaking populace, were replaced with a system of education promising Mayan children access to schooling in their heritage languages. DIGEBI has had an all-indigenous directorate since its inception. Within the workplace they have moved not only to prepare materials in Mayan languages for distribution to schools, but also to speak what they preach and teach. Signage in the building is primarily in a Mayan language, often K'iche'. All announcements and formal letters sent from DIGEBI offices include a salutation and closing in a Mayan language. Employees, regardless of ethnicity and descent, are encouraged to speak Mayan languages in the workplace to one another and to greet the public in a Mayan language. Classes and teaching materials are provided to help nonspeakers acquire a modicum of understanding of a Mayan language, if not fluency. The DIGEBI webpage provides a news story on the Kaqchikel class for their Spanish-language-dominant staff (see http://www.mineduc.gob.gt/administracion/dependencias/centrales/digebi/digebi.htm).

Just after the Acuerdo sobre Identidad y Derechos de los Pueblos Indígenas was signed in 1995, the Guatemalan Congress passed Governmental Accord 726-95, which affirms that girls as well as boys have a right to education, though an education tailored to girls' needs: learning about nutrition, hygiene, homemaking, sewing, cooking, providing a healthy environment for their children, and family planning. The Instituto Lingüístico of the Universidad Rafael Landívar designed, wrote, and translated into the majority Mayan languages a storybook/pamphlet recounting the story of "Manuela," a young Mayan girl who goes to school. In 1997 the program became the Seminario Nacional de Educación de la Niña, gaining United Nations sponsorship. The number of girls enrolled in grade school and continuing each year has steadily increased.

Also in 1995, Kaqchikel Cholchi', the Kaqchikel branch of the Academia de las Lenguas Mayas de Guatemala (ALMG), sponsored a neologism project. For the better part of a year, I worked with a team of three linguists, Ixcha'im Son Chonay, Ixkusamil Simón Apén, and Ixim Nik'te' Rodríguez Quiej, devising words that could concisely and transparently handle the topics of grades 1 through 4. Kab'lajuj Tijax, Lic. Martín Chacach, of the Instituto Lingüístico of Universidad Rafael Landívar monitored the project, dropping in twice a month to provide an independent judgment on the appropriateness of the lexical items and on their congruence with traditional Mayan tropes, cognitive categories, and worldview. A draft list of the vocabulary for the four basic school subjects, natural science, social science, language, and mathematics, was then submitted to a panel of community leaders, teachers, and day-keepers (ritual practioners). Words that seemed obscure or had tortuous derivations were rejected, revamped, and then resubmitted. Finally, an assembly of linguists and educators was called, including speakers of all nine K'iche'an languages. The lists of new words were disseminated to all participants, and cognate forms in each language were devised. These new words not only made it possible to teach all the basic subjects in elementary school without recourse to borrowings from Spanish and English, but also, by using cognate bases, reinforced the sense of unity and identity within the language group.

Also in 1995 PRONADE (Programa Nacional de Autogestión para el Desarrollo Educativo [National Program for Educational Development]) was set up with funds from the Center for International Private Enterprise (CIPE) and Entwicklungsbank. This program put the responsibility for building the schools, hiring the teachers, and overseeing the curriculum and instruction in the hands of local boards made up of parents and community leaders. In 1997 financing was decentralized, putting funds directly in the hands of the local committees. New schools sprang up quickly. By 2001, PRONADE had schools in 20 of the 22 departments of Guatemala. The year 2005 saw the addition of another department. The stated goal of PRONADE is to ensure that at least 70 percent of elementary-school-age children are attending classes. By 2005 this goal had been reached in all participating departments except Alta Verapaz (World Bank 2005). The World Bank's PRONADE report also notes, however, that "departments with the highest proportion of indigenous population have been slower in achieving full coverage" (World Bank 2005:5). Nonetheless, by 2003, 87 percent of the children in the targeted age group (7 to 14 years old) were in school, though all were not in their age-appropriate grades.

In 1998 the Ministry of Education inaugurated a new project: Edumaya. Edumaya replaced an earlier initiative by Universidad Rafael Landívar (PRODIPMA—Desarrollo Integral de la Población Maya de Guatemala [Program for Integral Development of the Mayan Population of Guatemala]), which ran from 1987 to 1993. PRODIPMA worked with basic literacy efforts, but also sought to train a cadre of Mayan scholars as professionals: doctors, lawyers, and business administrators. Edumaya was a similar government effort, with a heavy emphasis on training bilingual educators. The Universidad Rafael Landívar, with funding from the Agency for International Development (AID), collaborates in this effort, supplying a physical plant, teachers, and instructional materials.

Over the next several years, the Ministry of Education sought to increase its direct coverage as well, building schools in rural communities which formerly lacked them, adding grades 4 through 6 to grade schools previously truncated at grade 3, providing for more middle and high schools in non-urban areas, and establishing new technical and normal schools. In 2002, 17 new normal schools specializing in bilingual education were opened. In 2003 another 7 such teacher-training institutes were founded.

In 2001 and 2002 the Ministry of Education stepped up its in-service training programs for the teachers in the national school system. Plans called for "professionalization" of the teacher corps. Teachers were given half-day classes once a week or bimonthly (depending on the district). A major goal of these classes was cultural sensitivity training. Mayan culture and snippets of Mayan languages were taught in an effort to increase respect for the Mayan culture among the non-Mayas and pride in that heritage among the Mayas as well as to counteract disinformation, negative stereotypes, and common misconceptions held by all. However, this professionalization met with resistance. Juan de Dios de León López, regional supervisor for Sacatepéquez, reported (personal communication, January 30, 2003) that teachers complained about the lack of training or real understanding shown by their instructors. Mayan teachers felt they were being talked down to and misrepresented. Non-Mayan teachers felt they weren't given enough data with which to work and weren't taught enough language to be useful. Two non-Mayan teachers recounted their "language class" (anonymous personal communications): the instructor taught them to count to three in Kaqchikel and then told them to do the rest of the numbers to ten (not the vigesimal base 20 of Mayan languages) on their own. Frustrations ran high. But the professionalization program was not the only bugbear. Classrooms were often under-stocked; promised materials never arrived. The government school meal plan that provided needed dietary supplements for schoolchildren had been suspended. In January of 2003 the teachers went out on strike. They stayed out for 52 days, demonstrating in the capital, meeting with parents to explain their motives and problems, and running their own workshops. The teachers demanded improvements for their classrooms, access to the curricular materials developed by the Ministry of Education, distribution of these to all the schools, and some attention to the dietary and health needs of the students (especially in rural areas). They also asked for pay increases and adjustment of the sliding pay scale, recognizing time in service. Moreover, they asked that the professionalization not just be a token nod to political correctness, but that "Education Reform be put into practice that responded to both the spirit and the letter of the Peace Accords from which it was born" (Acevedo 2003). This included asking for real language training for those teachers in schools in Mayan-language-dominant areas who were not fluent in the language of their charges.

Also in 2003, the Ministry of Education was about to launch a new school curriculum. This curriculum had been designed by SIMAC (Sistema Integral de Mejoramiento y Adecuación Curricular [National System for the Improvement of Human Resources and Educational Curriculum]). A team of educators composed of international experts and Mayan scholar–educators devised a total curriculum for kindergarten through grade 12 that would be multicultural, celebrating the diversity of Guatemala's cultural heritage. The first textbooks at all levels were drafted in Spanish, the language held in common by the committee, but these materials would be translated into the Mayan languages of Guatemala as well as, eventually, Garífuna. As a first step in this translation process, neologisms were again to be created. Initially, DIGEBI sought to provide the necessary vocabulary to translate the books needed for the 13 language groups with at least 1,000 children attending government schools. However, due to lack of recruitable personnel, only 11 languages were included in the project: Q'anjob'al, Popti', Akateko, Q'eqchi', Poqomchi', Poqomam, Kaqchikel, K'iche', Tz'utujiil, Ixil, and Mam. I worked with this group for three months, moving through the curricular levels from kindergarten through grade 12. As with the early neologism project, proposals for new vocabulary were vetted by the group, allowing cognate bases and word formation strategies to be used. Validation of the proposed words was ongoing throughout the project. The neologists traveled to the regional offices of the Ministry of Education, sharing their proposals with the linguists working with the local schools and with the educators in the main offices. They also consulted regularly with the regional branches of the ALMG. Once the entire list of words, slightly over 2,300 lexemes) was created and had passed these initial inspections and revisions, the process of validation moved to the communities. Educators, students, and community leaders were invited to five-day workshops to review and approve or emend the lists. Each group took the task to heart, revising, arguing, and expanding the lexicon as related semantic fields required similar bolstering. The K'iche' group worked 17 to 18 hours a day to complete their task; the Tz'utujiil group went into extra days of meeting; all completed their revisions and approved the new set of words.

In 2004 DIGEBI finished their pilot CD and manual for teaching Kaqchikel as a second language (Maxwell et al. 2004). This CD with an accompanying CD player is to be distributed to teachers in government schools within the Kaqchikel area who do not speak the language of their students. The original Kaqchikel course is being used as a model to produce similar materials in Mam, Q'eqchi', and K'iche'.

In-service training continues for teachers in areas with majority Mayan populations, helping teachers, those who are speakers of the local language and those who aren't, to incorporate elements of Mayan culture in the classroom. Materials produced by the Instituto Lingüístico of the Universidad Rafael Landívar, by the Edumaya program, and by DIGEBI are distributed freely to the rural area schools. While DIGEBI is but 1 of 19 divisions of the Ministry of Education, Mayan education is also addressed in part by SIMAC and is the central concern of PRONADE.

The Bad News

Inevitably, economics is part of the bad news. Guatemala spends less than 2 percent of its GNP on education (Mingat and Winter 2002). Though in 2002 the Ministry of Education opened 17 normal schools for bilingual education and in 2003 added 7 more, there is still a shortage of bilingually trained teachers as well as bilingual classrooms for them. The projection for 2005 is to add 3 more normal schools and to increase the attention paid to interculturality (see http://www.mineduc.gob.gt/administracion/dependencias/centrales/digebi/digebi.htm).

Personnel are a big problem. DIGEBI is charged with providing bilingual education to all students speaking the 22 Mayan languages officially recognized by the government, but it cannot find native speakers trained as linguists and educators who can develop adequate materials in all these languages. The "big four" languages, Mam, K'iche', Kaqchikel, and Q'eqchi', have not only more speakers, but more trained linguists, educators with advanced degrees, and computer and graphics specialists. The 2002 neologism project was originally scheduled to include 13 languages, but qualified speakers of 2 could not be found. Similarly, AID-funded texts in Mayan languages produced by the Instituto Lingüístico of Universidad Rafael Landívar are first translated into the big four languages and then spread slowly, if at all, to the other languages.

The new curriculum, approved in 2003 and in the process of translation for the major Mayan languages in Guatemala, is still sadly ethnocentric. While celebrating cultural diversity, it relegates Mayan elements to the range of folklore and cultural patrimony. While working on the neologisms project for DIGEBI, I was disheartened to see the lack of respect for Mayan cosmology evinced by the text. The first kindergarten book, a pre-reader, showed pictures of rural scenes with certain elements anthropomorphized. There were no esoteric words to be cataloged for re-creation as neologisms; the text was wordless. But the teacher's manual instructed the teacher to have the children circle that which was *absurdo* (absurd) (Mineduc, teacher's manual, lenguaje 2003). The intent was to have the children circle trees, rocks, the sun, and other natural elements that seemed to be showing emotion. Mayan cosmology holds that all things in nature are sentient, are living beings. At home, Mayan children are instructed via aphorisms not to leave the *comal* (griddle) on the fire as it will burn and feel pain; they are taught to ask permission of the *rajawal juyu'* (the spirit or owner of the mountain) before chopping wood or hunting animals. To teach the children in school that seeing nature as composed of sentient beings is "absurd" contradicts the basic tenets of their traditional worldview.

This was but the beginning of the examination of the pilot materials for the new curriculum. I contacted my boss, the head of the linguistic division of DIGEBI, Rodrigo Chub' Ikal, and registered my chagrin. He asked me to keep a record of such problems, which he dubbed "impertenencias culturales" [cultural impertinence] (Chub' Ikal, personal communication). My co-researchers and I began a separate computer file for such gaps of cultural approximation. The list grew rapidly. The following are a representative sample.

Stories based on other places and climates

Aesop's tale of the industrious ant and the playful grasshopper is presented with the terms *winter* and *summer* used as they would be in countries with four seasons. In Guatemala, even for Spanish speakers, *winter* is the rainy season, May through September. *Summer* is the dry season, September through April. Of course, this was something that could be gotten around in translation, but it made a difference in how the word *winter* would be translated. It could be translated as "killing cold time" or as "rainy season." The latter would match Guatemalan Spanish usage of the word, but would make no sense in the story. The neologism team simply separated meanings, providing the extant terms for the local climatic conditions and creating terms for the seasons of the non-tropics.

Language conventions that show different social classification

In texts from grades 1 through 4 and in teacher's manuals, children are referred to with the phrase *niños y niñas*. This reflects new political correctness in Spanish. Rather than allow the masculine plural *niños* to subsume both sexes as has been the practice for hundreds of years, speakers and writers are moving to explicit mention of both genders. In Mayan languages there are gender neutral nouns that can be used. That is not a problem. However, if both genders are to be explicitly mentioned, the Mayan convention is always to mention the females first: *xtani', alab'oni'* (girls, boys), *ixoqi', achi'a'* (women, men), *te'ej, tata'aj* (mother, father). The Spanish text always puts the males first.

Lesson plans based on other cultural bases

The math lessons were all designed for base 10, even if set up to teach the numbers in the Mayan languages. Mayan mathematics uses base 20.

Lessons showing Mayan cultural institutions and practices as folklore

Mayan stories are not included in kindergarten or grade 1 lessons, though a section of *pura leyenda* (pure legend) does relate several Guatemalan-based tales. In grade 4, a section on music shows instruments from the pre-contact period, conch shell trumpets, long carved horns, drums; it also discusses the marimba. But it limits the Mayan contribution to music to ancient or folkloric pieces.

Lessons on Mayan religion as polytheistic and supplanted

All supernaturals are labeled *dioses*. Ancestors and spirit-owners of natural features are conflated. Reference to the flourishing modern practice of Mayan spirituality, under the guidance of *ajq'ija'* (day-keepers), is notably absent.

A particularly disturbing element of these materials is that the orthographic system that has been official in Guatemala since 1987 is not used. Instead, spellings follow the haphazard representations found in early translations of Mayan histories or the transliteration to near-Spanish used from the late 1940s until 1987, when the unified alphabet was approved by Congress. K'iche' is written as Quiché. The culture hero Q'ukumätz becomes Gucumatz. Again, these are problems that the translation team can fix, by spelling the forms correctly, but the Spanish version, complete with errors, was to be distributed to the many urban classrooms without a majority Mayan population or with no dominant Mayan language, leaving Spanish as the lingua franca across a polyglot student body.

The list of "impertenencias culturales" was duly forwarded up the administrative chain, reaching the director of DIGEBI, Raxche' Demetrio Rodríguez Guaján. He then spoke with his counterpart in SIMAC. The word soon came back down the line. We could change nothing. The translations had to be *exact* renderings of the Spanish, and the Spanish would not change. Luckily, not everything can be expressed in translation. However, the structure and content of the lessons still presuppose a western European cultural base. The respect offered Mayan culture is a nod to a historic past, a patrimony, rather than an ongoing vibrant element in the national society.

Now, in 2006, the new curriculum has been implemented. Bilingual education materials have been distributed to *rural* (read indigenous) schools, but teachers are often non-speakers or semi-speakers of the languages, unable to use indigenous-language readers. The indigenous-language autodidactic CDs plus Discmans, which were to be distributed to non-Mayan teachers and to Mayan teachers who were not fluent in the language of their school community, never got beyond promotional distribution to AID, the U.S. embassy, UNICEF, and a few of the regional education directors. However, there has been a sea change in the attitude of most rural teachers. Semi-speakers lament their lack of fluency in Mayan languages and are seeking aid on their own to improve their language skills, often with the express goal of being posted in their hometowns. Ladinos express regret at not having the language skills. The principals of many schools within the Kaqchikel-dominant departments have lobbied the regional directors for more and better language training as part of their in-service programming.

The scars of genocide still lie on the land. Huge population shifts have occurred, both directly and indirectly related to the war. Large numbers of Mayas migrated to the capital throughout the 1970s and 1980s. Those who fled napalm, death squads, and civil patrols to lose themselves in the capital generally tried to erase the outer markers of their ethnicity. Most did not teach their mother tongue to their children. The children of these internal refugees are just now receiving attention from DIGEBI. Before stepping down as director, Raxche' Demetrio Rodríguez Guaján began a pilot study of teaching Kaqchikel to monolingual Spanish-speaking children of Kaqchikel descent. The methodologies and materials used with bilingual and first-language Kaqchikel children proved ineffective, and a new vocational training for teachers and materials developers was outlined, though not yet implemented.

Similarly, a large area (1,575 square kilometers) in the Department of Quiché was designated as a municipality for returning external refugees and for internally displaced refugees who had not found safe havens. This municipality, Ixcán, is multilingual and multicultural. Nine Mayan language groups are intermixed within Ixcán, and 70 percent of the inhabitants retain native fluency in indigenous languages. Bilingual education in the area is hampered by the admixture of multiple languages in single classrooms. Teachers have no training in dealing with multilingual classes and so revert to monolingual Spanish instruction, though penalties for the use of Mayan languages on school grounds are not the Draconian punishments the parents of this generation of students experienced. Education within Ixcán is largely limited to primary school education, though not all communities have access to even these first grades. Official estimates place the illiteracy rate at 47 percent within this district.

For most Guatemalan grade school children today, the war is the stuff of their parents' nightmares, not part of their lived reality. But the war has inevitably shaped that reality. For some children, it was the war that brought their families to their current community; it was the war that made speaking Mayan languages a death sentence and extinguished its use even within their homes. For some children, the war disrupted normal family structures, leaving widows as heads of household, earning money in new markets through NGO-sponsored co-ops. These women are determined that their daughters will receive education alongside their sons. Government initiatives like Seminario Nacional de Educación de la Niña, mentioned above, helped foster community support for sending girls to school. In 1994, approximately 75 percent of the primary school-age boys were enrolled, while 67 percent of the same age girls matriculated. By 2004, the gap had narrowed to a scant 4 percent, with 87 percent of the school-age girls enrolled and 91 percent of their male peers matriculated.

As communities and community leaders try to deal with the psychological aftermath of the genocide, they are creating framing discourses for the violence, ways to both understand what happened to the social fabric and position themselves advantageously amidst the post-conflict negotiations of power. Schools are inevitably drawn into this positioning, as they are a primary tool for socialization, enculturation, and creating citizenship. The national curriculum designates each Tuesday as *martes nacional* (national Tuesday). The school day begins with presentation of the nation's flag, the salute to the flag, and all five verses with three refrains of the anthem. However, schools have also been engaged with the Murals for Peace project, in which large stretches of wall along town entrances or around key community structures have been designated as visual testimony sites. Historico-mythic illustrations, largely painted by schoolchildren, map trajectories of these indigenous communities, from an ancient, idyllic, maize-centered past through European contact, evangelization, and armed conflict to a present centered on education and economic gains. Not all war-torn communities have such murals, but all students within the national school system are presented with a vision of a new, unified, multicultural Guatemala, a vision projected by the new curriculum and new textbooks.

Education for All Guatemalans

Dr. Waqi' Q'anil Demetrio Cojtí Cuxil (1987, 1989) wrote that the Guatemalan educational system was designed as an instrument for ethnocide. He indicted each part of the system: the administration, the teachers, and the curriculum. The administration was set up so that promotion within schools and regional directorates and the central supervision were selected largely on the basis of kin networks and cronyism. Mayas were by and large excluded from positions of power, even as principals at the local level. This has changed over time. The self-founded Mayan schools and those founded by PRONADE are almost exclusively staffed by Mayas. DIGEBI has Mayas in all the head offices. Dr. Cojtí Cuxil himself was minister of education under Alfonso Portillo. Resisting the temptation of backlash, he did not sweep out non-Indian administrators and teachers; rather, he strove to be the minister of education for *"todos los guatemaltecos"* (all Guatemalans) (personal communication). This brief Mayan reign was ended with Oscar Berger's appointment of Ing. María del Carmen Aceña as minister of education. In 2008, we have Licda. Virginia Tacam de Tzul as vice-minister of Bilingual Intercultural Education.

Whereas past administrative policy resulted in few bilingual Mayas getting teaching appointments in government schools, the current government is actively recruiting bilingual teachers. From 2001 through 2004, there were 24 new bilingual-intercultural normal schools opened. Prior to the Peace Accords, not only were bilingual teachers seldom employed, but when hired by the government, they were typically sent to communities that spoke a Mayan language other than that of the teacher, assuring that Spanish would be the primary instructional tongue. Now, however, many community committees are hiring their own teachers and the government is trying to place bilingual teachers either in their communities of origin or within the same language area.

Teachers in the past generally prohibited the use of Mayan languages on the school grounds. Maya-speaking parents who have not passed on a Mayan language to their children typically cite the discrimination they faced in school and then in the workplace as a reason for speaking only Spanish to their off-spring (Garzon et al. 1998; Brown 1996; Cojtí Cuxil 1989). In 1990 Dr. Cojtí Cuxil gave a lecture to Oxlajuj Aj, a Kaqchikel Mayan Language and Culture seminar composed of ten Kaqchikel and ten non-Mayan scholars, expounding his theory of ethnocide via education. After his talk, the Kaqchikel man sitting to his immediate left rose, thanked Dr. Cojtí Cuxil for his insights, and then recalled his own school experience, during which both the teachers and his classmates ridiculed him whenever his Mayan background became fore-grounded. This testimony was followed directly by that of the next Kaqchikel seated in the semi-circle. Each of the ten Kaqchikel participants spoke, attesting to the concerted attack on the markers and practices of their ethnicity experienced while they were in school. While some teachers still do prohibit indigenous languages in their classrooms and within the school precinct, others are struggling to learn some words and constructions in these autochthonous "exotic" tongues. The denigration of indigenous language and culture within the school environs has been naturalized to the degree that a teacher (De León, personal communication) in a Kaqchikel village reports that when she occasionally wears *traje* (Mayan dress) her students, all native Kaqchikel speakers, ask her if she actually *likes* such clothing. The school in this village is staffed by five teachers (covering six grades); one of the teachers speaks some Kaqchikel. Three, however, would like to learn. The fifth refuses to even try to pronounce a word of the language. This same instructor sends her students to the principal to be deloused or to have menstruation explained, refusing to touch the children herself, believing them to be polluted and polluting.

The curriculum has come under heavy revisions. SIMAC has attempted two curricular reforms since Dr. Cojtí Cuxil's indictment. The last reform was designed to be truly intercultural, teaching respect for the Mayan, Garífunan, and Xincan cultures as well as fundamental Western knowledge. However, the approach to the indigenous customs and lifeways is essentialist and folkloric. Things Mayan are relegated to a glorious but remote past. The officially recognized spellings of the names of the Mayan languages and ethnic groups are not employed, rather the Spanish-based transliterations persist. Classic histories recorded in Mayan languages during the colonial period appear in upper-level classes, but names and titles of personages and spirits are not given in the indigenous original (nor in the modern transliteration), but are lifted from early Spanish translations.

Fortunato Pablo in a 1989 speech to Oxlajuj Aj listed the characteristics of a culture subjected to neo-colonialism: art is labeled "crafts," religion is called "superstition," and history and cultural practices are termed "folklore." The new intercultural curriculum evinces all of these traits. Mayan weaving shows up not as a life skill for the young girls, nor as the repository of historical knowledge, with designs chosen to reflect major events, nor even as a collection of major cultural symbols, but as a craft, producing pretty and marketable artifacts. Other Mayan art forms, such as sculpting, painting, literature, and poetry, are scarcely addressed. Mayan music is presented only in pre-contact forms, as represented by the murals of Bonampak, Mexico. Mayan cosmology is attacked from the first kindergarten exercises through the simplistic categorization of all spirits as "gods," presupposing a value system in which only monotheism can be true religion. Mayan history and lifeways show up in legend and folklore sections.

Huge advances have been made. The ultimate goal of bilingual education is no longer transition to a monolingual Spanish-speaking nation. Many schools no longer require indigenous peoples give up their languages in order to attend classes. Moreover, some non-Mayan Guatemalans are now considering learning a Mayan language and are exploring the cultures that share their national territory. DIGEBI is supplying teachers in Kaqchikel areas with language-learning CDs and planning similar courses in the other three of the big four Mayan languages. Interested private citizens regularly visit the DIGEBI offices to buy the CD and its manual. The ALMG runs classes in three Mayan languages for people in the capital; many students are of Mayan descent but either are no longer fluent or cannot write their languages, but there are also students of non-Mayan descent. The national university, San Carlos, offers Mayan language courses as well as English, French, German, and Japanese. The Universidad Rafael Landívar and the Universidad del Valle de Guatemala require students with majors in anthropology and in archaeology to study a Mayan language. On December 9, 2004, the Mayab' Nimatijob'al, Maya University of Guatemala, was inaugurated with a Mayan ceremony.

In March of 2003, the Guatemalan Congress passed the Ley de Idiomas, which ratified Mayan languages as official within their linguistic communities. The impact of economic advantages accruing to speakers of Mayan languages is increasing demand for training in Mayan languages, both by native speakers (who are often illiterate in their own languages) and non-natives.

While Guatemala may be moving toward a multicultural, multilingual future, its vision of this future is still blurred by naturalized understandings, the product of 500 years of Spanish language, and Euro-cultural hegemony. Nonetheless, schoolchildren may now be greeted in Maya by their teachers; they may have AID-funded free textbooks in their classrooms; they and their teachers are learning three-verse Mayan-language play-songs from peripatetic DIGEBI language promoters. Teachers and students alike may sport T-shirts that say, "Kojtzijon pa qach'ab'äl! Let's speak our language!"

7

Intergenerational Conflict in the Postwar Era

Jennifer L. Burrell

On October 28, 2003, during the annual *fiesta*, J. M., a young man in his early thirties, was killed by two members of the National Civil Police (PNC), the force charged with keeping order and guarding citizen safety after the signing of the Peace Accords. Police claimed that he was a *marero* (gang member) and a dangerous criminal; after an altercation on the street, the police fired eight shots into his chest and back, also wounding his brother-in-law in the process. He died of these gunshot wounds 30 minutes later. Following his shooting and death, Mayor Julian Mendoza Bautista asked the police to leave Todos Santos, citing concerns for their safety during the most important days of the All Saints Day fiesta, when many people drink to excess and every broken beer bottle becomes a potential weapon. The military arrived the following day to keep order until new police officers were assigned.

This murder, like the rise of *maras* (gangs) themselves, has been the object of local contention and has had an ongoing and polarizing effect in Todos Santos, with conflicts developing between those who believe this killing was unnecessary and others who side with the police, who claimed that they shot J. M. because they feared for the life of a fellow officer. At the crux of this conflict are community anxiety about rising rates of local crime, attributed to gangs, and a lack of understanding about why these young men have chosen this path. The young men themselves talk about the absence in the community of meaningful local roles or work that might take into account the new kinds of experiences, like migration, that they have had.

This state of affairs underscores how the conflict over maras and, by extension, youth culture in Todos Santos is central to the series of changes and ongoing processes of the post–Peace Accords era. In particular, the "youth problem" and what to do about it is rapidly rising to the forefront of national agendas throughout Central America. While intergenerational and age-associated struggles are a general feature of social life and are likely to divide

Fig 13. Main Street, Todos Santos Cuchumatán, July 2006. Photo by Jennifer Burrell.

people, age cuts across the social and economic processes of the post–Peace Accords era in particular ways, creating new divisions (over appropriate behavior and work, for example) and exacerbating others (such as the ongoing dilemma of how to be a respected community member). Equally important to consider is why there has been such a concerted effort at this moment to repress these conflicts in increasingly violent ways.

Criminalizing Generational Conflict in Postwar Guatemala

In this chapter, I explore how age-related conflicts are subsumed into the category of mara locally, while providing larger political, economic, and historical contexts for them. I examine the ways that local struggles over generation are now formed in relation to national and regional postwar anxieties over gangs. These anxieties are used to justify increasingly repressive displays of force, culminating in murder. Ongoing impunity, another factor central to this period, produces distinctive kinds of dialogues between state and local power. Community support for and justification of increasing repression is symptomatic of these relationships.

In the post–Peace Accords period, Rachel Sieder writes, the legal culture in indigenous communities throughout Guatemala consists of "a hybrid mixture of local adaptation and practices and elements of universalist or national legal norms" (1998:107; also see Handy 2004:557). In a post-Accords "irony of power," unexpected alliances are forming in the name of suppressing community youth rebellion (maras) in Todos Santos. Former civil patrollers and guerrillas mobilize under the umbrella of community security, utilizing the older and once state-sanctioned, but now illegal form of *comité de seguridad* (civil patrol). In the past, civil patrols served as a form of local power and a steady connection to the state for rural village men. Despite the fact that revitalizing these committees now brings repeated legal censure, it appears that it is a risk worth taking for Todosanteros. Conversely, the threat of judicial action may be without the teeth of state power, as the committees exercise growing power.

Mara activity, such as it is in Todos Santos, represents a choice for interceding in community processes made by both returning migrants and the young people who are heavily influenced by them. Through their participation in maras, some young men are channeling their education, experience, money, and time to less socially condoned activities, along a path differently weighted with the transnational baggage of images, consumption, style, and actions that surround young people. Gangs in Todos Santos hang out in the street until late at night, hassle one another and drunks, drink to excess, steal, have from time to time had long hair, and are rumored to take drugs. No one would claim that these activities never took place in the town before, but they were isolated or associated with fiestas, for example. Now, however, they are part of the daily lives of many young people.

Life cycles and age-related hierarchies, particularly religious ones such as *cofradías* (confraternity of the Catholic Church), have always been central to contemporary Mayan social life. These are frequently noted as sources of local conflict or the potential for it. Another generational focus of Mayan culture has been the close relationship to the *antepasados* (ancestors), who guide and watch over the living. I suggest yet another trajectory of contemporary generational conflict—how ongoing inequality and structural violence have lead to posing generational conflict itself as a threat.

Historical and Contemporary Perspectives on Maras

The problem of gangs is a postwar anxiety throughout Central America—and gang culture is arguably one of the most visible and brutal but least understood forms of violence following the signing of the Peace Accords in Guatemala. In a front-page article in the *New York Times*, Ginger Thompson recently wrote that "gangs have replaced guerillas as public enemy No. 1" (2004). She continued:

> Over the last decade, gangs have spread like a scourge across Central America, Mexico and the United States, setting off a catastrophic crime wave that has turned dirt-poor neighborhoods into combat zones and an equally virulent crackdown that has left thousands of gang members dead, in hiding, in jail or heading to the United States. (2004)

These groups are seemingly everywhere—in major cities, rural areas, and along borders—filling jails, corrupting youth, lowering life expectancy, and allegedly controlling drug trafficking, among other activities. Attempts to address the gang problem through legal, police, and prison reform have done little to stifle massive corruption among police forces. However, U.S.-influenced policies of zero tolerance and the expansion of the prison complex have contributed to the criminalization of loosely defined delinquency (for example, in Honduras and El Salvador young men with tattoos of any kind are assumed to be gang members and consequently imprisoned). Since the number of young people involved in gangs has steadily increased since the 1980s, despite a lack of reliable data as to the proportion of crime that is actually attributable to them, they have become a primary focus of public attention.

In mid-2003, the National Civil Police (PNC) in Guatemala reported that more than 100 thousand youth, both men and women, between the ages of 12 and 25, belong to different gangs or commit various types of crime. PNC director Oscar Segura sent the report to PAN (Partido de Avanzad Nacional [National Advance Party]) congressional representatives (who were in the process of gathering support for an anti-gang law that would try minors convicted of gang crimes as adults). In 1999, various reports (IADB 1999) measuring violence in Latin American cities noted an increase of homicides in Guatemala City in the years after the signing of the Peace Accords. Commentators (cf. Editorial 1999) attributed this to the increase in gang activity as well as the widespread availability of arms following the war.

Maras first came to public attention in Guatemala in September 1985, when they joined students from a Guatemala City high school to demonstrate against an increase in public bus fares. Over the course of several days, as thousands of teenagers rioted throughout the city, burned buses, and looted stores, the police came to call these groups *maras*. This name was embraced and over the next several years, some sixty maras were formed (AVANCSO 1989). Early urban mareros talked about their maras as fictive kinship groups and networks that often provided support missing elsewhere in their lives, but by the late 1980s their activities had become decidedly more criminal.

When Names Become Things

While regional urban gangs and urban gang violence are relatively well documented (Rodgers 2006; Washington Office on Latin America 2006, 2007), the emergence of rural groups throughout Guatemala is increasingly noted, often in villages that were formerly free of violent crime. Gang activity is often seen as related to military downsizing, which left many ex-combatants jobless and large numbers still armed. While some rural groups have allegedly become involved in drug trafficking and weapons running, what is happening in Todos Santos and in many other rural Mayan communities is a categorically distinct kind of activity from urban gang crime.

Yet the same word, *mara*—slang for and synonymous with the traditional Spanish word *pandilla* (gang)—is often used as a blanket term to describe very different kinds of activities, levels of criminality, and modes of participation, with only occasional distinctions made between urban or rural. As young Todosanteros noted after the death of J. M., using the same word to describe the activities of Mara Salvatrucha—the transnational gang active in Central American capitals and increasingly in the United States—and the locally based antagonisms between two groups of young men in one village is not only misleading but may, in fact, have shaped their activities. Put simply, the extreme local reaction to these groups of youth may have pushed them toward behavior that was more troublesome. Mara Salvatrucha arrived in Guatemala City in 1995. Also known as MS-13, it started in Los Angeles during the 1970s to fight the many pre-existing gangs hostile to Central Americans.

Eric Wolf's warning seems quite prescient in this case: "By turning names into things we create false models of reality. . . . Names thus become things, and things marked with X can be targets of war" (1982:6–7). Indeed, by not distinguishing what is meant by *mara* or, inversely, by insisting that *mara* means particular things, it can now be used to justify virtually any kind of zero-tolerance effort and the gradual remilitarization of rural communities.

The use and circulation of the word *mara*, which originally came from the Brazilian movie *Marabunta*, about the struggle between humans and red ants that devoured everything in their path (AVANCSO 1989), is leading to a set of worrisome local actions. The problem of gangs and the way that it has been unquestionably and solidly linked to youth culture and intergenerational conflict, especially in rural places, have led to a gradual, locally sanctioned and socially supported escalation in the violence used to deal with these groups. In Todos Santos, this includes the imposition of curfews, attempted lynchings, the (re)activation of security committees that closely resemble in both character and range of powers the civil patrols of the war years, and, ultimately, murder. Similarly, Beatriz Manz (2004) has also reported that gang-related activities have led to murder of alleged gang members in Santa María Tzejá. These measures are ostensibly invoked to protect citizens, who support these community-level impositions, and are the local manifestation of national and regional preoccupations with increasing crime, gangs, and anti-gang legislation now emerging (also see in this volume Goldín and Rosenbaum; Benson and Fischer).

Maras in Todos Santos

While urban maras initially tended to attract the poor, marginalized, and disenfranchised, the Todos Santos maras attract quite a different constituency. The young mareros of Todos Santos and other places away from urban areas are well-off by local standards, come from respected local families, attended secondary school outside of the village, and have fathers who are educated, run businesses, are teachers, and may be involved in local politics. Necessity, poverty, or escape from violent families (see Goldín and Rosenbaum, this volume) are not factors for these young men. In short, the original rivals and leaders of the two maras in Todos Santos—the Cholos and the Rockeros—were young men who had had every conceivable local opportunity to advance themselves, as did the young men associated with them. Members of both were well spoken and generally considered intelligent, at least until they started engaging in mara behavior and badly influencing others. In most cases, the labor of these young men as agriculturalists or elsewhere was not vital to the livelihood of their families. In other words, being a member of a gang, which is not a lucrative endeavor in Todos Santos, implies both resources and leisure time. The sons of poor or more economically marginal families cannot afford the leisure time it takes to belong to a so-called mara.

Yet, even given these circumstances, there is no denying the role of structural violence and the sustained lack of decent-paying jobs for young people in Todos Santos and throughout Guatemala and the way that this circumscribes futures, dreams, and desires. These ongoing conditions are symptoms of the lack of redistributive peace that Todosanteros noted when they commented on the signing of the Peace Accords: "We will not have peace until we also have work." Currently, a young man cannot dream of buying property, building and finishing a house, or sending his children to high school in Huehuetenango on the salary of a teacher, which was once considered a prestigious job (see Barrera Nueñz, this volume). Indeed, migration is quickly becoming the only option for most young men and, increasingly, women. The long-term and generational price of this state of affairs ultimately remains to be seen, but children who remain in Todos Santos while their parents work in the United States, returning to the town once every few years to watch Rambo videos with their children, may seek to meet particular needs by joining groups of so-called maras. In contrast, sufficient economic possibilities in other regions of the country, such as tourism, lake transport, export agriculture, and jobs in *maquilas* (factories or assembly plants) keep young men from migrating in such great numbers.

Generations are generally defined through life cycles or historical moments. Traditional civil-religious hierarchies that once ordered lives in terms of cycles have broken down in many places, contributing to fuzziness in terms of age or grade and what one ought to be doing at a particular point in life, roles that were formerly sharply defined. Instead, current generations are defined by the historical moments that have shaped their lives: war and counterinsurgency for parents and postwar and post–Peace Accords for their sons and daughters.

The generation of young adults to which the mareros belong is the first generation to come of age since *la violencia* (the intensification of the Guatemalan military's counterinsurgency campaign in the late 1970s and early 1980s). One of the consequences of this is that while they are "familiar with the local legacies of repressive violence, they have little firsthand knowledge of their parents' struggles for social justice and dignity" (Green 2003:63). The sense of social collectivity once experienced in many highland Mayan towns has been precipitously eroded, although in other ways Todosanteros engage in the maintenance and strengthening of community. Currently, youth strain against patriarchal control that is itself severely diminished in the face of years of war and structural violence. The lives of the current generation of Todosanteros, who are now between 25 and 35, are further bounded by ongoing impunity that has both structural effects—crime may and often does go unpunished—and psychological ones. Lucila Edelman, Diana Kordon, and Dario Lagos (1998) have noted impunity as a new traumatic factor in their work with the children of Dirty War survivors in Argentina. Not only is little or nothing done to achieve the symbolic reparation offered by justice, but impunity is also accompanied by the periodic reappearance of the same types of campaigns that caused trauma in the first place (Edelman et al. 1998:451).

Like the gang members in the Chimaltenango area of Guatemala that Linda Green has written about, mareros in Todos Santos gained access to "a modicum of local power and authority—features of earlier 'traditional' cofradía" (2003:67). However, while Chimaltenango gang members brutalize "their neighbors and kin with the same counter-insurgency tactics utilized by the army—violence, kidnapping and extortion" (Green 2003:67), in Todos Santos it is the community and authorities enacting these tactics to save themselves from the dangerous maras, the out-of-control youth among them.

From Bad Boys to Maras

Prior to 1996, people gossiped about groups of young men who would drink, fight, and occasionally steal, which, at the initial stages of my fieldwork, didn't seem that odd to me in terms of local male behavior. In fact, in a conversation having to do with sharing stories of the past with children, a cultural activist father of a number of sons and daughters commented, "The women have more freedom [*libertad*] to sit with their daughters but men [and boys] always spend a lot of time in the street" (field notes, January 2000). One of the things often done on the street is a visit to the cantina with friends. Public drunkenness on Saturdays after the market and during fiestas is especially prevalent, and this will often lead to fights. However, starting in mid-1996, when I moved to Todos Santos, I began to hear more about maras, and my field notes are sprinkled with comments about them. Mentions of mara activity and what they allegedly did or didn't do were always rather indefinite, talked about in terms of rumors, even (or perhaps especially) by the family of the so-called members. This had *not* been a feature of accounts of youth delinquency that I had heard between 1993 and 1995.

The Selective Use of the Label

I found the talk of gangs disturbing, but from my perspective, they didn't fit into any notions I held or read about gangs, and I wondered why they were called so and what was at stake. In a conversation with J. M. in early 1997, I brought up the topic of the maras and asked him about his alleged leadership of one of the groups. While he denied being a leader of a gang, he acknowledged that he was, in fact, a leader, commenting that some kids respected him and there was nothing wrong with that. With the benefit of hindsight, in this discussion he was, I now imagine, contesting the label of *marero*. However, he easily assumed the role of leader and was candid about the responsibilities and image management that it entailed. I noted in particular how he stressed the importance of protecting his position as leader and his reputation so that he could constructively parlay these into future community roles.

The word *mara*, in this case, seemed to reinforce the most negative aspects of what otherwise might have been understood as youthful rebellion or the legitimate questioning of formations of community-based power that no longer reflected contemporary needs and experiences. That is to say, in a particular local sense, the behavior came to justify the use of the label. Given this, it was practical to utilize the reputation of established and renowned gangs and gang members to provide a mystique for oneself. For example, one strategy J. M. used was to tell newly arrived tourists, especially those setting up businesses or planning to stay in Todos Santos for the long-term, that he was a member of a gang in Los Angeles, where he lived in the United States. He had never lived in Los Angeles, although his rival later lived there. He did not extort bribes, ask for protection money, or insist on free drinks (common practices among the police assigned to Todos Santos), but by mentioning this he situated himself in relation to an internationally known quantity of the category into which he claimed to feel forced. Through his manipulation of this category, he bought, at the very least, recognition, and perhaps even respect (at least among 15-year-old Todosanteros) for his role. As a social actor labeled in a particular way, he skewed and manipulated the category to fit his individual needs. These kinds of strategies and other more serious risks and displays of bravado, such as the murky incident with the police that finally led to his death, are what Roger Lancaster refers to as "the essence of machismo's ideal of manhood" (1992:195), and they contribute to the construction of such "outlaw" identities.

While the mareros' behavior was more youthful rebellion than dangerous criminality—hanging out, drinking, fighting, and hassling drunks on the street in the absence of job opportunities—their influence on youth was vast and mostly talked about as a growing and nearly intolerable lack of respect for their elders and for established forms of municipal and community-based authority. Community members commented that they no longer kept up particular community customs or celebrations because of the maras and their influence.

However, as local social life is increasingly differentiated, particularly due to migration, the one thing that potentially binds people together or unites them in the project of envisioning a common future is shared cultural practice, now under threat by young people and by evangelicals, who refuse to engage in them on religious grounds (see Philpot-Munson, this volume).

Bad Things Happen to Bad People: Escalations of Violence

An escalation in actions against J. M. and his activities continued. By late December 1997, just before Christmas, it was hard to deny the polarizing effect that the maras were having on the town. At the Saturday market on December 20, J. M. was nearly lynched in the town square by a mob that was urged on by the mayor after a confrontation between the two of them.

The mayor, as I recounted in my field notes from that morning, had publicly called J. M. and two other alleged gang members thieves, further commenting on his long hair and stating at some length that long hair on men was bad and set a terrible example for boys in the town. Some people took this as license to attack J. M. Apparently, several people started throwing punches at him; and when his younger brother tried to pull them off, they beat him, too. As the crowds surged around the altercation and more people started to join in beating him, J. M. was dragged out of the park and in front of the town hall, where people threw banana crates emptied on the spot, rotten fruit, and stones at him. Shortly thereafter, he broke free and managed to run the hundred feet or so to the weaving cooperative, where his father is president.

Although cooperative associates and the full-time employee quickly closed the door of the cooperative building and bolted it shut, a large unruly crowd quickly collected in front of it and on top of a bus parked across the street. As the crowd grew increasingly menacing, rumors circulated that there were plans to gather gasoline to burn the wooden building in an effort to force J. M. out. Some villagers went to place calls to the departmental offices of MINUGUA (Mission for the Verification of Human Rights in Guatemala, the UN peace-keeping force), and two other community leaders quickly caught rides to the departmental capital to collect police to help calm the crowds and safely remove J. M.

While this was happening, a friend and teacher walked past me with his son and commented, "Bad things happen to bad people." Shocked by his seem-ingly passive advocacy of what was happening to someone else's son, I turned away and my eye caught a few bloody quetzal notes that had slipped out of J. M.'s pocket when he'd been dragged down the street. Just then, another man directed his young son to pick up the bills. As midday approached, the buses rolled through town to take people back to their hamlets. The crowds dispersed somewhat, but people still remained in front of the co-op, calling for J. M. to come out or for his father to open the door of the building.

All afternoon, small groups gathered throughout the village, discussing what had happened, either supportive of the mayor's actions or strongly against them. One woman commented on what she referred to as the mayor's stupidity and his penchant for speaking unwisely and incautiously in public without thinking about potential repercussions. "One day," she said, "he'll get some-body killed." Others felt that J. M. had needed to be reprimanded, perhaps even publicly, if not quite in this fashion. Continuing to take advantage of the increased number of people present in the town center due to the market, the mayor allegedly issued a petition during the afternoon in an effort to collect 10,001 signatures or fingerprints (approximately 50 percent of the population plus one more) in order to lynch J. M.

J. M. remained in the cooperative until about 9 p.m. that evening, when a truckload of police officers came from Huehuetenango. They removed J. M.

and his father from the cooperative and brought them and two other family members to a hospital in the department capital. On Sunday, the following day, people flooded into town from the hamlets, perhaps to sign the petition or, alternatively, to finish their holiday errands. Although a town meeting was meant to take place in the central park, it did not materialize. Later, the petition was apparently dropped, although no one claimed to know why. Gossip circulating in the town center held that this near-lynching and the events following it were mostly caused by people from the *aldeas* (villages) (like the mayor) and not from the more civilized *centro* (urban center). I immediately thought of the aforementioned incident with the bloody quetzal notes, wondering how individuals construed their own tacit approval in such collective episodes by not using their influence in the community to attempt to put a stop to these incidents.

Following a lull of several weeks while J. M. recovered from his injuries and stayed out of sight, there was an incident that raised the hackles of the community and demolished any sympathy that might have been lingering after the near-lynching. Each year, on the Tuesday before Ash Wednesday, a big picnic is held in a high alpine meadow with various grades of children from the Urbana primary school and their teachers. Parents, tourists, and anyone else who wanted to come along did so. For weeks beforehand, children prepared *cascarones* (hollowed eggshells filled with confetti) that children would break over one another's heads. Buses and trucks were hired to bring everyone up to the meadow and dropped us off along the road where we walked in about one-half mile to an alpine meadow, the picnic site. Children played games, sang songs, and ate specially prepared food. Other carnivalesque activities included hitting one another with socks filled with lime or chalk dust.

After a number of hours, J. M. and a few friends, who had arrived in their own rented pickup truck with several cases of beer (which they had been drinking since they left town that morning), provoked an altercation with some of the teachers that resulted in a fist fight. One of the teachers of the younger children was injured and his glasses were broken in the fight. The children panicked and began to scatter and run toward the road. Terrified, some hid under bushes and behind rocks, and several were lost in the mountains overnight. Once most of the children had made it back to the road and the waiting buses and trucks, J. M. and his friends got into their pickup and began to throw beer bottles into the opened trucks. After they reached town, various teachers and parents ran to the town hall to report what had happened and file complaints. At one point, an older Ladino man I'd never seen before walked in to the street and started firing a gun. He apparently wasn't aiming at anyone in particular; rather, he seemed to be making a symbolic gesture. Shortly after this incident, J. M. returned to Michigan. The next we heard, he was in a hospital in Michigan, having been injured in a knife fight with another Todosantero at a bar in Grand Rapids.

Community Responses

In 1999, the PNC assigned several agents to Todos Santos and residents were happy to receive them, although some local business owners complained about the *multas* (fines) they were constantly required to pay. In late February and early March 2003, Mayor Julian Mendoza was called down to the departmental capital to meet with a supreme court judge, this time for the illegal actions of newly formed *comités de seguridad* (*Prensa Libre* 2003a, b, c, d). These committees, operating much as the civil patrols did during the 1980s and '90s, imposed and enforced a local curfew and were apparently clandestinely imprisoning their captives, holding people for up to several days with no legal recourse or rights. Mayor Mendoza claimed that that comités were necessary because of the forty gang leaders (although Todos Santos would be hard pressed to produce forty gang *members*) operating in the municipality. The reporter writing about the initial incident mentioned "how curious" it was that these comités operated in much the same way as the old civil patrols but without guns. Instead, they carried *lazos* and *látigos* (ropes and whips).

I asked Todosanteros about these comités, which many supported, seeing them as proactive and necessary in the community's ongoing fight to combat petty crime committed (mostly against each other) by young men: "What are these clandestine jails?" "*Community jails,*" I was told. "Where are they?" I wanted to know. "Usually in the outhouse—at the school or at someone's house, wherever," I was told.

In May 2003, this committee apparently threatened a local judge with death upon disagreeing with a one of his judgments. The judge reported that, fearing for his life following the threat, he now had to clear all of his decisions with the committee before making them public (GHRC 2003). At the end of this trajectory of escalating repression is the account with which I began this chapter, the murder of J. M.

Mareros in Chimaltenango, Guatemala, have learned that "the only power available to local men—since all others have been and continue to be repressed—is both the real and symbolic power of the gun" (Green 2003:67). As a result, they have developed ties to military and paramilitary networks of guns and drugs. In this region, where the acts are truly criminal (gun running, drug trafficking) and the threats are deadly, neighbors have not organized to patrol the streets, enforced curfews, or clandestinely jailed one another. In Todos Santos, the threats are of a different register altogether, and a different kind of dia-

logue is taking place about forms of local power and the state in relation to ongoing impunity and in relation to the past. But the stakes in Todos Santos and
the risks involved in regulating youth in such a way remain obscured.

Power Nostalgia

Among middle-aged Todosanteros, who are now reaching the time in their
lives when they might have taken on increased responsibilities, earning respect
from younger villagers, there is nostalgia for former structures of authority—
the very forms that were contested by those who ended up joining Catholic
Action as a way to address generational inequality and the tyranny of geron-
tocracy. Despite the economic costs and the strict hierarchies enforced through
these systems and some of the consequences, there seems to be a yearning
for the idealized kinds of individual and community identities that emerged
from these, especially in terms of social recognition, public initiation, and local sovereignty (cf. Watanabe 1992:126). This feeling is demonstrated in the following exchange between a middle-aged man (A), a middle-aged woman (B),
and young man in his late twenties that took place in a history workshop in
January 2000:

> A: But there was a system of authority here before that was very, very
> good, very, very, very good. Not years and years ago, only ten or fif-
> teen years ago.
> [Other topics are discussed and we eventually return to this.]
> B: Yes, everyone respected one another.
> A: Yes, and if one reads [Oakes's 1951 ethnography, *The Two Crosses of
> Todos Santos*] it's not mentioned. . . . [I]t reaffirms what other books
> say, for example, how social integration was experienced; how people
> rose through hierarchies to become principals; it wasn't because one
> chose to be there or there was a vote.
> B: Yes, they had to earn it [their positions]. They had to earn it little by
> little.
> A: . . . one could rise through the hierarchy to occupy a position of au-
> thority, so that you wouldn't fall into the temptations or errors that you
> might when you're very young. Yes, for me this was very good, a very
> intelligent form; you have to serve first, too, as an elder, as an *ixcuel*
> [apprentice]. [Quoted from transcripts]

The people involved in this discussion are already community leaders and acknowledged as such by many people. Their nostalgia for forms of power that
they could access through service and experience involves imagining an ideal-

ized version of the past, one that was so fraught with problems that conflicts around the costs of belonging to it led to its eventual demise.

Power nostalgia, I suspect circulates in different ways in relation to the postwar period. For some people, holding too much visible power is intolerable, a holdover from *la violencia*. Too much power equals the ability to exploit, amply demonstrated in the years during which the civil patrol operated. Perhaps this is the problem with gang members in Todos Santos: they wield too much power among youth and therefore comprise a threat.

In analyzing the kinds of conflicts that rise to the surface of communities in postwar Guatemala, generational conflict and increasing repression invoked to handle it may be the single struggle that will have the most devastating long-term effects in communities. Given a wider history of conflicts and community strategies for addressing their struggles with one another, the increasing repression of maras and marero activity in Todos Santos is, among other things, a strategy to counterbalance the diminishing authority of elders and the surging power of youth gained through economic alternatives such as migration. It may also indicate that there is a growing impatience with the Guatemalan state in transition, perhaps accompanied by nostalgia for yet another form of past hierarchy and prestige: the privilege of power through clandestinity.

8

Desires and Imagination

The Economy of Humanitarianism in Guatemala

José Oscar Barrera Nuñez

Emily was a 20-year-old woman from the United States who had many suitors in town. "Que bonitos ojos tienes!" men often said to her to make reference to the beauty of her eyes, or they made other compliments to allude to her straight brown hair or to the characteristic smile on her face. Her genial attitude and openness to talk with anyone seemed to captivate local men of similar age, such as the "the guys," a small group of Mayas and Ladinos who hung out with foreigners in the local Spanish schools. Adults also seemed to enjoy flirting with her. She was not insulted by comments but found them rather flattering. It was not just the men she befriended; her easygoing manner and attitude also enabled her to befriend many local women.

I first met Emily in the year 2000 when she visited Todos Santos Cuchumatán for a couple of weeks to learn Spanish in a recently opened Spanish school. She was hosted by a local family and participated in the activities that the school scheduled for students' "cultural immersion." This first experience was crucial for her ulterior engagement. Months later she returned to Todos Santos, inspired by reading *Pedagogy of the Oppressed* (Freire 1970), a book that she recommended and enthusiastically insisted that I read. In our conversations, Emily expressed how Paulo Freire's views of education gave her hope to address the inequalities in the world by giving people the weapons to reverse the impoverished conditions in which they are immersed.

Emily was an activist with a personal commitment to helping those whom she saw could benefit from education. She saw education as the means to empower Mayas and as a venue through which she could be part of such an enterprise. In the spring and summer of 2001, Emily intended to carry out a project with primary school teachers by encouraging them to implement storybooks in their teaching. Her idea was to use stories as a teaching device to expose students to new ways of thinking and seeing the world beyond their village. Her passion to empower primary school children and teachers through education intertwined with other desires that she also awakened in Todos Santos. While she was training teachers on alternative pedagogical techniques, she was also having a love affair with one of the guys. She had a good time with the guys, hanging out in the local tourist bar, drinking and dancing late into the night, and throwing parties occasionally at the Spanish school. One day, one of the neighbors went to the police to complain about the "scandal" that was happening inside the Spanish school, alluding to a salsa and merengue party that Emily was giving for tourists, Spanish learners, and others of her local friends.

Emily's story in Todos Santos is not just illustrative of the processes happening in Guatemala as a site of intertwined desires. In the aftermath of the civil war, Todos Santos has been transformed socially and economically more intensively than ever before due to the mutual desires between foreigners and Mayas. In the last twenty years, an increasing number of foreign organizations and individuals have appeared in Todos Santos. Tourists, volunteers, Spanish learners, activists, social researchers, nongovernmental organizations (NGOs), and many others bring their own imaginaries about themselves and the Mayas as they pursue their desires for the Mayas. The Mayas and Ladinos of Todos Santos have been adjusting to new conditions established by these exogenous forces. The lives of farmers, health promoters, teachers, hosting families of the Spanish schools, weavers, and migrants to the United States are closely connected to these foreigners and their desires. Love affairs, altruism, tourism, social research, and humanitarian intervention intertwine in ways that make Todos Santos a locale of intricate imaginaries and desires. This chapter is concerned with Mayas' and Western foreigners' imaginaries and desires. By focusing on Todos Santos Cuchumatán, I intend to provide a glimpse of the transcultural relations between Western foreigners and Mayas in post–civil war Guatemala. I argue that through their social interactions both Mayas and foreigners experience and reproduce each "Other" as they pursue the desires of their own imagination. In examining the mutual attraction that keeps the two together, I do not intend to evaluate whether or not the so-called international civil society makes a difference in Guatemala with its humanitarian efforts. Nor am I intending to judge Mayas appropriation of foreigners' agendas. Rather, I examine the social dynamics between Mayas and foreigners engaged in relations of mutual desires and reciprocal imaginaries (see also Barrera Nuñez 2005).

The Construction of Desire

When Emily first visited Todos Santos, she studied Spanish for two weeks as part of her university field trip to Guatemala. She was initially studying

Spanish in the city of Quetzaltenango, which, in addition to La Antigua Guatemala, is a major destination in the country for students of Spanish. After studying in Quetzaltenango for a few weeks, her class moved to Todos Santos. Here, she discovered the impressive landscape of the Cuchumatán Mountains and the beautiful scenery of the pine forest with houses scattered among the cornfields. Emily and her class were not alone, as Todos Santos attracts hundreds of backpack tourists going "off the beaten path" pursuing an "isolated" and "authentic" Mayan village. Many find the atmosphere in Todos Santos unique because almost all Mayas are dressed in their colorful clothing, which for many is an "objective" marker of "traditional" Mayan culture. Besides these tourists, Todos Santos also lures university students from North America, Europe, and Japan. Undergraduate and graduate research projects prevail in Todos Santos on all kinds of topics: history of the village, impacts of tourism, traditional Mayan culture, linguistics, postwar violence, Todos Santos' self-representations, artifact production, lynchings, and much more. There were about fifteen foreigners, including myself, conducting some kind of academic project during my uninterrupted 24-month fieldwork research (1999–2001). There were also volunteers from various organizations doing development work. Emily probably did not meet the two Peace Corps volunteers working in Todos Santos. They were withdrawn from town in May 2000 because it became a "dangerous" place. The lynching of a Japanese tourist and a Guatemalan bus driver drove away almost all tourists during that year, but it brought other foreigners, such as people from the United Nations, journalists, photographers, human rights activists, scholars, and many others investigating this event.

Emily studied in a language school that was recently opened. She and her university fellows were immersed into an atmosphere of "Mayaness" with colorful Todos Santos clothes, postcards, and photos hanging on the walls of the school for decor. She attended five hours of instruction every day and participated in the school activities. Foreigners interested in the activities are also invited to participate, and many of them do not pursue language learning. For many, Spanish schools are the most reliable way to penetrate into the life of the Mayas. The wide diversity of the Spanish schools' activities offers the opportunity for a mixture of foreigners to satisfy all kinds of desires, from those who are just interested in learning Spanish with little to no interest in interacting with locals through those who want a spiritual experience with Mayan shamans. It is for this reason that Spanish schools are the point of entry for many foreigners, including those who conduct social research. Teachers of the Spanish schools have become the main intermediaries between their community and outsiders.

The Economy of Humanitarianism

Studying in Todos Santos offered Emily the opportunity to learn Spanish in a place where Spanish is little spoken. Mam remains Mayas' prevailing language. Today, Spanish is mostly used in the relations between Mayas and outsiders and in the primary and *básico* (secondary) schools as well. Spanish schools immerse foreigners into a seductive atmosphere, constructing Todos Santos as the opposite to "Western" culture. Schools participate in what seems to be an economy of humanitarianism operating in Todos Santos and in Guatemala, characterized by helping, aiding, studying, and empowering Mayas.

Culture is a precious commodity emphasized in all aspects of these Spanish schools' advertising and activities. In one of the brochures it is stated, "Studying in this school is more than just learning a language or the art of weaving; it is a course on life in Todos Santos." Nevertheless, foreigners themselves helped to translate and put together this brochure. Spanish schools also present themselves as playing an active role in the development of the community while offering people like Emily the opportunity to participate in this social enterprise. Needless to say, this altruistic facade is common in other Spanish schools in Guatemala, such as the ones in the city of Quetzaltenango.

When Emily and her fellows studied Spanish in Todos Santos, they were informed about the recent opening of their school and of the social projects planned when funds became available. Projects would consist of scholarships for primary school children and a youth center where teenagers could learn skills such as carpentry, electricity, music, art, and so forth. Upon Emily's return to the United States after her first visit, she had not only raised funds for the schools in her hometown, but also created a website for the Spanish school, which a scholar from a U.S. university added to his website on Todos Santos. This website presents information on the three Spanish schools in Todos Santos as well as all kinds of information on projects where foreigners can get involved, such as projects on ecotourism, shaman groups, weaving cooperatives, and more.

Spanish schools are just one manifestation of larger processes in which both Mayas and foreigners are engaged in this economy of desires. The war brought all kinds of foreign individuals and organizations engaged in humanitarian intervention, including human rights advocacy, religious conversion, political activism, cultural revitalization, economic development, and health and education programs (see also, in this volume, DeHart; Maxwell; Stoll). Like other places in Guatemala, Todos Santos emerged as a locale where Mayas became objects of social reconstruction, recipients of charity, subjects of ideological conversion through human rights advocacy, "exotic" objects of tourism, objects of social research (primarily on topics involving violence), and subjects of all kinds of humanitarian intervention to "better" the life of the Mayas.

High levels of poverty, a large Mayan population, a violent history, a history of foreign intervention, the expansion of the market economy, and the spread of Western ideologies around the globe have intersected in a way that places like Todos Santos have turned into an economy of desires for the Other. The presence of the global civil society in the form of NGOs, volunteers, tourists, students, scholars, language learners, religious missionaries, and others has brought the explosion of organizations and peoples with good intentions to help Mayas.

Postcards, magazines, travel guidebooks, and all kinds of tourist paraphernalia are part of this economy of desires constructing Todos Santos as a "pristine" place that is threatened by both capitalism and political violence. This can be experienced through ethnographic films and even Hollywood films, such as *The Jury*, starring Demi Moore and Todos Santos Mayas.

Epistemological "curiosity" is also part of this economy. The devices that Spanish schools have appropriated to construct the experience of Mayaness makes evident the connections that the community has with other outsiders and how Mayas have inserted themselves in the reproduction of discourses about themselves. The teachers of the Spanish schools use films and ethnographic materials in their classes to introduce foreigners to Todos Santos. Two famous films, *Todos Santos: Report from a Guatemalan Village* (1982) and *Todos Santos: The Survivors* (1989), are the most popular films screened every week. These films narrate how Todos Santos has been violated by Western capitalism and the Guatemalan military, respectively. While many of these films were intended to raise awareness about Guatemala, Spanish schools have appropriated them to stimulate foreigners' imagination on Guatemala as contrastingly Other.

In this economy of desires both Westerners and Mayas are produced as commodities and in contrasting opposites. Todos Santos Mayas are found in literary texts, social theories, movies, documentaries, films, magazines, brochures, calendars, posters, university courses, productive projects, human rights campaigns, and more. They are the recipients of empowerment to be transformed into subjects of resistance or objects of scientific scrutiny to become subjects of ideological liberation. On the other hand, foreigners are constructed as active agents, subjects who record Mayas' testimonies, and as subjects, who provide Mayas with the means for their own social and economic empowerment. The binary construction of "Westerners" and "Mayas" fuels this economy of desires. Mayas and Westerners are both reproduced and the producers of the dichotomies of modern versus traditional, developed versus developing, empowered versus disempowered, and many others that they experience in their interactions.

Ethnographic films, written ethnographies, and even anthropological courses add to the orchestra of seductive forces that make Todos Santos a stimulating site for the imagination. In a conversation I had with a woman named Margaret about why she visited Todos Santos, she mentioned,

> I took an anthropology class in college; we read the book by Barbara Ted-lock [1983]: *Time and the [Highland] Maya.* We saw in class the video on Todos Santos. I really liked it a lot. Since then, I had so much curiosity to see what it was like. That was such a good class. I enjoyed it so much that I came to Guatemala.

Margaret is from the United States and was traveling with her backpack in Guatemala, where she found a volunteer job in Habitat for Humanity building houses in a Mayan village in the Western highlands.

Ethnographic videos, documentaries, and a wide ethnographic literature on Guatemala produced from the 1980s into the present have focused on the violence that communities like Todos Santos have experienced, whether by Western capitalist expansion or by the oppressive Guatemalan army. Violence as an icon of Guatemala has become appealing to foreigners, and academic scholarship has contributed to the lure. David Stoll has been severely criticized for contending that Rigoberta Menchú's testimony is not a totalizing account of Mayas' experiences of the civil war (Arias 2001; *Latin American Perspectives* 1999). However, it is important to also bring to light a point that has received little attention. In my understanding of his work, Stoll (1993) emphasizes how Western scholars have produced a discourse of Mayas as what he calls "all poor Guatemalans." He suggests that foreigners have produced themselves in oppo-sition to Mayas through this discourse. Academics often present themselves as "fortunate" and "empowered," a position from which they intend to give voice to the voiceless and power to the powerless. Nevertheless, I must point out that foreigners are not the only ones reproducing this discourse. Not only "Western" academics, journalists, tourists, activists, volunteers, or NGOs are involved, but also Mayas themselves (see also Stoll in this volume).

Seducing the Mayas

Not only have international and national organizations in Guatemala focused on the observance and monitoring of human rights, but in Todos Santos these entities and their mass of volunteers have introduced ideas about human rights, citizenship, development, and productivity. Some of the projects conducted include the supply of basic infrastructure, such as roads, electricity, water, sewage, school buildings, water tanks, and improved firewood stoves. Development projects have focused on the introduction of improved sheep for wool and meat production; irrigation systems, making possible the production of commercial crops such as potatoes and broccoli; wood looms for the production of commercial textiles; forestry; and micro-credits. Projects on health have been a priority also; these included training of health promoters and midwives, vaccination campaigns, and introduction of latrines.

The number of organizations working in Guatemala, particularly with Mayas, has increased over the years. According to the Council of Development Institutions (COINDE), there are 300 NGOs operating in Guatemala today. During the time of my fieldwork I recorded 43 organizations that have operated and some of which still operate in Todos Santos, such as the European Union, Veterinarians Without Borders, Peace Corps, Doctors Without Borders, CARE, and Summer Institute of Linguistics. Some of the funding agencies are the Organization of the Petroleum Exporting Countries (OPEC), USAID (U.S. Agency for International Development), Inter-American Development Bank, Dutch Cooperation, European Union, and United Nations Development Program. As a result of the work of these entities, dozens of local organizations have been created in Todos Santos, such as Mam Institute of Integral Development (IMDI), Pro-health Maya Association (AMAPROS), and many more. I should not omit the hundreds of individual foreigners who, on their own, have conducted and funded their own projects, from sponsoring education by giving money to their Todos Santos friends to buying materials for development projects.

Duplication of projects and programs is often a characteristic of this economy of humanitarianism. I often heard from NGO workers of their struggle to avoid doubling actions. NGOs have tried to establish better communication with each other to articulate their programs in the last few years. Humanitarian intervention has also created opportunities for "experts" in various areas to evaluate either the success of their programs or potential venues for further action.

The Power of Seduction of the Economy of Desire

Many travelers have come up with ways to get engaged in self-manufactured or already existing projects. Besides Emily, I encountered several people willing to help the Mayas during the time of my fieldwork, many of whom visited Todos Santos with other than altruistic agendas, such as traveling, sightseeing, touring, or experiencing Mayan culture. Many, however, were *seduced* by the humanitarian atmosphere of Todos Santos and Guatemala, in general, where helping the Mayas seems to be the "thing to do." I found well-intended travelers coming up with various projects. Juana, a traveler from Switzerland, for example, had envisioned a youth center where children and teenagers could learn job skills. She lived in Todos Santos for six months, searched for funding unsuccessfully, and could not get the interest of the people in the community. I even heard that a man from New York opened a "bar" for Mayas to teach them not only "how to drink," by exposing them to a diversity of liquors, but also how to drink in reasonable amounts, as the rumor of Todosanteros having a "problem of alcoholism" has spread among travelers.

The economy of humanitarianism has enabled people like Emily to get engaged in projects that "empower" Mayas. What is important to note, here, is that foreigners contribute to the construction of this atmosphere. They are seduced by an economy of tourism, NGOs, language learning, altruism, political activism, academia, and more, while at the same time they are also the primary architects of this economy by participating in or creating their own projects to empower Mayas. Many arrive with other agendas and later desire to get involved more actively.

Transformation of Ethnic Relations

Before the economy of humanitarianism consolidated in Todos Santos during the 1990s, Mayas were economically dependent on subsistent agriculture. Migrant labor was the main source of cash, primarily to coffee plantations in southern Guatemala and, in much less degree, in Chiapas, Mexico, where employment was also available on banana plantations.

Ladinos occupied key positions in the local municipality as secretary and treasurer. They also monopolized the most important aspects of the political life of Todos Santos. Ladinos were primary school teachers, store owners, and *habilitadores* (labor recruiters) and monopolized the sale of liquor. With the civil war, the ethnic relations in Todos Santos were radically transformed and the economic and politic hegemony of local Ladinos came to an end. The majority of the Ladinos living in the municipal center abandoned Todos Santos and sold their properties to the Mayas because of the dreadful living conditions prevailing in 1981 and 1982. The military's counterinsurgency campaigns and the guerillas' incursions killing military "allies" and "subversives" made Todos Santos a frightful place to live. Many Ladinos and Mayas fled to Huehuetenango and Guatemala City to save their lives, threatened by both armies. Very few Ladino families decided to stay. The majority only returned to sell their properties to Mayas.

Since 1982, Mayas, who have taken control of the local economy and politics, are filling the power vacuum left by Ladinos. They now own buses, stores, hotels, *comedores* (restaurants), and weaving cooperatives and have also become primary school teachers, tailors, habilitadores, and health promoters. Before the civil war, a few Mayas competed economically with Ladinos, such as a few habilitadores. In the aftermath of the war, Ladinos were not just a numeric minority, but their political and economic power was marginal.

In the municipal center and in some hamlets, several Ladino families live today in conditions as impoverished as the Mayas, and often even worse. The economic and social opportunities following the war as well as with the economy of humanitarianism increased for the Mayas. Ladinos, however, have been facing the negative connotations about them produced by this economy, which presents them as an "oppressive" and "exploitative" ethnic group against the Mayas. Even in some ethnographies and other academic texts, Western scholars despise Ladinos while showing their "solidarity" with the Mayas. Ladinos are aware of the attention given the Mayas in Todos Santos, which is more evident when Mayas have access to development projects and employment opportunities. "*Indígenas* have more opportunities than before," said Gastón, a Ladino dwelling in Todos Santos for more than 20 years. He added, "They are in advantage over Ladinos. They [Mayas] speak their [own] language and can easily get a job with an *institución* [NGO]. Things changed in Todos Santos with the war, but many *indígenas* don't want to see this." Ladinos are monolingual in Spanish and are not as marketable. One time Gastón had to strongly advocate for a single mother, a Ladina, to get a job with the local library. He was the only Ladino in the library committee and wanted to support this woman who was abandoned by her husband. He fell in love with a German tourist and left Todos Santos to live in Germany with his new partner. Ladinos are aware that they are not that attractive to tourists, Spanish learners, anthropologists, and many other foreigners who usually prefer to interact with Mayas. Ladino discontent on this issue is notorious. In the *aldea* (hamlet) of San Martín, which has the largest Ladino population in Todos Santos, a movement began in 2001 to become an independent municipality. San Martin Ladinos were in dialogue with the Guatemalan government to reach total autonomy. These Ladinos are unhappy that municipal funds are distributed in other aldeas of mainly Mayan population in addition to the aid they also receive from NGOs. San Martín is an area of coffee production, and Ladinos could benefit more if they had their own municipal funds.

Reproducing and Experiencing the Desiring "Other"

Emily had genuine intentions of using her skills and the means she had access to in the United States to improve the lives of the Mayas of Todos Santos. During her second visit during the spring and summer of 2001, Emily collaborated with another American woman, Patricia, who works as a coordinator. Together, they got materials for the school, such as grammar books for learning Spanish, a stereo, and a VCR. In trying to get money for the Spanish school in the United States, Emily realized that she could apply for funding at her university by forming a formal organization. She then gathered a group of her university fellows and created an organization through which she received a $1,500 grant to carry on her education project. With these funds, Emily and her fellows were able to buy storybooks, notebooks, and other materials for the primary school children.

In the summer of 2001, Emily returned to Todos Santos with three other fellows to conduct their education project. One of them, Cassandra, whom I met just once on the street, left after a few days. Emily told me that Cassandra did not adapt well; she could not put up with the living conditions of Todos Santos and the family with whom she stayed: "She said it is 'too rustic and poor.' She could not deal with not taking hot showers every morning, the food, or with the fleas in her bed." In contrast, Emily enjoyed Todos Santos and was happy that she was not alone conducting her project. Yet she was also struggling with the fact that she was the most fluent in Spanish while her fellows were studying Spanish in addition to their involvement as facilitators of their education project. It was a social dynamic of giving and receiving from each other. Todosanteros were teaching Spanish while their "students" were also their "teachers" by instructing them on creative ways to teach primary school children.

In the primary schools, Emily opted to work with the classes of the teachers working in the Spanish school. She knew these teachers well and had a good relationship with them. She initially intended to work with other primary school teachers who were not involved in the Spanish school. However, this meant building new relationships, which meant investing vital time, which she preferred to use working with the teachers she already knew.

Not all teachers of the Spanish school were participating in Emily's project since only a handful were interested enough to participate. Despite her enthusiasm and efforts, Emily and her fellows were frustrated with the teachers who were not that responsive to the project. Few teachers showed up for meetings to plan the activities for the primary school students. Emily and her fellows opted to work with just a few classes.

Nevertheless, Emily told me that even the teachers who were more responsive to her project did not do the work that was expected. Emily complained that some teachers used Emily and her fellows to leave the room and take a break:

> It feels like they are using us as an excuse to leave the room and do whatever they want; when, in fact, we want them to do it themselves. We are

there to assist and offer the little that we know. We are not teachers. We don't know. They are the teachers.

Emily was disappointed that teachers were not that interested in learning from them and in teaching ideas they intended to introduce.

What Emily was expecting from the teachers was more than creative thinking in teaching, it implied that teachers had to do more work designing lesson plans, evaluations, and creative activities. Planning and developing an extra curriculum added to teachers' already busy schedules teaching Spanish, attending to their families, and being involved in local committees.

A similar situation with regards to education occurred in 1996 with the organization Education Without Borders (EWB). Eustacio, a local, well-respected Ladino teacher, told me, "Education Without Borders worked in Todos Santos. They were people from Spain who came to improve [elementary] education." EWB focused its work building classrooms and providing teachers with professional training. Eustacio explained:

> Things went all right, but later [Todos Santos] teachers rejected them because they thought they [EWB] were monitoring teachers' work and, thus, would penalize them. The Spanish woman [working in this project] left very frustrated. She told me that "teachers don't want to work. They get to work on Tuesday [in remote villages] and want to leave on Thursday."

Furthermore, EWB tried to not affect children's morning classes by offering their training courses for teachers in the evenings. Teachers, however, claimed not to have time for training in the evening, but just during regular school hours. This irritated EWB people, who left Todos Santos earlier than planned.

One of the main problems that Emily found with teachers was her ambivalent position as a "coordinator" of the Spanish school and an "education advisor." A big part of that summer, she was a coordinator of the Spanish school, and her job was to be the liaison between foreigners and Spanish teachers. Teachers of the three Spanish schools, however, are used to a constant influx of foreigners desiring to help Mayas. In the way that it is presented by the teachers, the coordinator's role is to be an interpreter between foreigners and teachers to facilitate communication. However, coordinators do more than that; teachers depend on coordinators to keep their schools in business. They bring foreigners in to either learn Spanish or participate in the schools' activities. In many respects, coordinators are the main agents who bring revenues to the schools. I often saw the three Spanish schools closed at different times because there was no coordinator. In the three schools, I repeatedly saw coordinators angry with teachers because, in their view, teachers were not fulfilling their "responsibilities" to run "their own" school. Teachers often do not show up for work on time or don't show up at all, or they "forget" to arrange the logistics for school activities, stressing out the coordinator, who then has to arrange everything at the last minute. At other times, teachers leave coordinators to deal with any problems that arise between language learners and their host families.

Teachers are pleased with coordinators' performance if they bring students for language instruction. It is for this reason that coordinators' responsibilities constantly change; they are negotiated with teachers through daily interactions as coordinators also pursue their own desires for Todosanteros. Coordinators are appreciated by teachers if they pressure teachers to do their job running the Spanish school. A teacher stated:

> A good coordinator is strong, with a strong hand, [pause] but not with a strong hand against the teachers. Rather, one that tells them "get yourselves to work and be responsible"; and one who gives teachers strength. A good coordinator is also one who works painting the school building and conducts projects. That is a good coordinator. . . . A bad coordinator is one who just hangs out with friends instead of being in the school or searching for new students. It is also one who works for one school and then moves to another.

When I saw Emily on the street that summer, she told me she was tired of the Spanish school. She did not like the fact that teachers saw her more as someone who could bring business to the Spanish school than as a person who could help them to develop the education of children in Todos Santos. From that point, she announced to the teachers that she would quit as a coordinator of the school in order to focus just on the education project. Therefore, she went to the cities of Huehuetenango and Quetzaltenango to place an ad searching for a substitute.

Emily began to realize that things in Todos Santos do not work as they are presented to foreigners in the Spanish schools. She had a hard time when confronted with the Todos Santos she had constructed in her imagination. Emily recorded in her notes the inconsistencies of the discourse of the economy of humanitarianism that Spanish schools along with foreigners themselves reproduce:

> WHO [sic] makes up the [Spanish] school and what their roles are exactly, is somewhat ambiguous. . . . I was told it was a cooperative, that we all have voices in the decision making process, that the decisions must be

made with consent with everyone (Patricia, the coordinators, and I depending, though, on who is around and what kind of decision is being made). However, my own observations don't coordinate very well with this, as it seemed that work was not divided up very cooperatively, but rather that the coordinator did everything and made decisions regarding how the school was to be publicized and presented to the public.

Spanish school teachers have an ambivalent relationship with coordinators. By putting pressure on them, teachers irritate coordinators, but at the same time, they depend on coordinators to get foreigners involved in the schools. It is a relationship of rejection and attraction, detachment and dependency. Teachers often do not remember the names of coordinators, even after they have been working in the school for weeks. This also happens with Mayas who get involved in development projects. When I was visiting a family in the aldea of Tzunul, I inquired about the names of the organizations that provided them with latrines and training on wood looms. However, people only mentioned that it was an *institución* (institution). People seemed not to be interested in learning the names of the organizations that provide them with humanitarian aid. *Institución* is a generic term that encompasses all organizations that provide any kind of assistance in Todos Santos. Furthermore, it is often assumed that foreigners, such as tourists, who stay in Todos Santos for long periods of time are part of instituciones. As other scholars have pointed out, anthropologists in Guatemala are often seen as employees of organizations who could provide people with scholarships or develop projects (see Green 1999; Nelson 1999).

With the economic opportunities that emerged from humanitarian intervention and government programs, very few Todos Santos Mayas migrate to coffee plantations today. Since the 1990s Mayas have become involved in the agro-export of broccoli and coffee. Also hundreds of Mayas have migrated to the United States since the 1980s, awakening peoples' desires for economic success. When returning to Todos Santos, they bring their new trucks, build new houses, or buy coffee fields in the lowlands of Todos Santos or in the neighboring municipalities of Conception and Chiantla. Today, an increasing number of young Mayas, including women, migrate. There are about four thousand Todos Santos Mayas in the United States. Some of them leave the community after finishing their *básico* or *diversificado* schooling (junior high and high school, respectively). The expectation that they will have better job opportunities in the United States provides many Mayas with the incentive to finish their schooling. Some of these Mayas receive scholarships from NGOs, such as Proyecto Patojos from Spain. While the *padrinos* (godparents or sponsors) of this Spanish organization aim to empower Mayas through education, many

Mayas use the skills they gain to fulfill their desires by increasing their chances of finding a better job in the United States.

And the Story Goes On

After my fieldwork, Emily and I stayed in touch. She went back in the summer of 2002 to continue her education project with her university fellows. She was angry when we talked on the phone. Teachers of the Spanish school phoned her to ask her when she was returning to Todos Santos. They did not ask her when she was coming back to carry on her education project, but rather, they were desperate to get a coordinator for the Spanish school as the school was closed again. Emily said, "I'm going to have a serious conversation with the teachers. It's their school. They must take full responsibility and not depend on the coordinator to have their school running." Emily went back with six of her fellows to follow up with the education project. She, however, told me she was not that excited about going back: "I'm just going to have fun." Emily did not like that the teaching ideas she and her fellows intended to implement were put into action only when she and her fellows were there. It made her angry that teachers did not do things "on their own." It was her last summer in Guatemala; she does not want to return to Todos Santos to work anymore as she is tired of the education field: "I want to try something different." She mentioned that her next project was going to be in Ecuador, where she will work with her professor conducting research on public health.

Emily's experience in Guatemala made her come in contact with her own construction of Todos Santos and herself. She could not reconcile the imaginary of social justice and civil engagement that she learned in college with what she encountered in Guatemala. In her notes she wrote, "Doing my reading—*Empowering Education*—that is the easy part, to understand the theories and understand how things 'should' be done. But then to really do it, that's a whole other story. How to do it?"

9

Everyday Politics in a K'iche' Village of Totonicapán, Guatemala

Barbara Bocek

Tierra Blanca is a K'iche'-speaking village near the Pan-American Highway, in the western Guatemalan highlands. I lived there for three years in the 1990s while working as a Peace Corps extensionist and saw my neighbors' daily reactions to the social and political turmoil accompanying the waning years of the civil war. Though far less affected by the conflict than the Ixils interviewed by David Stoll (1993) and J. Jailey Philpot-Munson (this volume), Tierra Blancans similarly resented, feared, and blamed both the army and the guerrillas for the violence.

Most national events have little direct impact on the people of Tierra Blanca. They are poor, hard-working subsistence farmers who expect little from the world beyond their village. Some had heard of Nobel laureate Rigoberta Menchú, a fellow K'iche' ("Isn't she a *licenciada* (lawyer)? Didn't she win a prize from the government?"). Few were aware of the 1993 coup ("The president tried to steal the government"); of war refugees returning from Mexico ("Poor people! They ran from the army, and now they have no homes, no land"); and the ongoing peace negotiations ("The army, the guerrillas, their job is war; they don't want peace").

Tierra Blanca might seem a backwater whose inhabitants are in serious need of consciousness-raising. Yet their insularity probably makes them more representative of rural Guatemalans than the martyred dissidents, returning refugees, and heroic activists upon whom we focus most attention. Much of what they have to say contradicts the discourses of the Guatemalan Left and the Maya Movement that claim to represent them. Hence, their profound skepticism should be of considerable interest to those who want to build a broad opposition movement, win elections, and make Guatemala a more democratic society. In the interest of social realism, the villagers of Tierra Blanca speak for themselves in this chapter, insofar as possible. These conversations took place between January 1993 and December 1995, usually in K'iche'.

Fig 14. Mayas gather for a religious procession in Tierra Blanca. Photo by Barbara Bocek.

Bartolenses and Momostecos

A Tierra Blancan commented on a neighbor's deployment of identity politics: "You know Diego Ixcoy, his youngest child goes to school with the people of Momos. But years ago his children went to school with my children; they were Bartolenses then. It's said that *k'o kyeb' uwuj* (he has two identity cards)." The village of Tierra Blanca straddles the border between two *municipios* (counties or townships), Santiago Momostenango and San Bartolo Aguas Calientes, in the Department of Totonicapán. A centuries-old land dispute has slowly divided the population into overlapping Momostecan and Bartolense communities, both of which inhabit the space of an *aldea* (village) named Tierra Blanca. They speak the same dialect of K'iche' and have the same family names: Guox, Ajanel, Xiloj, Chanchavac. But their town halls and schools are conceptually and physically in the municipios of Momostenango and San Bartolo.

Bartolenses frame the division in terms of history: "A hundred years have passed! It's just that Momostecos keep thinking that San Bartolo is still theirs." The Momostecos' main concern is the land: "The fields, the water, they still belong to us! All that land was stolen by those thieves . . . [and] in the future the government (*q'atb'al tzij*) will return all of San Bartolo, every single village, to Momostenango."

The split has had at least three important consequences. First, because each household has been free to define (and change) its loyalties, there is no clear geographical division. On the single dirt road running through Tierra Blanca, the two schools and two town halls are within a few hundred meters of each other, and literally every other plot of land is in a different municipio.

Second, the tradition-minded Momostecos and the more experimental Bartolenses are steadily diverging, especially in religion. Bartolenses are primarily evangelicals who worship in numerous tiny household-based congregations. Momostecos are primarily Catholic, and many observe traditional Mayan religious practices as well. An evangelical told me:

> Years ago we were all Catholic. Now we've become evangelicals. We've accepted Jesus and we've baptized ourselves again. Only the people of Momos, . . . [i]n church they pray (*ke'q'ijilanik*) in front of wood posts; that's all those statues are. . . . Yes, over there in Momos they also burn copal incense when they pray in the hills, on those days when they use the old calendar.

Bartolenses deride Momostecos as *costumbrista* (old-fashioned), but they themselves have not completely abandoned Mayan religious practices. Both Bartolense and Momosteco place names include *mejab'al* and *sab'al* (the kneeling place and the burning place), and older Bartolenses are aware of the Mayan calendar. "Why are they setting off rockets over there among the Momostecos? Isn't it because today is Ajpu; it's an important day (*nimaq'ij*)?" Bartolenses point to electricity, piped water, and a refurbished town hall and school as signs of their community's development. Meanwhile, the small, aging Momosteco town hall and school sport broken windows and layers of graffiti that emphasizes vengeance. "Yes, the Bartolenses have a big new school and village hall," a Momosteco commented. "The Bartolenses . . . only have so much money because their sons go like thieves (*chelaq'al*) to Los Angeles, to Houston in the United States."

A third consequence is a history of violence and suspicion, not in the least alleviated by the passage of time. Most personal relations are peaceful. But during my stay there were fistfights, rock- and bottle-throwing, a gang rape, two shootings, and, during one notable week, gun-toting Momostecos closed the only road to some of their Bartolense neighbors.

Witchcraft accusations crop up in both populations but more often against the costumbrista Momostecos. A Momosteco explained:

> His chickens were getting killed every night but they were well closed in, no animal could have entered the coop, so he knew it was a *tz'u'm utiw* (coyote-skin) witch or a *wi'n*, a person-become-animal (*winaq uxinaq awaj*). How is the witch able to do it? The person prays to Evil (Itzel)

and rotates his head nine times, until his spirit leaves through his anus. Then this spirit enters any animal, like a coyote. It is done at night. . . . Then the person, now no longer really a person, can enter any house. It can kill animals, steal money; it can even enter a woman and leave its seed inside her; she won't feel anything. . . . Yes there are coyote-skins everywhere, but perhaps there are more here with us because some of our people truly know the old ideas.

The two sides also accuse each other of associating with the guerrillas. One day a local bus broke down near several Momosteco households. Ladinos on the bus were bored by the delay, but the Bartolense Tierra Blancans were joking nervously: "Here we are in the middle of the serpent Momostecos. What if we have to get off and wait here for another bus!" "They're not serpents; they're mountain lions, tigers," said another, raking his hand through the air like a claw. "Aren't they really the *guerrilla*?" said a third. "They'll take us up the mountain to the *subversión* (subversives); there they'll cut off our heads and steal everything we have."

Tierra Blancans and the Republic of Guatemala

A Tierra Blancan, hearing that President Serrano Elias had suspended the Constitution in May 1993, remarked, "It's said that the government has been stolen (*xelaq'axik*) by the president. This is really no good. Last time this happened all the prices went up and they haven't come down yet." Evangelical or Catholic, progressive or costumbrista, Tierra Blancans focus on local issues and day-to-day problems. Other than the school and barely functional health post, no national institution has a presence in the village. Radio programs are almost exclusively in Spanish, and news is broadcast at hours when few *campesinos* (peasants) are home to listen, even if their Spanish were adequate, which for the majority it is not.

Bartolenses and Momostecos are united in their general distrust of Ladinos: "Ladinos call us stupid Indians (*indios brutos*) but . . . it's they who can't understand us." Tierra Blancans disapprove of marital or business relations with Ladinos. Still, more and more young people are leaving Tierra Blanca to seek work in the capital. The lucky ones find low-paying, menial jobs. Most return as poor as when they left. An 18-year-old neighbor whom I saw in the capital said:

I'm sad here. I'm not at home here (*kuk'am ta nuwach waral*). I don't like it! There are so many cars, lines of cars! And so many people. There are lots of thieves here; they have knives, guns! . . . How much am I earning?

I don't know. My boss doesn't know how much to pay me because it's not yet clear how many hot dogs I'll sell.

After working 72-hour weeks for a month, this young man cleared about seventy-five quetzales (US$14).

In addition to those in the capital city, one of every three Tierra Blancan households has someone working legally or illegally in the United States. Short-term emigration can raise a family's standard of living, but the distance strains family ties. The money orders stop coming. A father of 13 children asked me:

> Could your family in the States help us find our son? He left seven years ago. . . . But it's three years now that we have heard nothing. He could be sick, even dead, in prison, maybe recruited into the army over there. Also it's possible that he is fine, that he just no longer cares for us. . . . If that's the situation we can get used to it. What we want is to know if he's alive, because we still care for him. He's our firstborn child.

Tierra Blancans are intimately familiar with village governance, but higher levels of government—laws, courts, police, and Congress—are lumped together as the *q'atb'al tzij* (word-cutting place). Weeks before the 1994 and 1995 national elections, party workers arrived at Tierra Blanca in pickups blaring *ranchero* (Mexican cowboy) music. They shamelessly gave away pens, hats, and other trinkets. The first to visit was the Union Centrista Nacional (UCN). My neighbors enjoyed the music and gifts and, henceforth, referred to all parties as "UCNistas." "Where did my rain cape and hat come from?" retorted a friend sporting the yellow and blue colors of the Partido Avanzado Nacional (PAN). "They were just given as presents by the UCNistas. . . . They parked in front of the village hall, gave us all this stuff, and told us to vote." When the New Guatemala Democratic Front (FDNG), a leftist coalition of popular organizations, visited Tierra Blanca, their workers spoke K'iche' and gave out promotional literature rather than trinkets. "It's good they spoke our language," a neighbor told me. "But I say that they are the party of the guerrillas, and, anyway, I am not going to vote."

To bring out the vote, political parties trucked village supporters to polling places at the municipios. Tierra Blancans were eager to accept free rides to San Bartolo or Momostenango. One voter remarked:

> We're going to market; the UCNistas are paying our fare. It's because of the elections. . . . Yes, possibly I'll vote, but I want to vote for each of them because who knows which is any good? We mark three or four I think. . . . I'll vote for one with the white dove [Unión Democrática],

then the rooster [Frente Revolucionaro Guatemalteco], then maybe the blue arrow [PAN]. Isn't there another one with a white arrow? I'll mark one for them too.

Despite free rides, few people voted. "Did I vote?" a former councilman responded. "The mayor cited us *principalib'* (elders), so we all went. It's necessary to show respect. But no, I didn't vote. Why vote? What use is voting? Aren't all congressional deputies thieves?"

With respect to voter apathy, Tierra Blancans may be extreme. But Guatemala's abstention rates, in general, are 40 percent or higher, reflecting an electorate with very low expectations. Tierra Blancans despair of the government when teachers fail to show up for school or the health post is closed day after day. Both are frequent occurrences. Yet widespread disillusionment with government has not translated into support for popular organizations or the Left.

One reason is that popular organizations, like the government, are outsiders. Another is fear of the guerrillas, an army propaganda line that popular organizations reinforce by being confrontational. Militants of the Committee for Campesino Unity (CUC) staged a roadblock nearby in October 1992, spray-painted slogans on vehicles, and harangued their occupants. They failed to win over my neighbors. One told me:

CUC isn't really the guerrilla. It's just the political party of Rigoberta Menchú, isn't it? But the army thinks CUC is the guerrilla. So when our bus was stopped and CUC was painted on the outside, I was afraid. I ran off. . . . What's bus fare when I was afraid for my life? If the army thinks that CUC is the guerrilla, it's good to have nothing to do with them.

The War and the Peace Process in Tierra Blanca

One Tierra Blancan commented on the civil war: "I think it's bad that children see dead bodies just thrown in the road as they're walking to school." One or two Tierra Blancans "disappeared" (*xil ta chi kiwach*) during the Lucas García regime in the early 1980s. At the village entrance on the Pan-American Highway, the mutilated bodies of people kidnapped elsewhere were flung out of cars with tinted windows. Like most of Totonicapán, Tierra Blanca escaped the worst of the violence, yet everyone knew of the massacres and razed villages elsewhere. One said:

I was here at home when helicopters landed on our soccer field. They flew over us first; they flew up and down, here and there; there were soldiers looking down at us. Oh God, I was afraid. . . . My husband was called by the mayor to the football field, but he didn't go. Thank God! We knew many people were being killed.

Although the guerrillas, army, and civil patrols were less visible than in other highland areas, they were subjects of fear and contempt. Most neighbors utterly derided both the army and guerrillas as *ajch'ojab'* (fighters): "Isn't fighting their job, all of them?" Guerrillas were, in addition, dismissed as thieves. "Aren't they all thieves?" a neighbor said. "They don't work; they don't plant milpa, so how do they eat? How do they live? They just steal whatever it is that they want; they steal from the rest of the people." In December 1994, a neighbor reported:

When I went up the mountain to our lands up there, suddenly I saw them, people I didn't recognize. . . . They had green painted clothes and hats; they wore boots; also they carried guns; they each had a gun. Clearly, they were the guerrilla. No, I didn't talk to them. Wouldn't that be dangerous? I said nothing; I just left. I ran away.

Tierra Blancans were worried to see guerrillas on their lands. Yet no one suggested informing the authorities. The army never managed to impose its system of counterinsurgency militias or civil patrols on Tierra Blanca—quite an achievement for the village, given how widely and brutally the army imposed this regime. "A long time ago, perhaps it was 1981 or 1982, we were all called to a meeting with the army, and we were told to patrol day and night," one man recalled. "But we didn't want to patrol; we all said we would not do it. We did not do it; and the army went away again."

Until late 1995, when the practice was ended by presidential order, the military was represented locally by men "commissioned" by the army. *Comisionados,* like civil patrol chiefs, have a fearsome reputation in human rights reports. But Tierra Blanca's comisionados were only mildly resented because they performed their duties with such an obvious lack of enthusiasm. One duty of comisionados was to encourage young men to join the army—an utterly thankless task in Tierra Blanca. Tierra Blanca's final comisionado was a 46-year-old father of 11 living children who, like his neighbors, had evaded military service in his youth. He told me, "No one here wants to join the army and I don't tell anyone to go."

Until early 1995, the Guatemalan army recruited young men by stopping buses and hauling away anyone remotely the right age. Every few months the army would occupy Cuatro Caminos, a major crossroads in the western highlands. Neighbors returning home would spread the word *k'o chapanik*—the army "was grabbing" boys off buses. The last instance of forced recruitment occurred in late 1994:

So the army went down to San Bartolo, but people there had already heard; everyone knew they were coming. When the army arrived, there were no boys anywhere. There was no one for them to grab. Not one had stayed in town! Where did they go? They went up the mountains, down in the canyons. They came up here and hid themselves with us. Next day the army came here to Tierra Blanca. It was just the same. No boys! They had gone down the canyons to San Bartolo.

Like everywhere in the highlands, youths in Tierra Blanca are full of stories about outwitting army press gangs. A 21-year-old told me:

The comisionado said to us, "Go on you Indians, go on; get up in the truck!" I was so frightened. . . . "Yes sir," I said. "Please just let me have a moment to urinate over there," I said. I went over by the tall weeds, I made like I was going to urinate, and then I just ran. I ran into the weeds; I ran this way, then that way, in case they came after me with bullets. Yes, they came after me. I didn't see how many men because I was running. I ran to the cliffs and I hid for five hours in the canyon. . . . I walked back to the highway; I got on another bus. Thank God that bus wasn't stopped by them, too; they would have seen me again and shot me for being a guerrilla.

In 1993, on a bus to San Bartolo, my irate fellow passengers prevented the comisionados from removing two young men. The bus driver, silent but sympathetic, slowed and finally stopped the bus in the middle of the dirt road while passengers berated the comisionados in a mixture of K'iche' and Spanish:

Pigs! Snakes! You're nothing but a pack of *putamadre* dogs! Get off this bus or we'll throw you off. We're all neighbors here. How can you do this to your own people? . . . See this box of chain saw parts the young man has? If I had a chain saw now I'd cut off your head! Get out of here; you're not grabbing young men in San Bartolo today.

Since late 1994 recruitment has been voluntary, in response to vigorous protests by the Left and pressure from human rights organizations. A 17-year-old neighbor showed me a recruitment flier from our hapless comisionado. He said:

The paper says there are all kinds of jobs in the army; one can be a baker or an electrician . . . and one receives food, clothes, and 600 quetzales a month. That's not true; it's a lie, I say. We won't be given tennis shoes, only army boots! . . . Wouldn't I have to go in the woods, up in the mountains, carrying with me a gun, to go fight them? So I told Norberto that I don't want to join. . . . What did he say? Nothing! *Utz ri', utz ri'* (That's fine, that's okay) is all he said. . . . None of us young men are going.

One morning in December 1992, slogans for the Guerrilla Army of the Poor (EGP) appeared on nearly every wall in the center of Momostenango. Months later, a neighbor asked, "Have you seen the walls over there? It's clear (*q'alaj*) Momostecos are nothing but guerrillas. In San Bartolo the mayor orders such words covered up. If not, there could be problems." There were indeed problems, because in May 1993 an army detachment arrived in Momostenango and sent soldiers from house to house "inviting" all residents to a community meeting. Surrounded by a dozen armed soldiers, about three hundred Momostecos sat in stony silence while a young officer gave an impassioned speech that lasted several hours. After a few words in K'iche' ("I am an indigenous person, as you are"), he switched to Spanish:

> When I arrived here and saw this town painted up, I said to myself and my men that Momostenango was a nest of guerrillas. We'll establish a permanent base if necessary to exterminate them, I said, and we will exterminate them! But now I've been here a little while; I've talked with people; I've come to know Momostenango. And I see this is a good town, a town that respects authority, a town of hard-working businessmen and artisans. What has happened here, like other parts of our country, you've simply been tricked (*engañados*) by the subversives. They have promised young men lots of money to join them, haven't they? And then they say they'll kill their families if they try to quit. We know! . . . Because we can see that Momostecos are not really guerrillas, because it's clear that what has happened is that some of you have been taken down the wrong road by the subversion, we have come to show everyone the right road. . . . If anyone wakes up in the morning and finds that the filthy EGP has painted their house or store, come to me. If you don't have money for paint, the army will supply it. If you are a woman alone and can't do the work, I'll lend the strong back and arms of a soldier to clean your walls. This way we'll see who the subversives are—and those of you listening know who you are.

The officer went on to provide physical descriptions—some very detailed—of individuals who he asserted were allied with *la subversión* (the subversion) in specific villages. The following day in Tierra Blanca, everyone at the Bartolense village hall had heard about the officer's speech. But instead of making their usual jokes about "Momosteco guerrillas," they hotly denied the accusations. During the last weeks before the November elections in 1995, URNG slogans appeared throughout San Bartolo and Momostenango. In December 1995, a small EGP contingent was still living in the hills above San Bartolo's hot springs:

> Didn't you hear that *ri pa q'ayes* (the ones out in the weeds) were in San Bartolo again? . . . They came while the electricity was off, and in two stores they bought all the coffee and sugar. . . . Yes, it was paid for. I say, there must be guerrilla supporters in San Bartolo, but nobody's giving away food for free. Surely some people know who they are, maybe even are related to them. It's said they are K'iche's like we are. . . . They wrote "EGP" on the police station, then suddenly they fled.

Those Tierra Blancans who were aware of the ongoing "peace process"— the negotiations between the government and the guerrillas—were doubtful that the war would end any time soon. Partly this reflects cynicism about all official efforts. But people also think the army just keeps fighting ("That's their job"), as do the guerrillas:

> That's what they do, the guerrillas—they fight. They don't have any other work, and they don't have land, so they don't plant milpa. Their lives are really difficult. But maybe the other guerrillas give them food and maybe also they are paid to fight. So if they stop the fighting, that's it; they'll be hungry (*k'o wijal kuk'*). They can't go back to their homes, because they don't have homes; they don't have families any more.

How Tierra Blancans View Popular Organizing and Human Rights

This is how a Tierra Blancan interpreted the spray-painted initials of the Committee for Campesino Unity: "What is CUC? You mean *kuk* (squirrel) don't you? It's an animal! [snickers] No, seriously, the CUC is a political party; it's from the government, isn't it?" Tierra Blancans have a strong sense of social justice, but justice as locally defined, interpreted, and dispensed. The mayor deals with delinquents as he sees fit, supported by the *nima'q taq winaq* (senior men). A tired young councilman sighed:

> It's necessary to respect the mayor. He is the one who commands. Right now, we're tired; it's 5:30; the day's gone. We're hungry; we want to go home. But the mayor hasn't yet "given us the road" (*maja' kuya b'e chaqech*). They're just sitting in there talking. If I just left by myself; if I went home? He would send me to jail for an hour tomorrow.

About twice a month the mayor orders a neighbor fined or locked up in the little basement jail. Offenses include drunkenness, fighting, beating or frightening one's children, denying the obvious paternity of an out-of-wedlock baby, and cussing out the mayor (*kuk'yaq itzel taq tzij puwi'*). There is no due process, and these summary judgments clearly violate Tierra Blancans' constitutional rights. Yet there is widespread support for the mayor. Released prisoners profess shame, not resentment. A 33-year-old neighbor explained:

> Yes, I was in jail for two days. It was hard. I was hungry, even though my wife sent my food to me. And it was cold. But I was in jail because of fighting. I fought the *ajch'amiyab'* (councilmen) when they put me in jail.... It's because I drank so much *tzam re siwan* (liquor from the canyon, or home brew). I was a drunk; that's why the mayor ordered the men to put me in there.

When 12-year-olds were caught pick-pocketing in another town, the mayor of Tierra Blanca sentenced them to a week of hauling rocks, and the neighbors heartily approved: "It's good that they work. They'll work hard all week, so that they have time to think about their sin, so that they know that here there is law."

Law and order as understood in Tierra Blanca do not necessarily extend to crimes as defined by the penal code. A neighbor was caught with 2,700 marijuana plants in his milpa above the Pan-American Highway. A neighbor related:

> I was going up to my upper milpa; it was early, 5:00 in the morning, when I found myself with a policeman on the trail. A policeman up there on our land in the dark! That was frightening. He saw me; he spoke to me and asked whose land was that over there? I was afraid, so I said I didn't know. The policeman said, "Isn't that Rubén's land?" "Maybe it is; I don't know," I said. It is his land, of course! He planted marijuana because he was told that he could make a lot of money.... I don't know where the seeds came from, from Ladinos or maybe Mexicans.... Then later more police came and Guardia Hacienda; they seized him and took him and his nephew, too. They burned some of the plants right there. The rest they took, almost 2,000 plants were carried off by them. I say they are just going to sell it themselves.

Many Tierra Blancans were unaware that planting marijuana is against the law, despite billboards along the Pan-American Highway and radio announcements. At least half a dozen neighbors expected I would stock seeds for marijuana just like vegetables and trees. "Can't you get some?" they badgered. "How is planting marijuana against the law?" So they were shocked to learn that Rubén could be in the slammer for a long time. One of them observed:

> It's true then that to plant marijuana is prohibited. But Rubén hadn't known that; he just planted it because one makes a lot of money. Isn't it better to be poor like the rest of us? He's gone to prison; he'll never come out of there now. And he has his wife, his children. . . . It's said that if he paid a lawyer to go before the judge and present papers for him, he could get out. But that takes a lot of money. If he had sold the marijuana he would have the money now.

Despite acute concern over their lack of land, Tierra Blancans do not sympathize with land seizures elsewhere in Guatemala by campesinos like themselves. Owing to a pervasive distrust of outsiders, they are suspicious of the organizers' motives. A 53-year-old neighbor was looking at newspaper photos of demonstrations by CONIC, the Coordinadora Nacional Indígena y Campesina, in February 1995:

> These people don't have land, they say. And now their baby has just died! They have no homes, they say, and of course the baby got sick and died, living in the street under the sun during the day, in the cold at night. Their lives are so difficult (*k'ax ri kik'aslemal*). But why are they staying there in front of the National Palace? That's dangerous. More people could die. They went because the CONIC came and told them to go to the capital and cry out for land. That's no good. We would never go do such a thing. Who is CONIC? Does anyone know them? Better to stay here with what little one has. If one goes with those groups, one could lose everything.

Perhaps organizations like CONIC fare better where land shortages are even more acute than in Totonicapán, although that is hard to imagine. The people of Totonicapán lose land to erosion and their numerous siblings, but few have been forcibly dispossessed because the land is just too high and cold to be very profitable. Tierra Blancans count their unfruitful patches of mountainside as the most precious of their possessions, a gift from God and an inheritance from their parents. The idea that land could be a right granted by the government has yet to occur to them, perhaps because they have so little reason to expect anything from the state. "Those women are in front of the National Palace screaming because they want to be given land as a gift," a 38-year-old Momosteco said of CONIC demonstrations in Guatemala City. "But the CONIC just wants the government to give land to them. What a bunch of crazy people (*e'mox taq winaq*)."

Human rights was increasingly in the news after a mid-1993 constitutional crisis led to the selection of Ramiro de León Carpio, human rights ombudsman, as president. The United Nations, the European Community, the Catholic Church, government agencies, and popular organizations all mounted efforts to promote human rights, some of them in Mayan languages as well as Spanish. Even in Tierra Blanca, "human rights" began to enter the popular consciousness.

Back in 1993, when the Tierra Blanca school director tried to organize meetings on the subject, some neighbors were hostile to the idea:

> The teacher is talking about human rights. These days there are too many human rights—even thieves have rights, people who kill have rights. Before, there was law. If you stole, you yourself were killed! So there were no thieves. It's different now. Now you might steal, you might kill, but you don't even go to prison. That's what human rights is.... Other ideas, like the right to have schools, to own land, to speak our own language? But our school doesn't really accomplish much any more (*ma kachakun ta chi ri'*). And if you don't have land, you're just poor. We're all poor here.... We already know the government doesn't help us. We're not waiting for gifts; we know how to work; we're not thieves.

By February 1995, in contrast, Tierra Blancans were starting to see the point. As happened frequently, the Treasury Police halted our slow, overcrowded bus and claimed to be looking for contraband—while hitting up the driver for a bribe. We were already very late. Usually, passengers are resigned and only grumble a few complaints. This time I was surprised to see a neighbor stand up and loudly tell the driver that we would denounce the Guardia to Derechos Humanos (Human Rights). Even more surprising, there was general agreement: "*Sí hombre,* they're only looking for money for themselves, not contraband!"

One of my neighbors associated the name of Rigoberta Menchú with human rights for indigenous people, though, as Victor Montejo suggests, Menchú's text and its deconstruction by David Stoll (1998) are largely irrelevant for indigenous people (Montejo 2005:101). The neighbor said: "Yes, she won a prize for writing her book, a book about us K'iche's. She asked the army and the guerrillas to stop killing our people. And she is a K'iche'; she is one of us. Now people everywhere know how it is here with us and with the Ladinos in Guatemala."

After the October 1995 massacre in Xamán, where soldiers killed 12 resettled refugees, neighbors condemned the incident in the strongest language I had ever heard in Tierra Blanca. "The army is killing our people again," they said, gazing at newspaper photos of the bodies. "First they drove them from their homes and stole all their things. Now the refugees have returned and they are being killed. The army is evil. Who will stop the killing?" Impressed that they described the dead as *qawinaq* (our people), I asked: "Who are the deceased? Where are they from?" "They are all *naturalib'* [from *naturales* in Spanish, for indigenous], K'iche's, Q'eqchi's, people returned from Mexico."

Are Tierra Blancans Mayas?

This is how a Tierra Blancan reacted to the multilingual radio program *Mayab' Winaq:* "What does this mean, *mayab' winaq?* . . . Those people, they all died long ago (*najtir konojel xekamik*). There are no longer Mayas. There are only us K'iche's, the Mams, the Tz'utujils. I don't know anyone called a Maya." On the basis of ethnological science, anthropologists refer to Guatemala's indigenous people as Mayas. So do most foreigners and the Guatemalan indigenous professionals, activists, and elders striving to revive Mayan culture and ethnic identity. Matthew Restall (2001), among others, has observed that until recently it was rare for Mayas to think of themselves or act collectively as such. The label has yet to make much impression on Tierra Blancans. Following an age-old tradition of municipio-based identity, they see themselves as Momostecos or Bartolenses first, as K'iche's rather than Mams or Kaqchikels, and as indigenous opposed to Ladino. But they do not see themselves as Mayas. There is no collective term in K'iche' for Mayas other than *mayab'*, borrowed recently from Spanish. The mayab' are the *ojer taq winaq* (people of long ago), who are not necessarily related to anyone today. The naturalib', in contrast, include Tierra Blancans and other contemporary or recent indigenous people.

Tierra Blancans are so localistic that they rarely acknowledge the connections with other indigenous peasants that the Left and the Maya Movement might expect. Perhaps owing to long-standing land conflicts with other K'iche'-speaking neighbors, they see people like themselves as competitors rather than allies. They distrust Ladinos even more, but there are too few locally to assume the dimensions of an ethnic enemy as visualized by the Maya Movement. As for the Guatemalan elites against which the Left would like to organize Tierra Blancans, this presumed class enemy is even more remote.

Tierra Blancans have definite ideas about ethnicity, human rights, and social justice, but these reflect a deeply religious and conservative view of themselves and their place in the world, not the urban ideologies advanced by the Left or the Right. Even if political discourse is well-intentioned and to the point, it occasions deep suspicion among people who distrust outsiders and whose immediate concern is feeding large families by farming tiny plots of land. To my neighbors, the ethnic and class-conscious groups trying to organize them are barely distinguishable from Guatemala's political parties and have as little credibility. As for the guerrillas, my neighbors equate them with the army as "fighters" and "killers," not because they can't distinguish between the two but because they dismiss the civil war as irrelevant to their most immediate, pressing problems.

At the same time, there is evidence that the people of Tierra Blanca are broadening their perspective on the world. Forced by relentless poverty and population pressure to emigrate, seasonally or permanently, more villagers are coming in contact with non-K'iche's, Ladinos, even foreigners. Education levels are slowly improving as, year by year, first three, then five, then eight students manage to complete sixth grade. Rigoberta Menchú has become an icon to Tierra Blancans for bringing recognition to K'iche' villagers like themselves.

Pinning their hopes on a faltering peace process, Guatemalan organizers and their foreign supporters are promoting a political culture in which human rights discourse is increasingly legitimate. If current levels of violence abate, there will be new opportunities for the Guatemalan Left to work with rural indigenous communities. But the Left and its international supporters must go beyond "revolutionary nostalgia" (Montejo 2005:90) and help villagers like Tierra Blancans leave the war, the army, and the guerrillas behind. What is needed is an agenda that accepts villagers on their own terms—as Momostecos and Bartolenses, not as Mayas—and focuses on the issues that matter to them: land, income, and family.

Acknowledgments

I am indebted to the people of Tierra Blanca for their honesty, humor, patience, and generosity.

10
Fried Chicken or *Pop*?

Redefining Development and Ethnicity in Totonicapán

Monica DeHart

In the summer of 1996, my fieldwork with the Cooperation for Rural Development of the West (CDRO) took me to the organization's self-declared star community: San Pedro. Given that this trip occurred at a relatively early moment in my 12-year history of ethnographic research on indigenous development projects in rural Totonicapán, I was not yet a regular visitor to San Pedro or the two other rural K'iche' communities where I would come to work. Upon hearing that I had never visited San Pedro, Emilio, a CDRO program director, eagerly offered to take me to see the *Pixib'al Ja* (community hall) they had built there. We set off in one of CDRO's many four-wheel-drive Toyota pickups with the trademark CDRO logo—the K'iche' *pop* (woven mat) image—on the driver and passenger doors announcing our passage. Along the bumpy two-mile drive over the mountainous landscape, Emilio lauded the many development achievements that this star community had achieved, noting that it was definitely the most advanced of all the CDRO affiliates. Indeed, he cited the community hall that we were going to see as the best example of that progress.

We eventually pulled up to a black metal gate which enclosed a large, cement-block, two-story yellow building set off by a dirt playground and parking area. I remember being impressed, as the building communicated a formal institutional persona rarely seen in the rural communities at that time. Once inside the building, however, that formality was shattered by a hall full of playing schoolchildren. After a moment of confusion, Emilio and I were greeted by an earnest-looking man in his mid-thirties who Emilio briefly introduced as Juan García, CDRO's local council president. Juan offered to take us on a tour of the building and eagerly escorted us up to the second story, where he pointed out different rooms and offices for my benefit. Then he led us to the roof, where construction of a third story was currently underway. Finally, Juan brought us back to the community council's designated meeting room, where he took a seat at the front desk, flanked by two men who had also accompanied us on the tour.

Emilio politely introduced me to our hosts and explained, in Spanish, that I was a North American anthropologist studying CDRO's development program. Nodding enthusiastically throughout the introduction, Juan barely waited for his cue before addressing me. He thanked me for my visit and then launched into a description of the community hall's functions, mentioning that it hosted a primary school, a shoe-making apprentice program, a typewriting training program, and an office for the local authorities. The community authorities are made up of a body of obligatory, elected positions dedicated to community administration and the execution of local law (see Barrios 1998a, b; and Tzaquitzal et al. 1999 for the history and organization of Totonicapán's local authorities). Judging by the glowing image that Juan presented, Emilio was not alone in considering the community hall to be CDRO's crowning development feat. Juan finished by mentioning the council's current plans and needs, most notably, efforts to finance a prospective computer lab. Then he paused, leaned forward a bit, and asked, "Which international foundation did you say you represented?"

This impromptu meeting with the council members in San Pedro left no doubt in my mind why this had become CDRO's showcase community. In addition to the monumental development feats it housed, its council members were clearly accustomed to unannounced visits from international passersby who sought a glimpse of the progress the organization had made. Furthermore, these council members seemed to know all too well how important these visits were to securing new development funds. The fact that I was an anthropologist studying development initiatives, rather than a donor or aid organization representative, was a distinction of little importance to them.

Therefore, it was no small irony when, three years later, the same Juan García who had been our gracious tour guide sat with me in a private interview and disparagingly compared CDRO to a fried-chicken fast-food restaurant chain whose sole interest was to expand its franchises rather than to promote real development. He and other local critics claimed that CDRO's "pop" concept represented a savvy marketing strategy rather than an authentic Mayan development method. Their critique challenged the validity of CDRO's ethnic development program and its difference from Western capitalist corporations. In essence, they implied that pop was just another item on CDRO's fast-food menu. I was thus left to ponder whether CDRO's ethnic development was about fried chicken or pop?

In this chapter, I draw on the CDRO experience to explore the complex relationship between Mayan culture and development in post–Peace Accord Guatemala. In Totonicapán, an area which escaped the worst of the violence of the 1980s, development work has served as an important arena for defining identity politics, both within the rural indigenous communities and in relation to a global Western modernity. Therefore, I analyze how shifts in global development policies have correlated with the aims and methods of local indigenous initiatives like CDRO's, shaping ideas about what constitutes authentic ethnic development versus insidious capitalist enfranchisement. Furthermore, I show how development projects serve as a powerful framework for articulating class differences and local politics within the indigenous community.

*Pop*ularizing Local Development

By the late 1990s, CDRO was one of the preeminent indigenous development organizations in Guatemala, working in over 40 different indigenous communities and managing an operating budget of over a million dollars. Much of its success, however, derived from its unique grassroots origins. The CDRO initiative emerged in the early 1980s when indigenous community leaders from rural Totonicapán initiated a pilot project in San Pedro. By 1984, the association CDRO was formally established with the participation of 25 members. These founding members established an organizational system based on traditional Mayan culture which they envisioned as a vehicle for facilitating community self-development.

CDRO's efforts to promote a development project rooted in Mayan culture explicitly sought to address ethnic development needs and interests in a way that other projects—including urban Ladino insurgencies and authoritarian state development models—had not. In the context of the state's violent repression and "scorched earth" tactics of the early 1980s, CDRO publicly positioned itself as a neutral, non-politicized organ promoting proposals rather than protests, even though consciousness-raising and local autonomy were among its goals. Its founders drew upon Mayan oral traditions, historical documents, and community customs to formulate the institution's unique vision of the Mayan worldview and its relevance to the development process.

Central to this worldview was the woven mat, or *pop*—a K'iche' concept with dense cultural significance within the rural Totonicapán communities. According to CDRO, the woven mat refers most literally to the sacred place where K'iche' community elders would traditionally sit at ritual social gatherings. At a more symbolic level, the mat's round shape represents the cyclical, continuous notion of time and space that are held to guide K'iche's worldview. Finally, the mat's weave points to the interconnectedness and interdependency that characterize Mayan collective traditions. Building on the *pop*'s many meanings, CDRO has used the woven mat to represent the organization's development methodology, its institutional configuration, and its au-

RI POP WOKOJ
ORGANIGRAMA HORIZONTAL
CDRO

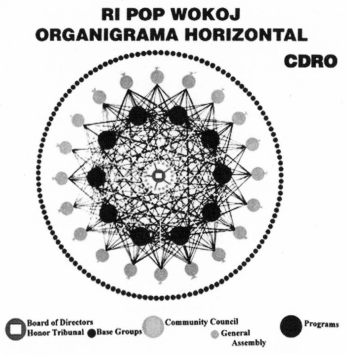

Board of Directors
Honor Tribunal ●Base Groups

Community Council
● General
Assembly

● Programs

Fig 15. The Cooperation for Rural Development of the West logo. Courtesy of Cooperación para el Desarrollo Rural de Occidente (CDRO), 1995 (original modified).

thentic Mayan identity. CDRO graphically depicted the "pop" concept that serves as its organizational logo in a circular, web-like structure composed of multiple, color-coded, overlapping, and interwoven lines.

In this form, the pop icon became a ubiquitous image in the Western highlands during the 1990s. Frequently seen on the doors of CDRO's numerous four-wheel-drive vehicles as they traveled through the rural communities and also prominently displayed at the entrance to CDRO's administrative and training buildings, the pop became an important source of institutional "branding." Through the icon, CDRO established public recognition and legitimacy through an easily-identifiable logo.

As an organizational form, the pop reflects the numerous layers of participation that constitute the organization. The outermost circle represents the base communities, which are connected to the community councils and to specific programs such as health, infrastructure, or handicraft production. All of the aforementioned entities participate as members of the general assembly, from which the board of directors is elected. In CDRO's graphic rendition of this structure, all of these spheres are coded vis-à-vis primary colors for easy identification. The lines that form the weave are interpreted as diverse forms of relation and coordination that exist in the system (CDRO 1997:7).

CDRO has used the woven mat trope not only to depict this unique organizational structure, but also to represent its development method. Specifically, CDRO has used the pop emblem to reference three main cultural tenets informing every project: total community participation, mutual support, and horizontality. In essence, these concepts refer to a development process that is universal, inclusive, democratic, and egalitarian, mobilizing the community as a collective protagonist of development through the promotion of reciprocity and equilibrium. While CDRO has mobilized the woven mat to reference a communal, egalitarian Mayan culture, other scholars have interpreted it as a hierarchical symbol of kingship or elite privilege (see Robicsek 1983; Freidel et al. 1995; D. Tedlock 1985). While local residents articulated the importance of the pop as an important Mayan cultural artifact and symbol, they did not perceive CDRO's icon as embodying that concept.

We can see examples of these principles at work in the woven mat structure itself. The pop organizational scheme reflects multiple levels of representation and authority that are interconnected in a complex system of checks and balances. Specific individual and group interests are balanced at the community council level, encouraging total participation and mutual support. Representatives from the community councils are elected to serve on CDRO's board of directors, thus maintaining "community" control over the development process and indigenous leadership of the organization at all levels; however, two-year service terms ensure that these representatives go right back to working at the community level, applying their experience for the greater good rather than toward individual social or economic advancement.

Despite CDRO's invocation of traditional Mayan culture, its program and goals were still compatible with global capitalism. In its successful microcredit program, for example, CDRO's methodology allowed community members to place some conditions on their participation in the market and to mitigate its negative consequences by reinforcing collective over individual risk or gain. Nonetheless, these same microcredit initiatives also simultaneously extended and deepened the role of modern financial institutions within the rural landscape. Therefore, rather than undermining or opposing Western capitalist practices, CDRO's ethnic development selectively appropriated and retrofitted them for community use. In many ways, this strategy reflected the historical complementary between Totonicapán's of local ethnic identity and a "well developed *Indian* market economy . . . [that] provides the material basis for Indian cultural autonomy and Indian political resistance to the state" (C. Smith 1988:215), a point to which I will return below.

These examples present us with several reasons why CDRO's methodology became so attractive to the global development industry. In the wake of 1980s structural adjustment policies in Latin America—characterized by state downsizing, cutbacks in social welfare, and the privatization of services—community-level projects like CDRO's came to represent the best of both worlds. On the one hand, CDRO's projects were community-based and culturally appropriate, promoting participation, sustainability, and equality. On the other hand, they were privately funded, locally managed, and complementary with market incorporation. Consequently, in many ways CDRO's bottom-up, social enterprise development efforts complemented neoliberal economic reforms as well as satisfied international humanitarian goals. These reflected how development capital flowed directly from private and multilateral funding agencies to specific local constituencies on the ground, repositioning beneficiaries as development agents and stakeholders. Compared to 1970s cooperative efforts, this newer phase of community participation involved the privatization of the development on a much larger scale. Various scholars have critiqued how these local, participatory strategies shifted the burden of development from states to the poor (see Annis 1988; Rahnema 1992; Reilly 1995; Paley 2001).

By 1998, CDRO had proposed a regionalization project that aspired to use the CDRO woven mat methodology as a model for stimulating self-development among non-indigenous community organizations across seven departments of western Guatemala (CDRO 1998a). As I will discuss later, it was the perceived similarity between this replicable pop model and a fast-food franchise expansion that has made CDRO suspect among some of its community affiliates.

Development through Difference

In addition to satisfying neoliberal development priorities, the pop method also proved attractive to the international development industry because of its explicitly ethnic roots. For example, at the 1997 Inter-American Conference of Mayors in Miami, Florida, Charles Reilly, a former Peace Corp director and Inter-American Development Bank representative used his closing speech to single out CDRO and the pop as the most promising example of local governance:

> Of course, highland Guatemala is not Asuncion, Buenos Aires, Kingston, New York, Quebec, Rio de Janeiro, Santiago de Chile, or even Guatemala City. But the mayors of those cities and thousands of other towns and everyone in the development business might learn something from the *Pop*. . . . Because universal policies are seldom universal, they are

supplemented by "targeted" policies. CDRO, with its woven mat, is far ahead of us. Inspired by the ancient Mayan document *Pop Wuj*, it insists that advancement requires that "no group be left behind." This high-land organization weaves together interdependent villages, towns, and representatives in an extraordinary social, economic, and political tap-estry rooted in Mayan culture. That single sphere, woven from the many threads of polity, economy, and society to form a pattern of local devel-opment, was for me the compelling message from Miami. (1997:7)

As Reilly's quote reveals, the pop's appeal comes from its ancient origins and the holistic, egalitarian, participative alternative they represent. Despite that uniqueness, it was a strategy from which "everyone in the development in-dustry might learn." The Guatemalan government also validated the CDRO method, awarding the organization its National Order of the Guatemalan Cultural Patrimony award in 2000. These acts of recognition show how state and global development trends have legitimized ethnic community activists as both an alternative to top-down, state-run development precedents and a ve-hicle for promoting Western capitalist modernity. In this context, CDRO's pop logo not only identified the organization as an effective local initiative, but also affirmed CDRO's cultural authority as a legitimate Mayan organization relative to other groups.

However, CDRO's efforts to substantiate its Mayan roots have not been limited to associating itself with the pop; the organization has also asserted its legitimacy by contrasting itself with what it is not—namely, the West. CDRO's general advisor, Benjamín Son Turnil, provided an eloquent example of this type of self-representation when he contrasted CDRO to a Kaqchikel organization in a neighboring town (see DeHart 2008). Son Turnil critiqued this Kaqchikel organization for adorning its offices with Mayan artifacts, cre-ating an external appearance of indigenous authenticity even as its program re-flected an "eminently Western capitalist" mindset. Son Turnil used this story to lament indigenous organizations' reliance on exotic cultural artifacts to com-municate their identity. He saw these organizations as orienting themselves to-ward the past rather than seeking to develop the mundane practices of everyday community life—i.e., particular forms of conflict resolution, emergency sup-port, and reciprocity—as productive tools for the future. Son Turnil's experi-ence in Chimaltenango reflects how grassroots indigenous organizations have struggled amongst themselves to define the terms of Mayaness in a context characterized by multiple and often competing formulations of Mayan culture (on the Maya Movement see Bastos and Camus 1993; Fischer and Brown 1996; Warren 1998). Son Turnil critiqued the Mayan artifacts he encountered as cul-tural commodities and evidence of Western capitalism rather than as proof of an authentic indigenous identity—a distinction also elaborated by José Oscar Barrera Nuñez in this volume.

This effort to represent Mayan culture in opposition to Western traditions was also present in CDRO's institutional *Uk'ux Wuj* (the founding document). Therein CDRO describes the source of Mayan knowledge in distinct contrast to Western liberalism: "The global focus is based on the Mayan worldview, which is different from the liberal Western vision that separates out problems and studies them in a specialized way, thereby losing sight of their interrelatedness as causes and as effects" (1998b:18). In these juxtapositions between Mayan and Western approaches, CDRO has framed Mayan culture as an internal essence that is defined by its difference from Western ways. CDRO differentiated between the two cultural spaces by juxtaposing a unique Mayan moral economy defined by collective property and mutual support against the private property and individual accumulation of Western society. CDRO also distinguished between Mayan ways of knowing, identified as a holistic understanding of cause and effect, and the positivist, scientific method used in the West.

There is nothing especially novel about CDRO's efforts to position Mayan culture in opposition to Western traditions; indeed, the notion of ethnic difference hinges on that very distinction. CDRO's efforts are unique, however, in their insistence that Mayan development methods are more efficient, effective, and, thus, legitimate than Western initiatives. In other words, they assert that Mayan techniques provide a more useful means of achieving development within the rural communities because of the refusal to "separate out problems" in favor of exploring the "interrelatedness" of the causes and effects of underdevelopment. It was exactly this purportedly superior, holistic approach that Reilly praised in his glowing assessment of the CDRO project and which made CDRO a poster child for indigenous development efforts. When CDRO embarked on plans to build a regional training center in 1999, the center's blueprints were admired by Spain's Queen Elizabeth, who visited CDRO during her trip through Guatemala. When CDRO's training center was completed a year later, its inaugural event was attended by the Spanish ambassador to Guatemala and representatives from the United Nations, the Inter-American Foundation, and the Soros Foundation.

However, the same qualities that made CDRO attractive to global development agencies produced problems for CDRO's local cultural authority. Indeed, conflicts between CDRO, its council members, and traditional authorities in San Pedro show how community members have debated what counts as authentic Mayan culture and whether the pop—as a development method—can be considered a legitimate example of it. These debates were important to community members because, ultimately, they determined who could speak for the indigenous community and who was entitled to control over the resources that community development projects captured. These struggles present a clear picture of how neoliberal processes, such as corporate franchise expansion and privatization, shaped local understandings of the development process. In these discussions, the distance between a collective Mayan community and a profit-driven Western capitalist becomes difficult to measure. I would argue, in fact, that it is not so much the substance of these two positions or the distance between them that is important, as both positions were mutually imbricated. Instead, what was important was the ability to locate oneself on the side of the community in order to claim to occupy the moral high ground of indigenous authenticity.

Fried Chicken or *Pop*?

Ironically, in the Totonicapán community where the pop method was perhaps proven most successful, it also served as a point of contention among local organizers. In many ways, it was the pop's fame as an innovative community development model that was responsible for creating these tensions between CDRO and a few of its community affiliates in San Pedro.

I got a glimpse of these tensions firsthand when I went to interview Juan García at his home in San Pedro on a rainy June day in 1999. By this time, Juan had retired from the community council president post that he had occupied when he led me and Emilio on a tour of San Pedro's community hall several years prior. Now, although he remained active in the community council, he had changed his tune about CDRO considerably. We sat in a storeroom located just off the main production room of his large house. While we talked, I watched his four employees stretch printed cotton-polyester fabric over long work tables, preparing to make the polo shirts that Juan—a successful merchant—sold in markets throughout central and eastern Guatemala. Juan shifted back and forth on his makeshift chair (a bundle of freshly sewn and packaged shirts) while he talked about the council's work, but when I asked Juan about his relationship with CDRO, he became visibly agitated:

> CDRO is like Pollo Campero [the Guatemalan equivalent to Kentucky Fried Chicken]. CDRO found a good business and went out looking how to expand without thinking about the problems it might cause. CDRO comes to the communities and constructs an organizational framework but doesn't resolve the problems of the communities and, thus, leaves them in an awkward state of confusion. Our village succeeded because it took the opportunity and knew how to get ahead, but even so it lacked the resources to do everything it wanted.

In this provocative analogy, Juan, the quintessential rural capitalist, was accusing CDRO of having a capitalist mentality that equated development with "good business." Therefore, he was accusing CDRO of seeing its affiliates as nothing more than franchisees. These were strong charges given the fact that CDRO's entire program was oriented toward promoting community self-development and the revival of local Mayan culture. More ironically still, CDRO had represented Juan's community as its "star" community.

When I asked another San Pedro council member—who, notably, was also a successful merchant—about how CDRO was using Mayan culture, he corroborated Juan's critique, responding, "Oh, that's just how CDRO paints the organizations for the gringos."

In these two cases, San Pedro council members challenged the authenticity of CDRO's ethnic development program, calling it more of a global marketing strategy than a reflection of legitimate community ideals. Their critiques demonstrate the powerful role that development processes have come to play in mediating community politics and class positions in post–Peace Accord rural Totonicapán. (See also Smith, this volume, for more on intra-community political conflicts.) So, as I asked above, Does this mean that pop is nothing more than an item on CDRO's fast-food chain menu?

In answering this question, we should notice that the terms that these two council members used to critique CDRO look suspiciously familiar. After all, by talking about "the community" versus the "Western capitalist," Juan and his colleague were repeating the distinction that CDRO itself had used to validate its own vision of authentic Mayan culture; however, in the council members' critique, CDRO itself was the organization charged with being nothing more than an "eminently Western capitalist" institution.

In thinking about the meaning of these labels—community versus capitalist—we might also note the irony of their juxtaposition here. Carol Smith's study of local market production in Totonicapán in the 1970s revealed the region to be the home of intense petty capitalist production for regional markets. More importantly, Smith demonstrated how this petty commerce was a central ingredient of Totonicapán ethnic identity since the 19th century (see C. Smith 1988, 1990a). Consequently, community and capitalism have certainly not been mutually exclusive in recent history. What's more, many of the community council members like Juan García were part of a fairly wealthy local merchant class that sold products to larger urban and national markets. Consequently, their use of the capitalist critique must be seen in strategic terms.

To begin, the council members' critique of CDRO sought to reduce the pop method to nothing more than a marketing strategy so that council members could then highlight their own individual contributions to San Pedro's development. In their eyes, it was not the franchisor, but rather the local franchisee that actually made things happen.

However, council critiques of CDRO's capitalist mentality went beyond just writing off CDRO as the responsible party for development; they also hoped to distinguish local council members as more moral and authentically indigenous development actors. In this sense, the council members were reproducing the difference between local ethnic moral economies and global capitalist moral economies that both CDRO and admiring development officials had made before them.

Council members alleged that CDRO employees' semi-professional status, international travel experience, and fixed salary distinguished them as a local professional class relative to their community counterparts. This class difference was exacerbated by rumors that "CDRO employees' salaries come in dollars." The idea of dollared salaries and the sight of CDRO administrators driving brand-new, four-wheel-drive vehicles emblazoned with the pop logo contributed to community perceptions of CDRO as a different kind of capitalist; the pop "brand name" marked CDRO associates as corporate managers rather than organization employees.

By singling out CDRO as a bad capitalist entrepreneur, council members deflected critiques that they themselves constituted an exploitative capitalist elite. As successful merchants and powerful members of the local community council, Juan and his counterparts had come to control significant resources within the community, not least of which was the impressive community building and the development programs it housed. This put them at odds with elected local authorities who charged that Juan and his crew were essentially trying to privatize communal goods (DeHart 2008). In the context of state efforts to privatize industry and social services throughout Guatemala, the perceived threat of corporate expansion within the community was all too real for community members. Many Guatemalans complain that privatization, rather than stimulating price reduction and service diversification, has instead brought price gouging and irregularity with serious negative consequences for large sectors of society, principle among them the already economically precarious rural indigenous populations. The fact that the council had undergone a process of legal incorporation without first notifying community members of its plans had heightened fears that the council itself had corporate aspirations in the capitalist sense of the word. In an effort to neutralize these fears, council members like Juan aimed to redraw the community's boundaries, repositioning themselves firmly within the community moral tradition. In doing so, they reinstituted themselves as more authentic ethnic actors and averted critiques that they themselves were the entrepreneurs working on behalf of global capital.

Coming Full Circle

This chapter has explored how ethnic development—and its embodiment in the "pop" concept—has been central to defining indigenous community politics both internally and in relation to global capitalist institutions in the wake of 1996. I have argued that global development assumptions and strategies brought groups like CDRO into favor as authentic, local, egalitarian, and sustainable development models (see DeHart 2001, 2003). The "pop" concept, in particular, played an important role in organizing CDRO's innovative community development model and symbolizing its unique cultural roots in a way that has brought CDRO both global notoriety and local critique. Interestingly, even though both CDRO and its council affiliates represented petty capitalist themselves, their efforts to frame themselves as authentic, ethnic development alternatives were expressed in opposition to Western capitalism. Rather than actually being in contradiction with capitalist market integration, these actors were all trying to redefine ethnicity as a more appropriate and effective vehicle for development. What was at stake in their competing representations of ethnic authenticity was access to the moral authority and material resources that came with local development initiatives. CDRO's story thus demonstrates the importance of changing local and global contexts for defining the relationship between ethnicity and development. In other words, the pop method's ability to draw such international celebrity status as an authentic grassroots development solution while being simultaneously analogous to a fast-food restaurant chain looking for franchise expansion highlights the complex way that neoliberal development trends have relocated and re-signified ethnic difference.

Acknowledgments

This research was funded by the National Science Foundation, Fulbright-Hayes, the Inter-American Foundation, Stanford University, and the University of Puget Sound. Special thanks my colleagues at CDRO and community members in San Pedro for their generous collaboration. I am grateful to George Collier, Paulla Ebron, Akhil Gupta, Lisa Hoffman, Jennifer Hubbert, Diane Nelson, Anu Sharma, Carol Smith, and the volume editors for their important critiques and recommendations.

11

Neoliberal Violence

Social Suffering in Guatemala's Postwar Era

Peter Benson and Edward F. Fischer

"Things are better now," it is commonly said in Guatemala, "not like before." The present is compared to *la violencia*. In this era after the wide-ranging Peace Accords, the 36-year internal armed conflict has become a touchstone for measuring and evaluating an ordinary sense of things. Dangers and uncertainties of a previous era, vividly remembered by many, are no longer an overwhelming presence in social experience. That particularly overriding and totalizing kind of violence is now, thankfully, said to be part of the past. Things have changed. The number of disappearances and deaths has decreased, massacres and wholesale destruction of villages has waned, the average income of Mayan peoples has risen, and average education levels have increased. But there is also deepening socioeconomic inequality brought on by uneven patterns of economic development. And lasting peace has proven elusive. Violence has become commonplace. On average, 250 people are murdered each month in the capital city alone (OCAVI 2007). Tabloid newspapers are canvassed with images of bullet-ridden cars and bloody corpses, tucked a few pages inside more respectable dailies. Violent crimes are rarely successfully prosecuted. Clandestine terror squads attack individuals in ways meant to look like common crime. The gang violence that now overwhelms the capital is creeping into more rural regions. While the army presumably hunts drug traffickers and cracks down on heinous crimes, political violence continues apace, as seen in the 1997 assassination of Bishop Juan Gerardi Conedera and campaign-related killings in recent elections (Thomas and Benson 2008). There has also been a resurgence of right-wing political activity and a former dictator's return to power. Because all of this is not categorized as "war," there is the sense that the "something better" promised for so long has been realized in the postwar period (Fischer and Benson 2006).

In this chapter, we document how emerging forms of violence influence a sense of place and social engagements that define everyday life in rural and

Fig 16. Youths hang out in front of a store in Tecpán. Photo by
Peter Benson.

urban Guatemala. Drawing on the medical anthropological concept of "social suffering," we analyze a clustering of lived effects and delineate structural
conditions that underpin disparate forms of violence (Bourdieu et al. 2000;
Farmer 2004; Kleinman et al. 1997). This literature emphasizes the institutional and structural dimensions of suffering, including the role of markets and
governments. Scholars have contextualized the origins of suffering and violence amidst sociopolitical and economic conditions and analyzed experiences
of violence in the context of everyday attitudes. They have emphasized that
in modern societies and capitalist economies suffering tends to adversely im-

pact poor and marginalized groups because of the uneven distribution of material, social, and symbolic capital (Farmer 2003). Likewise, we emphasize the fundamental role of the aggressive program of liberal economic reform that arose alongside the Peace Accords (as outlined in this volume's introduction and other chapters) in fostering new forms of violence and vulnerability. While violence is most commonly explained in terms of individual actions (not just in Guatemala, but in other contexts dominated by a neoliberal zeitgeist, where gang members and other unsavory types are blamed for violence), we instead locate agency in structural conditions themselves, the very processes said to be Guatemala's path toward progress and lasting peace.

The decentralization of markets and politics has involved an attendant "neoliberalization of violence," the simultaneous dispersion of violence into everyday forms and the distribution of blame onto individuals, which deflects attention away from systematically exerted aspects of violence. Violence "not only traumatizes individuals," Angelina Snodgrass Godoy writes about Guatemala's armed conflict, "but in some cases may transform the social fabric of entire communities, thus explaining the persistence of its effects even in settings where all those who survived the initial violence have departed or died, or where new non-state forces predominate in decision making processes" (2002: 641). Like Godoy's concept of the "democratization of terror," which emphasizes how new forms of violence and terror involve expanding segments of the population as either victims or perpetrators (or both), our view addresses the paradoxical way the outsourcing of violence away from a state monopoly contours civil society and political participation in such a way that actually fuels state power. By implicating neoliberal ideologies and policies in the production of the new violence, we complicate simple assessments of the Peace Accords' successes and failures and challenge the guiding premise that unfettered market forces are necessary for achieving peace and security.

The ethnographic setting for our study is Tecpán, a town of about 10 thousand located 80 kilometers west of Guatemala City. Tecpán has a reputation in the region as a progressive and affluent place. In the city proper, about 70 percent of the residents are Kaqchikel Mayas, although the Spanish-speaking, non-Indian, Ladino minority has historically exerted disproportionate control over local government and commercial institutions, buttressed by racist ideologies and colonial inequalities. But Tecpán is also home to an exceptionally strong indigenous bourgeois class that has long supported ethnic consciousness, the value of education, and economic experimentation. In the past few decades, this group became increasingly assertive in local and national politics (Fischer and Hendrickson 2002; Fischer 2001; Hendrickson 1995). Since the late 1990s, Tecpán has undergone major social transformations. There has been an influx of foreign popular culture fare along with various kinds of economic restructuring, including a shift away from traditional milpa agriculture and toward nontraditional export crops in the outlying rural hamlets and entrepreneurial activities in the town's regionally known apparel industry. In both industries, economic production is a powerful means of social and class mobility for Mayas. Entrepreneurial activity in Tecpán has partially been fostered by (or at least emerged within the context of) the aggressive program of privatization and liberal economic reform and a new attitude toward Mayan peoples in the postwar period. Yet, opportunities for social mobility and economic advancement have gone hand in hand with the partial erosion of economic control and security for many people (C. Smith 1990c). International and national trade reforms entail significant pressures related to market access and competition (Fischer and Benson 2006; Fischer 2004; Goldín and Asturias de Barrios 2001; Goldín 1996; Thomas 2006). This context of shifting economic practices and mixed outcomes is one important part of the larger picture of insecurities and inequalities that shape contemporary forms of violence and how people think about and react to them.

El General Returns

General Efraín Ríos Montt (see also Fischer and Benson 2006) talks to God. To hear him tell it, they are good buddies—two old, privileged white guys sharing their disgust at the state of affairs today, from the rise in crime and corruption to the decline in family and faith. This deity speaks in Old Testament tones, calling for vengeance rather than forgiveness, the need for discipline more than compassion. This God told the former military dictator, head of Congress, and born-again evangelical Christian to run for president in Guatemala's 2003 elections. Prior to this, in 1989, he founded the hard-line conservative FRG (Guatemalan Republican Front) party and in 1994 was elected to Congress, where he served as majority leader. Through that summer, the legality of his candidacy was in doubt. A quaint section tucked in Article 186 of the Constitution bars those who have participated in coups from being president (a military junta brought Ríos Montt to power in 1982). On this basis, the Supreme Electoral Tribunal ruled in June 2003 that he was ineligible, a decision at first upheld by the Constitutional Court. Ríos Montt, however, continued to campaign, confident he would prevail.

On July 24, "Black Thursday" as it came to be known, the campaign organized demonstrations that shut down Guatemala City and cost millions in property damage. Thousands of rural supporters were bused in and armed by campaign workers with machetes, sticks, tires, and gasoline; organizers, cell phones held up to their black ski masks, directed the protesters toward targeted government buildings and private businesses, a number of which were looted while police looked on, unwilling to intervene. As smoke from burning cars and buildings filled the skyline, Ríos Montt announced to the press that he would not be able to control his supporters, that they must be heard and their will heeded. Now, even the Constitutional Court overruled itself and, citing international accords, decided that retroactively applying the 1985 Constitution to his 1982 actions would violate his human rights.

One would hope that such a mantel would be uncomfortable for El General, as he likes to be called. Human rights monitors hold him largely responsible for the displacement, torture, and death of tens of thousands of noncombatants during the height of the armed conflict. Because the victims were overwhelmingly rural Mayas, the United Nations Truth Commission declared the violence a case of genocide. But, paradoxically, in 2003 it was poor Mayan peasants who formed the base of his popular support. As the majority leader of Congress, he cultivated allegiance by pushing huge subsidies for fertilizer, increasing the minimum wage, and making large payments to those who served in the country's notorious army-led Civil Auto-Defense Patrols of the early 1980s.

Organized in Civil Auto-Defense Patrols, villagers were charged with protecting their towns from "subversives," often given quotas of suspects to hand over to the local military garrison for "questioning" (see Carmack 1988). The civil patrols were responsible for thousands of extra-judicial killings (as the Guatemalan legal code delicately phrases it), working with the army to instill a quotidian terror in Guatemalans that we can scarcely imagine, even in this age of terrorist threats. Yet, the civil patrollers were also victims, forced into their position under the threat of persecution and death themselves. Poor Mayan farmers were forced to turn on their neighbors and friends, also poor Mayan farmers.

In June 2003, Ríos Montt spoke in Xenimajuyu, a small hamlet on the outskirts of Tecpán. Over a thousand people gathered in a large field on the edge of the village, many because they were promised information about the next installment of promised payments. Ríos Montt was campaigning on a platform of greater security to combat the wave of crime that has swept through the country. He arrived in Xenimajuyu in a red helicopter, accompanied by a fanfare of firecrackers and campaign songs ("My mommy votes for Ríos Montt; my daddy votes for Ríos Montt"). He roused crowds with the fervor of an evangelical pastor. He railed against corruption: "I am not a rich man. I am where I am today because of my hard work. But I am not rich." And he inveighed against political patronage: "Who does your mayor work for? Who does your congressman work for? Who does the president of the Republic work for? You, that's right. And so why should you have to enter their offices with your head bowed . . . to beg for . . . favor? This is wrong. You are their boss."

The day after his visit to Xenimajuyu, Ríos Montt made an ill-timed campaign stop in Rabinal, a Mayan town in the K'iche' region. Forensic anthropologists had been working there, excavating clandestine graves and identifying victims' bodies to document what happened there during the violence and bring some sense of closure to still-grieving families who never knew for sure the fate of their "disappeared" loved ones. On the day Ríos Montt arrived, several bodies were being reburied in marked graves. The presence of the man many hold responsible for these deaths was too much for some townspeople. They arrived at the rally with a coffin painted black and began to jeer at Ríos Montt. Not heeding the advice of his security team, he took the stage to calm the crowd but was met with a barrage of bottles and rocks. After getting hit with a stone, he retreated to his helicopter holding a handkerchief on his bleeding forehead.

The reasoned editorials of the national press that followed stated that it was foolish for Ríos Montt to have gone to Rabinal that day. They also condemned the protesters for using tactics of intimidation in a free election. But who can blame them? The media contextualized culpability for violence on the side of protesters only, localizing agency in the present and detaching a legacy of state-sponsored violence that, in this case, clearly fed into popular uprising. Such representations bolster Ríos Montt's vows to end crime and corruption through force, depicting the masses as a threat to the integrity of democracy and in need of the order of a firm government. Historical forgetting is a precondition for the sustenance of a system of structural violence that, paradoxically, couples a patriarchal view of government with the erosion of services and government functions and effaces the collective political and moral meanings that undergird the use of violence in the context of a social protest. In the end, Ríos Montt's bid did not carry the day. He finished in third place in the presidential race. "I don't care what he says," declared a Mayan man at the Xenimajuyu rally. "We remember who he is and what he has done. We have suffered enough. I will never vote for him no matter how much money he promises."

Violence's Social Course

In June 2002 thousands of residents of Tecpán marched into the municipal center to protest a new property and estate tax passed down as part of structural adjustment programs mandated by the International Monetary Fund (IMF). Estimates range from 3 thousand to 45 thousand protesters. Whatever the number, it was a remarkable show of public dissent that would have been suicidal not long ago. The leader of the demonstration was a Kaqchikel-speaking human rights worker who lives in the municipality. In late 2001, he began organizing opposition to new taxes that, as part of the Peace Accord implementation, were devolved from the Ministry of Finance to local municipal governments, a neoliberal approach to improve accountability while empowering local populations. But many Tecpánecos rightly believe that local government is no less corrupt than the national level. They see the new house and shiny red BMW of the mayor, a member of Ríos Montt's FRG party. Said one community leader in Tecpán: "The mayor treated us poorly. We tried to discuss the tax with him. We told him it was impossible to afford, but he was rude and would not hear our demands."

The cohort marched into town and inhabited the central park in front of the municipal building, carrying banners and documents demanding the mayor's resignation. In front of his office they were met by a phalanx of local police. Even if the crowd was growing frustrated and anxious, no one anticipated the violence about to erupt. A youth, said by all to be a gang member, hurled a rock through one of the town hall's windows. Other protesters immediately followed suit. "The only thing certain was that nothing was certain," said one, "and I heard the first window shatter, then others, and all of a sudden it was out of control. No one knew what was going on."

Many participants abandoned their pacific intentions and torched the municipal building, the police station, and the mayor's home. His car was flipped on its head and set ablaze. Police reacted by throwing tear gas bombs into the crowd, and protesters readily recovered those bombs and returned them to their senders. Many already had knowledge of these weapons, especially those from outlying hamlets, having had extended military training with the Guatemalan army years before as part of the civil patrols (Fischer 2001:58). Rumor has it that protesters used their phones to coordinate looting and relay information about the location of police, who were eventually stripped naked; their firearms were stolen and their bodies were beaten, bloodied, and dragged through the street. The mayor hurried to his getaway vehicle, protected by his bodyguards, while rioters pegged him with stones—some trying their best to kill him.

Despite the creative ways that protesters subverted police authority and established momentary control of the town center, no one wanted June 10 to turn violent, except perhaps those eager to steal televisions, appliances, and food from houses around the park. It is also clear that "gang members" were not the only ones looting and torching. "Many say that the mayor mistreated the protesters, that he was rude and would not hear their demands," said one community organizer. "That is why the people got angry. Many say that it was just the gangs that were acting violently during the protests. But if the mayor was treating the protesters badly when they went to see him, then they had their own reasons for becoming violent." Protesters lamented that the *Prensa Libre* later dubbed their well-intentioned event "chaotic" and that they were portrayed as incorrigible and undemocratic. "We were interested in resolving real political issues," said one participant, becoming noticeably upset as he added, "The gangs are to blame, not the protesters. But everyone ended up losing. We didn't start the violence in this town; the violence has been here, but we are blamed and we are the ones who suffer."

Gangs and Rumors of Gangs

We were up late one night, sitting around the kitchen table talking with a friend in Tecpán and decided to run to the store to get a few beers. The corner store was closed, and the closest place with what passes for cold beer was off the central park, a leisurely five-minute walk. We were heading out the door on foot when our host stopped us with his warning: "You should take your car." At first we thought he was just commenting on what gringo idiots we were for having a car and yet choosing to walk. Then he explained: "It's better not to walk after ten o'clock," he said. "The gangs come out, hanging out on the corners looking for victims. They would spot you blondies [*canchitos*] a kilometer away. You should take the car." So we did, doors locked, eyes peeled for shady characters in the shadows cast by the intermittent streetlamps and houselights. We saw a few groups of teens standing around or walking down the street. They could be gang members, we thought, and we had seen the spray-paint tags popping up on walls around town.

Locals seem certain of gang activities. Some have an idea about their members; some have witnessed their vandalism; all have seen the graffiti signatures (Diamantes, Salvatruchas, Calle 18, Batos Locos, Patojos Locos) that increasingly demarcate territorial hegemonies. There are wild rumors of gangs robbing shoppers and vendors. On one Tuesday, market day, about a week after the June 10 protests, we heard stories that gangs were taking advantage of the narrow passageway running alongside the cathedral where fruits and vegetables are sold. One woman was robbed for 700 quetzales (about US$90) and spent the afternoon sobbing on the church steps, attended to by relatives and friends.

Ten years ago, domestic violence, municipal graft, and petty theft were Tecpán's most pressing crime problems. Today, the perception is clearly that Tecpán is a much more dangerous place. Gangs have become a scapegoat for discussing violence. Tecpanecos say that gang leaders are local youths who went to live in the capital, looking for more opportunities than this small town offers and finding community in the street gangs. There are also youths who have moved to town, living here with no visible means of support. It is said that one gang leader runs a brothel on the town's outskirts.

Gangs are no doubt real, and their presence is menacing. On a national level, some estimates put gang membership higher than that of the national police force (Painter 2007). But they have become larger than life in Tecpán. The category "gang member" can serve as a useful container for popular feelings of anxiety, stress, and despondency, especially when the whole pueblo is being labeled chaotic and violent, as after June 10. Think of the category as an ideological limit point within the communicative sphere of Guatemalan civil society, where violence becomes explicable (Fischer and Benson 2006). Here popular feelings of blame and complicity are disavowed; responsibility is attributed to a group that is defined in nebulous and vague terms, its identity often no more than graffiti writing.

This ideological field is evidence of a fundamental shift in how violence is imagined and talked about in contemporary Guatemala. Among violence's key existential qualities are often lack of clarity and ubiquitous uncertainty. As seen in the Rabinal uprising as well as Tecpán's June 10 protests, collective forms of violence arise out of a murky confluence of economic, political, and existential processes: "The only thing that was certain was that nothing was certain," said one protester. As in the CEH findings, the discourse about gangs and delinquents transforms this murk into objectified categories involving a clear attribution of blame. Such an orientation might then enable various forms of governance, ranging from formal military intervention to the disciplining effects of everyday rumor circulation. On multiple levels, violence gets framed as a "local" phenomenon, indigenous or not indigenous to a given area (or street corner). In Tecpán, residents struggle to delocalize gang violence as something inherited. Some blame the globalization of Western movies and other popular culture, bringing images of gang violence to the highlands (Fischer and Benson 2006). Others blame a political economy of boredom, saying that there is nothing to do in town and so delinquency is understandable (Benson 2004). Still others blame this on a breakdown of the moral structure of community. Blame, it seems, has become an ironic partner of "reconciliation" in these postwar times.

Coercive Harmony and the Limits of Reconciliation

In the aftermath of the protests, a reconciliation process with the mayor left many protesters feeling blindsided. The efforts point to a number of contradictory processes at work in the postwar era. In an emerging democratic public sphere where being seen or heard can be politically empowering and potentially dangerous, forms of symbolic violence structure discourse insofar as some voices are valued more than others. Ideals of empowerment and compromise are, in practice, seen to be limiting, since it is often the case that the kind of compromise that is reached favors established interests.

Democratic town hall meetings took place in Chimaltenango, the department's capital city, between the mayor, protest organizers, and the departmental governor. "We got what we wanted," said one protester, "a chance at a meeting with the mayor, a chance to talk. At least we got that." This is a common term, *por lo menos* (at least), used among protesters to describe the meetings. "The protests didn't work out as planned," said another participant, "but at least we can sit down with the mayor." The opportunity for having a reconciliation process itself, regardless of the outcome of such meetings, is put forth as an object of desire, a goal that will be used to determine the putative success of the protest. In effect, the protesters are saying that the protest was successful because it brought leaders of the indigenous community to the table with the Ladino leadership, even though, as it turns out, the deck was already stacked. Returning to the concept of "limit points," we see here how political commentary had stopped at a certain point, por lo menos, that established a horizon at which critique could comfortably rest and political action could be deemed a success, even apart from any real evidence that social structures were changed. The limit point allows political subjects at least some sense of enfranchisement, while this concession paradoxically limits the very terms of freedom that it purports to enable.

Indeed, at the reconciliation meetings, the mayor was able to co-opt protesters' sentiments and largely define the idiom through which political critique could emerge. "We are all completely in agreement," he said during one meeting. "You have the right to protest. I helped write those laws, remember. But what about those honorable people screaming, 'Kill him, kill him.' I want to work with these honorable people, but I don't want to lose democracy." One protest organizer responded:

> We too want a dialogue, but with no direct accusations or blaming. Because when you look at the press, it says we have no law here, that there is chaos in Tecpán, and that we the organizers are to blame, that there is no difference between what we did and what the gangs did. The same problems we are discussing here right now, we already met with you about this.

Quickly the mayor stood up and moved toward the center of the meeting hall. The documents brought to him on June 10, he claimed, were not official and he could not sign them. He insisted there was nothing he could do about the tax. It was his duty as mayor to carry out the task of decentralization, not to call it into question. "The law is the law and the tax is the tax," the governor reinforced his position. Here as always, local authorities in Tecpán must occupy a "tenuous position between constituent mandates and state authority" (Fischer 2001:57). It seems to the mayor that the protesters are now laying the blame on him. The organizer must respond again: "We are not here to accuse you. When we're talking here we are on an even level, in dialogue; it is a democratic process." The organizers, not wanting to be blamed by the mayor or the media for the violence, are forced to limit their critique so they themselves do not appear to have a "finger in the wound" (Nelson 1999).

While discourses of harmony and reconciliation are ordinarily perceived as being advantageous to the "little guy," providing at least a foot in the door, such gestures—by strategically eschewing behaviors and beliefs categorized as "trouble making"—almost invariably favor established interests in a fashion that encourages active acceptance by the opposition (Nader 1997). The protesters, if they do not embrace the mayor's rhetoric, are seen as stubborn, unwilling to listen. This was their critique of the mayor all along! The same protester that was so enthusiastic about the meeting opportunity beforehand admitted afterwards: "I am disappointed. The mayor just kept talking about his bad character. Yeah, that's a problem. But we all know that. That's why we protested in the first place."

Mano Dura: The Wild Zone of Power

A neoliberalization of violence is currently underway in Guatemala, like other places in which spiked levels of violence and crime have accompanied economic privatization and the erosion of state functions (from education to law enforcement) or their displacement to the private sector. As befits our global era, there has been a semi-privatization of coercive powers, the outsourcing of a function once exclusively claimed by the state. This loosening up of violence creates quandaries of representation for ethnographers, advocates, and other observers. In the 1980s, in the terminal Cold War zeitgeist of the day, it was obvious who the bad guys were (the army, the government), making their actions easier to oppose in representational form (if also with more deadly consequences). The quest was to shed light on and turn the world's attentions to the atrocities going on in Guatemala, the genocide of Mayan peoples. It was one of those instances where anthropologists could employ their on-the-ground understanding to uncover and expose various forms of injustice. But a few things have happened since then to destabilize this ethical terrain. The signing of the Peace Accords created a climate in which the state now partners with civil society and the private sector to ensure lasting peace (which, conveniently, also pries open the possibility that the state is not entirely to blame for the reality of lasting failures). Meanwhile, in a new media world the "perpetrator" is now represented as a more anonymous and diffuse specter of "crime," usually equated with gangs and delinquency (Benson 2004). Delinquents become that segment of the population not effectively or integrally partnered with the state and other groups to achieve peace and security.

One result is that the deaths and suffering get washed away in the larger flood of violence overwhelming the country. It is the best cover for political violence. This is not to divert blame from the state and its armed services. The military is widely and credibly believed to be tightly connected with drug traffickers. In 1990, members of the notorious presidential guard killed anthropologist Myrna Mack. Government forces have been involved in other acts of intimidation and coercion. Yet, the majority of politically motivated killing in recent years seem to have been carried out by private death squads, while the sustained wave of common crime is largely the work of freelance criminals working for profit rather than for politics (except when politics are profitable).

Far from a waning of power, the state benefits from relinquishing its monopoly on force in several ways. Foreign observance and attention of the social situation can decline because the kinds of suffering that emerge in the wake of genocide do not, perverse as it may be, carry the cultural capital or marketing potential as warfare. In the 1990s, foreign military aid to Guatemala dropped precipitously. After 1996's Peace Accords, military aid dropped further and the Guatemalan government began a major reduction in the size of its armed forces. Although the Peace Accords mandate that the military focus exclusively on external threats, recent presidents have invoked special powers to keep the army deployed to help fight the nationwide wave of violent crime. The social production of fear through rumor, images, and empirical experience allows the state to position itself as *mano dura* (an iron fist), something that civil society needs to function properly.

Important social implications of the narrow focus on "security" issues were seen in the national political campaigns of 2003 and 2007. Most leading candidates adopted a "tough on crime" platform and portrayed themselves—in stump speeches and roadside billboards—as eager to stamp out crime and eager to potentially utilize force and coercive power in the process. One right-wing candidate's slogan was *"seguridad total"* (total security), giving the impression of an ensuing clampdown. Viewers of campaign propaganda are not supposed to fear that the state might victimize or violate them or their civil rights in order to achieve aggregate safety and security. Viewers are supposed to imagine that those who will be stamped out are delinquents, never the interpellated voting subject. The state claims to categorically distinguish within the fabric of civil society itself and treats subjects differently. While "gang members" are targeted for punishment, innocent citizens are presumably protected. But here lies the problem with such a politics, a problem that is at once philosophical and practical. The state represents the "people" in aggregate and, at the same time, makes sometimes less than fine distinctions based on such factors as race, class, background, and geography. The rub of "security" campaigning is that such a position inevitably pits the government against the public electing a particular candidate. The state and its functionaries are positioned in opposition to the "people," assuming a hybrid role as protectorate and punisher. Susan Buck-Morss eloquently describes this aporia of democratic political entities as follows:

> From the perspective of the end of the twentieth century, the paradox seems irrefutable that political regimes claiming to rule in the name of the masses—claiming, that is, to be radically democratic—construct, *legitimately*, a terrain in which the exercise of power is out of control of the masses, veiled from public scrutiny, arbitrary, and absolute. Modern sovereignties harbor a blind spot, a zone in which power is above the law and thus, at least potentially, a terrain of terror. This wild zone of power, by its very structure impossible to domesticate, is intrinsic to mass-democratic regimes. [. . . As] regimes of supreme, sovereign power, they are always already *more* than a democracy—and consequently a good deal less. [2000: 2–3]

In politically representing the nation on whole, the state also comes to protect that body politic from internal elements, warding against aspects that are deemed dangerous though they reside inside the nationally imagined public itself (Nelson 2001).

The present moment in Guatemala (as much as the larger globalized war over security and peace) is marked by a most pressing danger, the tendency of violence to compound and fester under the duress of images of insecurity, instability, and mayhem and circulating discourses that personalize blame, targeting select groups rather than structural conditions or social relations. The social production of fear makes security an opportunity and a technology for state agencies, a vehicle for seeking or maintaining political power, emphasizing a heavy-handed militaristic approach, and justifying neoliberal policies premised upon a philosophy of individualized responsibility.

Current political struggles in Guatemala largely comprise struggles over the meaning and uses of violence. Today, more than ever, image control is a central function of violence. Whereas before, in the war period, the effort was focused on secrecy, now it is just as often focused on media spin and a particular framing of violence (as seen in Ríos Montt's speeches) as the doing of thuggish delinquency only. It is this irony that was on the minds of the rabble rousers that day in Rabinal, the fact that Ríos Montt's campaigning about peace and security completely deflects attention from his own role in broad-scale violence and military action. The current spike of common violence serves the authoritarian proclivities of state actors, who are shielded from the consequences of their decisions by bodyguards and high walls and bulletproof Sport Utility Vehicles. As attention is diverted to the terrors of violent crime, they can loot the coffers and fill their Panamanian bank accounts to ensure a comfortable retirement in exile, away from the havoc they have sown.

Violence as Symptom of Structural Conditions

In Guatemala's postwar era, neoliberal reforms compound and foster forms of violence on multiple levels. This case study speaks to similar processes taking place in other parts of the world (from intelligence contractors in Iraq to private prisons in the United States). In such cases we see the politicization of security as a proxy for militarism and the iron fist of mainstream political parties as well as extremists. To understand ethnographic dimensions of this shifting sociopolitical landscape of violence and responses to it, we need a theoretical framework that links an anthropological analysis of the inherently collective and deeply contextual nature of suffering to a social theoretical analysis of power and market reforms. We find the concept of "social suffering" to be useful for thinking about violence in contemporary Guatemala. The concept refers to the clustering of social and public health problems in particular localities and under the weight of large-scale structural and societal forces (Kleinman et al. 1997). Against a dominant tendency to reduce suffering to biological or psychological dimensions, the concept emphasizes the inherently collective nature of suffering, the fact that suffering is usually informed by social forces and played out in community settings in which people are differently positioned with regard to the material, symbolic, and social resources they can muster to pursue life chances, negotiate survival strategies, engage in entrepreneurial opportunities, and come to grips with perceived threats and uncertainties of restructuring.

This conceptual framework is relevant for thinking critically about ethnographic implications of neoliberal reforms because it pushes us to consider the role of liberal models of accountability, as expressed in official reports and informal rumor worlds, in shaping local forms of social experience that are overwhelmed and challenged by violence. What we find is that the circulation of rumors—the storied world of what happened and who is to blame—dovetails with neoliberal ideology and practice in a few key ways. First, new forms of violence in Guatemala are explained within the context of a moral economy bent on individualizing responsibility and depicting the culpable agents as presumably rational actors isolated from historical and social processes. Second, this image world depicts violence as something that is fundamentally urban and youthful, typified in the stereotype of gang members, which helps translate structural problems having to do with rural economic dislocation, industrialization, the rise of export sectors, and waves of rural-to-urban labor migration brought about by neoliberal reforms into cultural problems having to do with moral decline. Hence, folks in Tecpán do not regard gang violence as something that is indigenous to the highlands, but rather as a phenomenon essentially organized on the streets of Guatemala City and diffused to outlying regions. Third, this vision of culture war gives rise to a biopolitical logic that seeks to eradicate and control those segments of the population that disrupt economic and governmental efficiency and detract from the country's marketability vis-à-vis development programs. Finally, although violence would presumably hinder economic growth, the emerging violence industry and private security sector are evidence of a more complicated relationship between violence, economy, and society.

Anthropologists are sensitive to the material and symbolic value of violence in neoliberal times. Alan Klima's (2002) look at meditation practices and mortuary rituals in Thailand shows how images of death and violence have been put to political use by the country's radical democratic movement and invested with moral meaning in the context of religious protests against state-sponsored persecution. Klima also emphasizes the sensational component of violent imagery and the commoditization of violence in the mass media, a process that tends to inoculate the public against the cutting edge of resistance movements that seek to socialize and historicize suffering. Ellen Moodie's (2006) work on social suffering and insecurity in El Salvador has likewise called attention to the power of cultural representations to frame a dominant view of violence as random and deviant, turning attention from the role of structural forces in enabling the very conditions in which violence and crime are fostered.

With Moodie, we find that stories of danger and violence in Central America tend to express broader concerns about social fragmentation, rapid urbanization, economic insecurity, and the failures of democratic reform. The pressing danger is that as sensationalized violence becomes a quilting point for diffuse feelings of insecurity that are systematically generated, collective responses will fail to address underlying causes of social instability. By conceptualizing violence as a variety of social suffering, we can explain this dynamic process in terms of a feedback between what Arthur Kleinman (1999) calls "first order" and "second order" social dangers. The many social problems that affect ordinary Guatemalans comprise a first-order set of dangers that are responded to via strategies of privatization, militarization, and scapegoat explanations—these being some of the second-order dangers that potentially make things worse.

Guatemala teaches us that the relocation of coercive power from the state to private agencies—the neoliberalization of violence—does not entail the erosion of state power in a simple way. Rather, the reorganization of violence (through the distribution of responsibility onto individuals or groups and the increasing presence of private security forces) plays to the state's claim to sovereign power and the strategic promotion of an emergency mindset to shield the state's lasting participation in and failure to ever redress violence against the "people." Guatemala thus also teaches us that the measures implemented to bring about security are very different from those needed to achieve lasting peace.

12

Harvest of Conviction

Solidarity in Guatemalan Scholarship, 1988–2008

David Stoll

This volume's contributors are, like other Guatemala scholars, in search of moral direction. True north used to be the 1954 CIA coup and the army-guerrilla conflict that drove Guatemala's history to the 1996 Peace Accords. Like any good narrative of commitment, the army versus the people paradigm that defined so much scholarship was both a plausible description of empirical reality and a moral charter for taking action. Solidarity with victims was uppermost when the first *Harvest of Violence* appeared in 1988, and the monster-combine responsible for most of the harvest was clearly the Guatemalan army. The army committed or sponsored a large majority of the mayhem, it did its best to implicate peasants in the murder of suspected guerrillas, and it was the main target of two truth commissions in the 1990s, the Catholic Church's Project for the Recuperation of Historical Memory (REMHI) and the United Nations–sponsored Commission for Historical Clarification (CEH). Sixteen months after the Peace Accords were signed, the shocking murder of REMHI's director, Monsignor Juan Gerardi, gave new life to the narrative that had guided scholars for so many years. The assassins' obvious intent was to send a warning to anyone who contemplated indicting army officers.

Eventually, a Guatemalan court convicted three military men—two of them on President Alvaro Arzú's (1996–2000) presidential military staff (EMP)—of complicity in Gerardi's murder. The human rights movement hailed the convictions. But the evidence against the three was very shaky, and now a detailed account of how they were framed has been provided by the journalists Maite Rico and Bertrand de la Grange (2003). Rico and de la Grange conclude that Monsignor Gerardi was murdered by (1) a gang of colonial church art-looters, led by the daughter of an influential Catholic priest, which was set up by (2) a clandestine army network seeking to discredit the Arzú administration. Not coincidentally, this was the same network that returned to power in 2000 with the electoral victory of former dictator Efraín Ríos Montt and his Gua-

Fig 17. Amajchel reunion on May 12, 1994. Photo by Barbara Bocek.

temalan Republican Front (FRG). If Rico and de la Grange are correct about authorship of the crime, Gerardi was assassinated to disgrace the Arzú administration precisely because it was trying to honor the peace agreement. If so, Guatemala's most-respected human rights organization, the archbishop's Office on Human Rights (ODHA), was gulled by Ríosmonttistas who, once they took power, subverted crucial peace accords on the police and judiciary (for a defense of the prosecution case and an attack on de la Grange and Rico that fails to respond to much of their evidence, see Goldman 2007).

To recover from the fiscal ruin of the FRG years, in 2004 the Oscar Berger administration (2004–2008) chopped the army almost in half, to 15,500 troops—below the level required by the Peace Accords. Unfortunately, networks within the officer corps continue to operate by the old rules, under even more layers of mystery and denial than before. Demobilizations have fed former fighters into criminal enterprises and security firms. Thanks to the U.S. war on drugs, partnering with Colombian and Mexican mafias has become Guatemala's most profitable industry. Because criminal organizations often have ties to the security forces, or at least retired members of same, even human rights groups are reduced to referring helplessly to "occult powers" (e.g., Peacock and Beltrán 2003). No one has figured out how to reverse the underlying penetration of the state by criminal organizations.

Political activists have made Guatemala a synonym for human rights violations by focusing on crimes committed by the state—this is what distinguishes such abuses from other kinds. Yet if these were the only kinds of violence that mattered to Guatemalans, their country would be only a template for grant proposals, not an actual society. Human rights groups have a professional obligation to focus on state complicity, but Guatemalans have to deal with many forms of violence in which the state is not the most obvious culprit. They have to live with each other their entire lives, not just for a brief period of research, and they have the intimate knowledge needed to trace the mazeways of human responsibility. So while they can blame a power structure or a history of colonialism, just like social theorists do, they also blame each other, as described by the contributors to this collection.

Given all the different kinds of crime experienced by Guatemalans and wholesaled over the airwaves (car-jackings, ransom-kidnappings, home-invasions by gangs dressed as police, home-invasions committed by gangs who *are* the police, youth-gang homicides, homicides that seem senseless because the perpetrator was on drugs or the motive is unclear, mob lynchings of crime suspects), no single institution could be responsible for all the havoc. In the army's manifestation as uniformed and predictable troops, it is the only credible force in the country, and it is accountable in a way that criminals and lynch mobs are not. This is why, in the eyes of many Guatemalans, the army is not just part of the problem; the army is also part of the solution to the rampant insecurity that they feel.

What about the former guerrillas of the Guatemalan National Revolutionary Union (URNG)? Where do they fit in? When the first *Harvest of Violence* appeared in 1988, guerrilla killings of civilians were sufficiently fewer, or at least less visible, such that no contributors felt compelled to excavate the subject. Most survivors inside Guatemala were under army control, limiting their ability to express their point of view. This narrowed the range of credible voices to refugees outside the country and to insurgents, which is why the story told by Rigoberta Menchú (Burgos-Debray 1984) became so compelling. To what extent did the guerrillas actually represent the Mayas and other repressed Guatemalans for whom they claimed to speak? Some scholars took the URNG's legitimacy for granted; others regarded it as unknowable. Twenty-five years later, the question is still so politically sensitive among Guatemala scholars that the only polite way to frame it is, Which answer do you prefer?

Consider the story of Diego (a pseudonym), who survived the war only by switching to every possible side. In 1979 Diego was an evangelical pastor and assistant military commissioner in an area where an underground network was surfacing, asserting authority, and executing village leaders who opposed it. The network belonged to the Guerrilla Army of the Poor (EGP), one of the four guerrilla organizations of the URNG. When two EGP cadres arrived at

Diego's door to determine his loyalties, he convinced them he was harmless. Soon their local committee fell apart, and guess who ended up leading the new one. Over the next five years, the capable Diego became the EGP's person in charge for 900 civilians hiding from army offensives. Like most internal refugees, eventually they had no choice but to surrender, which for Diego meant two months of interrogation in an army compound. The only way to survive the experience was to join the army's civil patrol and its counterinsurgency sweeps. Not wanting to meet old comrades with an army rifle in his hands, Diego was one of the first local men to brave army threats and stop patrolling.

"After going with the guerrillas and being under their control, after going with the army and being under their control, I don't want to be with the guerrillas or the army," he told me in 1995. "This is why I've arrived at the conclusion that the army has to sign the peace agreement, and the guerrillas have to sign the peace agreement, because we're tired." When I met Diego, he was a local coordinator for the Consejo Etnico Runujel Junam (CERJ), a network of conscientious objectors helping conscripts drop out of the army's civil patrols. In a few years he and his local group were at loggerheads with CERJ because CERJ's leader, Amílcar Méndez, did not want his affiliates to dissipate their energies in development projects.

Now then, with which of Diego's personas do you wish to be in solidarity? The evangelical pastor, the guerrilla cadre, the civil patroller, the leader of a popular organization, or the development coordinator? Classifying him as "complicit" or "suspect" echoes the EGP's and the army's shared assumption that they had the right to demand his loyalty and, if he betrayed them, kill him. Regarding his moves as contradictory runs the risk of replacing his assumptions with our own. Fixing on any of Diego's manifestations as the most significant carries the risk of underestimating the others. But if we trace his steps on the different paths that came open to him and other Guatemalans, we can avoid idealizing some of the decisions he made and denigrating others.

Our Staircase to Moral Authority

Once scholars decided that value-neutrality would not suffice to deal with bloodbaths, once we tried to make a deal with the ghosts of the dead in order to continue doing our research with a clear conscience, we began to run up and down staircases of empirical, political, and moral issues. Once declarations had been made from the balcony, it became impossible to welcome all the new information marching up the steps. Think of the staircase in the following terms: (1) Empirical issues that, through examination of the evidence, should be resolvable to the satisfaction of reasonable parties. Chronologies of events, property lines, and responsibility for homicides fall into this category, regardless of how many contradictory versions we collect. Even if the rumors about a homicide are endless, and even if the victim's friends are all postmodernists, they still want to identify the murderer. (2) Empirical issues that require so much selection and interpretation of evidence that reasonable parties can come to different conclusions. For example, to what degree did Mayan peasants support the guerrillas? (3) Politically and morally loaded issues that determine our obligations as scholars. Was the insurgency against a dictatorship a popular uprising? Was it an inevitable reaction to oppression as the guerrillas claimed? If Mayas blame the guerrillas as well as the army for starting the violence, have they turned against their liberators only because of army repression? Or because of guerrilla "errors"? Or do such explanations serve as moral alibis for the guerrillas, to excuse them from sharing responsibility for escalating violence?

Only at the end of the 1980s, when the Maya Movement began to accuse the guerrillas of using peasants as cannon fodder, did these questions have to be faced. In the case of my own research (Stoll 1993 and 1999), in the *municipios* (county seat) of Ixil country and Uspantán in northern Quiché Department, the controversy is whether Mayas should be considered victims only of the army or of the guerrillas as well (Hale 1997; *Human Rights Review* 1999; *Latin American Perspectives* 1999; Manz et al. 1999; Arias 2001; Morales 2001). Of the people I interviewed, most had harsh words for both sides. Throughout Guatemala the army versus the people narrative has lost credibility, as has the very idea of political solutions.

Among Guatemalans the usual presumption is that politicians are liars, that their only real aim is to line their own pockets, that government is a form of robbery, and that political competition leads to violence. Ideologies and parties are viewed as vehicles for the personal ambition of leaders, who will reliably plunder government funds at the first opportunity. If survey research is any guide (Azpuru and Seligson 2004:11), cost-of-living, crime, and corruption are more pressing issues for most Guatemalans than justice for victims of army abuses or human rights guarantees, which they tend to view as loopholes exploited by criminals to avoid punishment. Hopes being invested in church or migration to the United States are far more obvious than hope in the political Left.

But the army versus the people narrative is not dead. It was echoed by the two truth commissions as they built an irrefutable case against the army. It is still voiced by ex-guerrillas who experienced a wave of popular support in the late 1970s and early 1980s. It is defended by U.S. scholars who vindicate the insurgency as an inevitable reaction to oppression, hence, a last resort for Guatemalans who had no choice but armed struggle and, therefore, a popular struggle. It is picked up by consultants who come to Guatemala on the wings of international aid, to push reforms envisioned by the peace process. The army versus the people paradigm will continue to attract anyone who wishes to comprehend Guatemala in terms of a simple moral narrative of struggle against oppression. Translated into the language of human rights, the army versus the people polarity provides a compelling rationale for international involvement in Guatemala. Even now that the army has been downsized, those occult powers which seem to preserve the army's prerogatives make the army versus the people a rationale with no end in sight.

NGOs Minus Electoral Movement Equals Missionary Work?

The peace process of the 1990s was successful in two important ways. First, it ended the army-guerrilla confrontation and removed uniformed combatants from Mayan areas. Second, political violence became a small fraction of what it once had been. These are not minor accomplishments. But after a brief period of confidence, when the 1996 Peace Accords seemed like a blueprint for a more equitable Guatemala, human rights activists are once again looking over their shoulders. They are leading a much shorter parade than they expected. They may have moral ownership of the Guatemalan case on the international level, but not within its borders, even among the peasants and other lower-class Guatemalans whom they wish to represent.

The peace process was supposed to give the demobilized guerrillas, the rest of the Left, and the Maya Movement the space they needed to overcome their distrust of each other, develop new leaders, and become an electoral force. Unfortunately, electoral results have deflated the Left's claim to speak for a broad range of Guatemalans. The URNG and the rest of the Left peaked at 12 percent of the vote in 1999, declined to half that in 2003 (split between five different parties), and fared about the same in 2007 (split between three different parties). As coalitions dissolved in acrimony, so did the URNG's claim to represent the Guatemalan people—and the political pressure needed to institutionalize the Peace Accords.

For a revolutionary project on which so much blood and ink was spilled, this is a sad end. One of the strategies in a UN-brokered peace deal is to flood a political system with money to win over key players and build democratic institutions. Encouraged by international aid flows, human rights became the common denominator for the guerrillas and their allies; for their competitors in the Maya Movement and other civil sectors; for a parade of diplomats and aid initiatives from the European Union, the United States, and the United Nations; and for international nongovernmental organizations (NGOs) and their burgeoning local counterparts. Through the language of human rights, Guatemalans who lacked representation in the political system could use NGOs to hook up with anyone in the international community who wanted to help them.

The resulting political triangle (Guatemalan activists, international funders, and the Guatemalan state) became institutionalized in the Assembly of Civil Society, a parallel forum in the government-URNG peace negotiations. According to Susan Burgerman (2001, 2005), never have NGOs influenced peace negotiations quite like they did in this case. Unfortunately, it was the very weakness of the guerrilla movement and Guatemala's return to democracy that gave the NGOs their leverage. Since the idiom of human rights allows survivors, activists, and lawyers speak for others, NGOs claimed to represent broad sectors, but without elections or other consultative mechanisms that could substantiate their claims.

Since the 1996 Peace Accords, the URNG has fared so poorly that it exists more at the level of international aid channels such as the Guillermo Torriello Foundation than as a party of elected politicians and their supporters. Internationally financed NGOs are even more evident in the Maya Movement. As Richard Adams and Santiago Bastos (2003:275–276) document, foreign funders have shown a strong preference for Indians over non-Indians; in this collection Judith Maxwell, José Oscar Barrera Nuñez, and Monica DeHart show just how pervasive NGOs have become in towns and spheres that attract foreigners.

Because NGOs are the channel for so many aspirations that now bypass the state, they are fraught with consequences. The funding they provide is a privilege rather than a right, which continues only if recipients meet the conditions of donors. Because even long-term funding is relatively short-term, leaders tend to become more responsive to their foreign funders than to their domestic constituencies. Neighbors who do not benefit directly tend to become jealous of the financial flows, as if these were unfair windfalls cornered by the local coordinators. Thus, NGOs frequently aggravate competition between local subunits of the larger collectivity that foreign donors wish to support. The most obvious result of community-building can be community-splitting.

At the level of organizations rather than communities, the Maya Movement consists largely of NGO networks competing with each other for funding. The factionalism that results is hardly new. There is much experience with this sort of thing under a different heading, that of missionary work. A typical dilemma in Christian missions is that establishing congregations requires a flow of resources, producing a patronage structure, which is monopolized by the first converts. Were the first converts to become the fervent evangelists envisioned by missionaries, they would have to share the benefits with newer converts. The conscious or unconscious result is opportunity hoarding, a characteristic problem of top-down schemes to achieve change (Schröder 2003:442).

In the case of evangelical churches, whose astounding success is the envy of the Latin American Left, they usually do not begin to mushroom until local leaders chase away the missionaries.

Missionary work does not have to be so idealistic that it backfires—but it can do so easily, like any utopian scheme. In the case of the evangelical mission I studied (Stoll 1983), adaptation to the thorny realities of the field was often slowed by the need to fulfill the romantic expectations of U.S. supporters. But the mission was not just an innocent victim of homeland naïveté. To attract recruits and funding, it encouraged unrealistic expectations about the transformative power of Bible translation. Mission publicity backfired when star converts reverted to polygamy and shamanism. I detect similar tensions in the conflicting requirements of activism, scholarship, and NGO imagery in Guatemala. The simple moral polarities that confirm preexisting assumptions, attract attention, and raise funds (e.g., the army versus the people, Maya versus Ladino, rich versus poor) are a poor guide to the paradoxes of an actual country. To prevent contradictions between fund-raising imagery and field conditions from embarrassing the enterprise, sub-rosa rules and inhibitions develop. When events flout expectations, the result is panic.

Consider the periodic alarms over Efraín Ríos Montt, the born-again Protestant general who seized power in 1982 and defeated the guerrillas with an Old Testament combination of moralism and massacre. Elsewhere in this volume, Abigail Adams, Peter Benson and Edward Fischer, and J. Jailey Philpot-Munson attest to his startling charisma for many Mayas. Because army killing of suspected guerrilla supporters peaked under Ríos Montt (Ball et al. 1999:37–38), the human rights movement wants to put him on trial for genocide in both Guatemala and Spain. Yet the general or his surrogate candidates won two presidential elections, in 1991 and 1999, and came close to winning a third in 1995. In 1999 voters chose Ríos Montt's candidate and party to lead the country only months after the CEH truth commission's finding of genocide against his 1982–83 administration. Ríos Montt's strongest support came not from Guatemalan Ladinos, who presumably helped him commit genocide, but from Mayan peasants in the same departments (Quiché, Baja Verapaz, Huehuetenango) where his army committed the most massacres.

Truth Commissioners versus Civil Patrollers

Why didn't the CEH and REMHI truth commissions have more impact on how Guatemalans perceive the violence? The "historical memory" that the truth commissions hoped to establish was, like the army versus the people paradigm, both an empirical claim about reality and a charter for action. Historical memory would presumably incorporate many different experiences yet, because a large majority of the killing was committed by one side, focus on the army. As this collection attests, Guatemalans have far more to say about the violence than can be compressed into a single collective memory.

Nowhere is this more apparent than in polemics over the army's *patrullas de auto-defensa civil* (PACs), the huge militia into which the army conscripted all the men under its control. Consider the differing assessments of the civil patrols by Adams, Benson and Fischer, and Philpot-Munson in this collection. The patrols disbanded officially in 1996, but ex-patrollers and ex-patrol chiefs continue to bedevil human rights groups and populate their press releases. Unfortunately, the same oppressed Mayan peasants whom the Guatemalan Left wants to represent, and who are supposed to welcome human rights as their friend, are also ex-patrollers whom the Left and human rights NGOs demonize whenever they fail to behave the way they are supposed to.

There is no question that the civil patrols contributed to the death and destruction. The shares of violence that the CEH attributed to government forces (93 percent) and, specifically, to the civil patrols (18 percent) are much larger than the share that the CEH attributed to the guerrillas (3 percent). But the guerrilla forces were so much smaller that, per capita, the average guerrilla could have committed more abuses than the average soldier and patroller. In 1997 the URNG demobilization of 2,959 members and their children produced an estimated 800 to 1,000 combatants. In 1981 and 1982, estimates Yvon LeBot, there were 6,000 full-time guerrilla combatants plus "some thousands provisionally and precariously armed" from a support base of more than a quarter million people (1995:195). But if the URNG was defeated for lack of weapons, as is frequently argued, then many of the 6,000 full-time combatants either were not fully armed or did not exist. During the same period the army reached a strength of 36,000 soldiers and as many as 900,000 patrollers. Thus, if there were ever 6,000 full-time guerrilla combatants and 10,000 part-time Fuerzas Guerrilleras Locales (FGL), which is a generous estimate (Schirmer 1998:41, 47), they would have been outnumbered 58.5 to 1.0 by 936,000 government counterinsurgents. Yet if the guerrillas and their FGLs committed 3 percent of the violence, their share of the violence would have been outnumbered only 31 times by the government's 93 percent share of the violence.

This did not prevent peace negotiators from agreeing on concessions to the guerrillas. The civil patrollers fared differently. Because they were junior partners in the army's crimes, and because they were not represented directly in the peace talks, they did not receive the modest severance packages that the guerrillas did. As former patrollers observed aid flows to returning refugees and guerrillas or heard exaggerated and envious accounts of same, they began to demand payment for their many months of militia duty. Human rights groups decided that, because patrollers were human rights violators, compensating them would be an abomination. And so the former patrollers became the bad conscience of the peace process—constantly invoked to explain why Mayas have failed to cooperate as planned.

The most sophisticated analysis of the civil patrols is Paul Kobrak's (1997) doctoral dissertation about K'iche' Mayas on the heights between Aguacatán and Ixil country. These are people who live at the upper edge of habitable altitude, making them very marginal but not particularly land-poor. The EGP organized some of the K'iche's but antagonized others, creating an opening for the army to force the latter into its patrols. After massacres by both sides, the army drove the EGP from the locality. Ten years later, the civil patrols were not just frightened conscripts being ordered around by army despots. Instead, they were determined local institutions that many villagers regarded as guardians of community solidarity and local control.

How could this have happened? How could survivors of army repression view the patrols as their own institution when it was brutally imposed upon them? Kobrak reminds us that solidarity among peasants is an ideal, and sometimes an achievement, but not a sociological given. Peasants compete with each other as well as with outsiders, and the Cordillera of the Cuchumatanes above Aguacatán is one of many places where land conflicts with fellow peasants are more common than conflicts with large landowners. The EGP wanted to unite villagers against external class enemies, but such foes were too far away to be very meaningful. So instead of uniting the population, the EGP factionalized it even more. Once the army demonstrated superior force, Kobrak reports, "the civil patrols helped manage and suppress these divisions by establishing a collective village response to the war"; this is how an army strategy became a community institution (Kobrak 1997:6). By the early 1990s, villagers viewed their patrolling as a form of armed neutrality that protected them from both sides (Kobrak 1997:136). Keeping the EGP away also kept the army off their backs. Contrary to the army versus the people paradigm, which assumed that the more organized a village was the more likely it would be revolutionary, Kobrak's patrollers felt that the more organized a village was the less likely it would fall victim to guerrillas or soldiers (1997:199).

Memory-Redemption versus Moral Economy

Like the French sociologist Yvon Le Bot (1995) and my own analysis of Ixil country (Stoll 1993), Kobrak puts the local experience of the violence in sufficient context that guerrilla organizing loses the claim to be a redemptive last resort for a population with no other alternatives. But that subverts the structure of feeling that has drawn so many scholars and activists to Guatemala. And that is patently immoral and dangerous—consider Victoria Sanford's

(2003) indictment of myself and Le Bot as apologists for genocide, with back-cover endorsements from Michael Ondaatje, Ariel Dorfman, Philippe Bourgois, and Arturo Arias. Hence, there has been a warm welcome for several local histories that refurbish the guerrilla movement as a popular struggle—for old-timers, for newcomers, for funding networks, in short, for anyone who feels the need to continue using Guatemala for its now well-established function as a human rights horror story.

Daniel Wilkinson has published the most eloquent of these works in *Silence on the Mountain* (2002). Making up for scholarly neglect of the war in the coffee piedmont above the Pacific coast, he finds survivors who can explain connections between the 1952 agrarian reform, its destruction by the 1954 CIA counter-revolution, and the appearance of the Revolutionary Organization of the People in Arms (ORPA) two decades later. Beatriz Manz (2004), based on long-term contact with the Ixcán colony of Santa Maria Tzejá, documents the rise and fall of EGP organizing and Santa Maria's rebirth as an NGO-subsidized migration pole to the United States. Greg Grandin (2004) excavates the buried history of labor organizing and the Guatemalan Worker's Party (PGT) in Alta Verapaz from the 1920s to the 1978 massacre at Panzós. In a dissertation that has yet to become a book, Carlota McAllister (2003) uses her fieldwork in the EGP stronghold of Chupol, Chichicastenango, Quiché, to show that this was a popular struggle—at least in Chupol.

By rousting survivors out of hiding and persuading them to talk, each of these scholars has recovered experiences and memories that might otherwise be lost. Each was in the right place at the right time to enrich our understanding of the violence at the local level. However, each is also editing a wider repertoire of social memory in order to resuscitate the last-resort paradigm, that is, enshrinement of the insurgency's redemptive claim to represent the Guatemalan people. That after 1954 the Left was prevented from competing in national electoral politics—of this there is no doubt. That peaceful mass organizing also became impossible—of this, too, there is no doubt. That large numbers of Guatemalans supported the guerrillas in some areas—there is no doubt about that. What cannot be demonstrated is that a majority or plurality of Guatemalans, let alone of the Mayas, regarded armed struggle as their best alternative. While support for the guerrillas was strong in some areas, it was weak or non-existent in many others.

Because army versus the people scholars continue to enjoy such handsome funding and legitimacy, I suggest that we clarify our value judgments in terms of moral economy. For present purposes, let us say that "moral economy" is how different factions use ritual exchange to produce competing ideas of moral authority. For example, when human rights groups accuse Ríos Montt of genocide against Mayas and when Mayan voters elect Ríos Montt's political party to run their municipal governments, competing moral economies are probably at work. Paul Diener was the first to introduce moral economy to Guatemala scholarship in his neglected analysis of "a saint which preaches revolution" among the Ch'orti' Mayas (1978:109). Greg Grandin analyzes the moral economy of revolutionary peasants in Alta Verapaz, only to stop at the point where moral economy turned against the guerrillas (2004:124).

Why not extend our analysis of moral economy in order to compare the agendas of different factions in Guatemalan society with our own agendas as scholars and activists? This collection's rich postwar ethnography is a good place to start—consider Philpot-Munson's account of how Pentecostals have defined the peace process in Nebaj. Such groups would appear to have a very different moral agenda than foreign political activists do. Next consider Barrera Nuñez's "humanitarian economy" in the tourist town and NGO hub of Todos Santos Cuchumatán, which is generated by an underlying "economy of desires" in which foreigners and Todos Santeros turn each other into commodities that they hope will satisfy their very different expectations. Given the short distance between self-interest and moral agenda, this is a good example of how moral economy operates. Evidently, our wish to turn Mayas into a source of moral authority for ourselves, by helping them in ways that we deem appropriate, leads to idealizing them in ways that overlook what they want.

A second theorist who can help us situate ourselves in terms of moral economy is Steven Sampson (2003) with his analysis of international trouble spots. Sampson describes three kinds of actors competing for power: the state, projects funded by the international community, and bandits. Where the state becomes so weak that bandit society and project society compete openly for sovereignty, the result is a "complex humanitarian emergency," "collapsed state," or (Sampson's term [2003:326]) "white-jeep state," in which foreigners drive around in white jeeps and attempt to perform state functions. When bandits succeed in turning the state or project society into a source of private enrichment, the result is a mafia, which can be defined broadly to include political parties as well as crime syndicates. If the Guatemalan state has always been a source of private enrichment, and if it is now being undermined by "occult powers," Sampson's framework can help internationalists situate ourselves in the picture more realistically than the army versus the people paradigm does, with its tendency to degenerate into grandstanding.

A third theorist who can help us understand our position in Guatemala is James Ferguson (1999), with his portrayal of World Bank discourse in Lesotho. Ferguson shows how a powerful international institution defines a country in order to fit what the agency is designed to do. In the case of Guatemala, scholars and human rights groups do not have the power of the World Bank, but we do have a certain amount of leverage, and to preserve that leverage we select elements of a complex situation that serve to justify our continued involvement in the country. The army versus the people cult has produced a simple fundable version of Guatemala, but at the cost of institutionalizing disappointment with Guatemalans—they are never quite good enough, as illustrated by Julián López García's (2001) witty analysis of the buzzwords *capacitar* (to train or educate) and *capacitación* (training). Because the Mayas postulated by this moral economy are ideal constructs, the real McCoy is always a disappointment, of the kind that requires further funding.

Solidarity as Conversion Narrative

In recent decades the two largest streams of activists and scholars coming to Guatemala have been from the United States and Spain. The coincidence with empire is not a coincidence. Solidarity with Guatemala is the Left's inversion of what Renato Rosaldo (1988) called imperialist nostalgia. Referring to another wrecked country that enchants foreigners, Joan Dayan observes that books about Haiti are conversion narratives (1995:xi). So are books about Guatemala. Because of the Spanish conquest and the U.S. role in overthrowing an elected reformist government in 1954, Guatemalan history seems very recognizable to visitors who are looking for an opportunity to do penance for their country's sins. Because familiar villains play paradigmatic roles, little time needs to be invested in the destabilizing experiences of disorientation and learning (Napier 2004). You can become a hero on your first visit. By getting into graduate school and submitting the right tropes to funders, you can turn a conversion experience into a career.

Like any other choice of story line, the revolutionary vision carries a price that someone will pay. Turning Guatemala into a pilgrimage for redemptive hopes has definite implications for what foreign funders are told to expect, what they decide to pay for, and what Guatemalans are expected to do in order to qualify for further funding. If the funders and their eyes and ears among Guatemala scholars engage in moral boycotts of Guatemalan feelings that violate our own sensibilities, we do so at the expense of the people we want to help. And so foreign scholars construct our own interpretation of Guatemala, fortified with many subtle defenses against how Guatemalans perceive their country and, therefore, a poor guide to how they feel. Since most actual Guatemalans are not equal to the solidarity narrative, the scholars and activists who feel most inspired by this narrative have had no choice but to substitute themselves as its guardians. Should we be surprised that so many Guatemalans feel no ownership of the results?

This is how solidarity interpretations of Guatemala as a grand political opera pitting the army against the people have contributed to parochializing the

Guatemalan peace process. What began as an undeniable empirical description of a human rights crisis—the army's indiscriminate violence against presumed guerrilla supporters—became a theology protecting an insurgency's assumptions from the scrutiny these deserved. Translated into the language of funding proposals, the result is a set of expectations that cannot be met by most Guatemalans. As a result, the peace process has shrunk to procedures, consultations, and demands that can be managed by NGOs, their international funders, and Guatemalan constituencies. The goals may be laudable, but this is a process from which many Guatemalans feel excluded. Foreign scholars did not create the solidarity interpretation of Guatemala. Instead, we picked it up from survivors of a repressed and factionalized Left, in the form of appeals that were persuasive to our ears. But when we allow army versus the people experiences to enshrine the insurgency's assumptions, we replace the spectrum of social memory with a narrower and rather idealized redemptive version of that memory. We replace the people with the guerrillas, and the guerrillas with ourselves, in the kind of substitution that made Vladimir Ilyich Lenin famous and that the guerrillas repeated with disastrous results.

My purpose is not to suggest that human rights in Guatemala is a lost cause. It is, instead, to point out the price of hitching scholarship to moral dualism, which then encourages the demon move against critical thinking. I doubt that the army's many crimes will be punished until justice for these crimes becomes quite separate from solidarity with an insurgency that lost its popular base more than two decades ago. If justice is ever achieved, the time frame could easily be measured in additional decades. If the Augusto Pinochet experience (see Stern 2006a, b) is any guide for Guatemala, what brings its own top criminals to justice will not be nostalgia for the guerrilla movement.

(For the complete version of this essay, including a literature review, contact the author at dstoll@middlebury.edu.)

Conclusions

Robert M. Carmack

In order to truly assess developments in Guatemala with respect to its Mayan peoples since the original *Harvest of Violence* was written, it will be useful to review precisely why that volume was necessary, what it revealed about conditions in Guatemala at the time of writing, and the key issues it raised that are relevant to the *Mayas in Postwar Guatemala:* Harvest of Violence *Revisited* volume.

The eleven anthropologists, geographer, and political scientist who contributed chapters to the original *Harvest* volume were motivated by their belief that the U.S. government and public, in general, did not understand what was happening in Guatemala at the time. The goal of the book was to inform the U.S. government and its citizens about the significance of the civil war in Guatemala and to insist that official policies be changed in order to protect the millions of innocent peoples whose very lives were in mortal danger.

It was widely thought at the time in U.S. governmental circles that the violence was caused by communist intrusions (inspired by Fidel Castro's Cuba), whereas economic exploitation of the Indians by the dominant Ladino class and clandestine governmental ethnic cleansing appeared to be the more significant forces at work. The *Harvest* authors further perceived that the U.S. government had not understood the dire conditions under which the Mayas were living, conditions that, in fact, had taken the form of a protracted genocidal program.

The *Harvest* authors argued that to an important extent the distorted official view of what was occurring in Guatemala was the result of faulty methods being employed in the gathering of information about the ongoing violence. Documents from the American Embassy in Guatemala indicated that information was being obtained largely by military and other ill-prepared officials who lacked the language skills and cultural understanding needed to clarify the true nature of the unfolding events in the country. The authors of the *Har-*

vest book, in contrast, had lived among the Indians for long periods of time, knew their languages and cultures, and therefore were in positions to provide more valid accounts of what had been happening in this important Central American country.

The first *Harvest* book focused on events associated with the civil war itself. The chapters were organized according to the planned counterinsurgency agenda of the Guatemalan military. Some chapters described events occurring in "red" communities, where, according to the military, "subversives" allegedly had infiltrated and, therefore, indiscriminate killing of Indians was required; pink and yellow communities were thought to be inhabited by a mixture of subversives and loyalists, and, accordingly, only selective violence should be applied; finally, green communities were said to be relatively free of subversion and, therefore, simply had to be kept under surveillance. Two additional chapters were devoted to refugees: one on refugees internal to Guatemala and the other on refugees outside Guatemala.

General Comparisons between the Two *Harvest* Volumes

Before summarizing the responses by the authors of this volume to specific questions raised by the first *Harvest* volume, some general comparisons between the two volumes should be noted.

We may begin with an obvious major difference between the conditions in Guatemala under which the two accounts were prepared: the *Mayas in Postwar Guatemala:* Harvest of Violence *Revisited* authors write at a time when the civil war in Guatemala has ended, and the genocidal campaign against the Mayan population by the state officially ended almost ten years ago. As a result, Guatemala is no longer the subject of intense scrutiny by the U.S. government or other organizations of the international community. Accordingly, the authors of the present volume do not write with the same urgency as the scholars who authored the original *Harvest* volume. Furthermore, there is no indication that the present volume is intended primarily as a wakeup call to U.S. governmental agencies, but it seems more designed to provide a general account aimed at the scholarly world, the educated public, and, only in a general way, the national and international governmental and nongovernmental organizations.

Although the chapters of this volume make clear that very serious problems continue to afflict the Mayan peoples of Guatemala, the horrors of the civil war period are no longer the main topic of interest. As mentioned by David Stoll in the commentary to this volume, the focus has shifted from the war itself to other urgent matters: namely, implementing the Peace Accords, coming to grips with the findings of the "Truth Commission" on whom to blame for the past violence, attempting to implement international human rights, working with NGOs to promote socioeconomic development, incorporating the insurgents (URNG) and counterinsurgents (Efraín Ríos Montt) into the democratic political system, and, perhaps most serious of all, controlling vicious cycles of corruption, crime, and delinquency. In different degrees and diverse ways, all of these profoundly serious matters are discussed in the chapters of this volume.

The authors of this volume, like their predecessors who authored the original *Harvest* volume, hope to reach a broad sector of the educated public on the urgent matters just mentioned. For that reason they rely heavily on narrative accounts and generally employ prose that is readily understood. Theory is mentioned in most of the chapters, but is central to none of them. As with the first *Harvest* volume, the authors of this volume are primarily anthropologists who obtained their information through long-term ethnographic participation in the communities on which they report.

Field techniques appear to be similar for the authors of both volumes, although fieldwork was a much more dangerous undertaking for the original *Harvest* scholars. One of the consequences of the more peaceful post–civil war setting, perhaps, is that the present ethnographers have been able to obtain better knowledge of the different Mayan languages spoken in the communities under study than was the case of the scholars who produced the first *Harvest* volume. It is worth noting, too, that more than half of the authors are female, whereas only two of the eleven authors of the original *Harvest* volume were women. As a result of this fact, we learn more about women than we did in the earlier volume, especially Mayan women (for example, see the discussion of "machismo" in the chapter by Liliana Goldín and Brenda Rosenbaum).

Although, as mentioned, theory is not stressed in either volume, the reader will detect a modest "postmodern" bent in this one. Specifically, one finds in the present chapters more self-reflection by the authors on their relations with the people under study and the potential impact of their writings on the latter's well-being. Rather than the search for "explanations" of developments through the analysis of socioeconomic factors, we find greater concern with giving voice to the Indians themselves, understanding how the Indians interpret their own conditions, and adopting moral positions relative to the issues being described. These tendencies vary somewhat from author to author, but the overall picture portrayed is of a highly polarized Guatemala in which the traditional neocolonial relations that have for centuries subjugated the Indians are giving way to rapid change and new ways of being "Indian" (or Maya).

The local community continues to be the primary subject of study in *Mayas in Postwar Guatemala*. As with the first *Harvest* volume, a (far from representative) series of Indian communities are described for the Huehuetenango,

Totonicapán, Ixil, Lake Atitlán, and Verapaz regions. One of the important omissions in the first *Harvest* volume—an account of civil war events in Guatemala City—is partially rectified in this volume by a description of a neighborhood community in this urban capital (although the Indians are not the focus of this account). A study in this volume of a vendor community in the Antigua area also provides a description of Mayan merchants, a social category largely absent in the earlier volume.

As with the first *Harvest* volume, regional and national developments are woven into the community stories herein. It is noteworthy that in both volumes the communities are placed in their national context, although in the original *Harvest* volume this context was defined almost entirely in terms of state and insurgency armies competing at the national level. The linkages between the local communities and the state in the present volume are much more complex in all sociocultural dimensions. Furthermore, international ties are far more robust, involving numerous NGOs, UN commissions, evangelical churches, and national indigenous programs in language, law, education, and government. These expanded national and international relations give a more dynamic "open" quality to the communities under study than in the original *Harvest* volume. This opening of the supposedly "closed" communities of Guatemala, both Mayan and non-Mayan, is no doubt an accurate reflection of dramatic changes taking place in recent years throughout Guatemala.

Addressing Specific Issues Raised by the First *Harvest* Volume

The concluding chapter of the original *Harvest* book, written by Richard N. Adams, summarized not only the dimensions of the violence taking place in Guatemala at the time but also its possible impact on the future of Guatemala, in general, and the Indians, in particular. Adams's discussion of the primary sociocultural factors involved in the civil war and their consequences for the future of Guatemala and its Indians is particularly relevant for evaluating present conditions in Guatemala as revealed by the chapters that constitute this volume.

Adams called attention to the relevance of historical relations between the Ladinos and Indians, especially the many forms of exploitation of Indians by Ladinos, and the largely nonviolent nature of past Indian resistance to this exploitation. He noted, however, the Indians' massive mobilization against the violence of the civil war and predicted that Indian resistance would continue in the future, the next time with a new political awareness. Adams further reminded us that, historically, the Indians have been viewed as ignorant and socially retarded, whereas, in fact, through time they have adopted many features of the modern world. No doubt this trend would continue in the future.

Adams also pointed to the tendency for Ladino and Indian ethnic conflicts to be dressed in ideological clothing, particularly the "democratic" versus "communist" ideologies associated with the civil war. An ideological orientation would likely continue, even though for the Indians their cultural identity as Mayas would probably remain primary. Adams claimed that it would be difficult to predict the impact on identity, whether ethnic or ideological, caused by the many Indians who fled into refuge outside Guatemala but who would someday return to their home communities.

Finally, Adams questioned whether the Indian communities could recover from the violence and political intervention (such as the formation of the militant civil patrols) that accompanied the civil war. He reminded us that social "recovery" in the Indian communities would vary with the kinds of violence the different communities experienced during the war (whether red, pink, yellow, or green). For example, he anticipated that the most difficult areas in terms of recovery would be communities in the Ixil, central Quiché, Chimaltenango, and Verapaz regions. In such communities, a key issue would be whether survivors were able to cope psychologically with the knowledge that their families had been killed without cause. Perhaps an even more crucial issue would be the extent to which the military continued to dictate governmental policies toward the Indians and other peoples at risk in such communities.

Based on specific issues raised by the original *Harvest* volume, the following series of questions seem particularly pertinent for any attempt to draw conclusions based on the chapters in this volume:

To what extent is the kind of violence perpetrated during the civil war period still being carried out in Guatemala?

What has been the impact on particular Indian communities of their having experienced widely different levels of insurgent and counterinsurgent violence?

How well have the Indians and other victims of the civil war coped psychologically with the effects of past genocidal violence?

What is the role today of the army and other governmental agencies in the political life of the Indian communities?

To what extent do ethnic distinctions between Ladinos and Indians continue to define social life in the Guatemalan communities?

What are the internal and external sociocultural factors most influencing developments among the Indians of Guatemala today?

Stoll, in his commentary to the *Revisited* volume, raises an additional question worth addressing in this final section: What new perspectives, if any, on the nature of the civil war have emerged since the writing of the first *Harvest* volume; and, in particular, to what extent have scholars continued to rely on a paradigm that enshrines "the insurgency's redemptive claim to represent the Guatemalan people?"

How the authors of this volume address the specific issues raised by the above questions will now be briefly summarized.

Continuation of Violence

All the authors of *Mayas in Postwar Guatemala* make it clear that the genocidal violence of the civil war period has ceased in the communities under study. Nevertheless, a more diffuse form of violence such as common criminal activities, lynchings, gang activities, and disruptive demonstrations are reported for virtually all the communities. Peter Benson and Edward Fischer argue that a high level of violence can be found throughout Guatemala, and specifically in the Kaqchikel community of Tecpán. While this violence is much less state sponsored than in the past and is diffused widely throughout the diverse social sectors of the Guatemalan society, it is said to be connected in complex ways to the violent legacy of the civil war period. A similar indirect connection between the civil war violence and the recent generalized violence in Guatemalan communities is suggested by Liliana Goldín and Brenda Rosenbaum for the lower-class urban communities of Guatemala City and by Jennifer Burrell in connection with the gang activities and local official responses to them in the Mam community of Todos Santos, Huehuetenango.

Impact of Past Violence

Not all the authors attempt to describe the respective communities' situation during the civil war period, but those who do generally describe "red" communities that experienced high levels of violence in the past. This is the case for Todos Santos (Burrell), Tecpán (Benson and Fischer), Coban (Adams), Nebaj (Philpot-Munson), and Sololá (Smith); in all of these communities the civil war violence was of code red type. It is probably significant that the chapters on communities less affected by the civil war violence (code green), such as Totonicapán (DeHart) and Tierra Blanca (Bocek), make little reference to violence there. The vendors' community in Antigua is a special case, given the fact that the ongoing violence there consists largely of a specialized form of commodity theft and marketplace intimidation. It is likely that similar violence occurred within the Indian marketplaces during the civil war, but we lack specific information on this point.

Residual Psychological Problems

It is noteworthy that none of the authors of this volume deal directly with the issue of residual psychological problems caused by the violence of the civil war. This is somewhat surprising, given the "postmodern" tendency to take account of individual psychic and cultural states. Benson and Fischer, the most post-modern of the authors, are highly reflective about their study and tend to focus on the motives and cultural ideas of those affected by the violence. They also consider the question of "suffering" associated with violence, which they interpret as being profoundly "social" and a motivation for the continuing violence in Tecpán and elsewhere.

Undoubtedly, psychological problems resulting from the trauma of the civil war violence are endemic to the Mayan communities, despite the absence of serious consideration of it in the chapters herein. One indication of this from Nebaj (Philpot-Munson) is that 37 teenage suicides have been reported there during the past six years.

Continuing State Intervention

The army continues to exercise influence in those communities that were hit hard by the violence and ended up with a heavy military presence. Thus, in Todos Santos (Burrell), Tecpán (Benson and Fischer), Coban (Adams), and Nebaj (Philpot-Munson) local civil patrols have been reconstituted, and the police are said to be operating with excessive force. The continuing military influence in these communities is also indicated by the strong support the local peoples have shown for the presidential candidacy of Ríos Montt, the national leader who remains a key symbol of militarism and civil war violence.

On the political level, state intervention seems to be increasingly insignificant compared to the role now played by local officials (such as the mayors). The pivotal role of local authorities is specifically emphasized for the communities of Todos Santos (Benson and Fischer) and Sololá (Smith) and for the vendors of Antigua (Little). In the case of the neighborhood communities of Guatemala City (Goldín and Rosenbaum), neither the state nor the local government has paid much official attention to the people there or to their dire socioeconomic needs.

Indian and Ladino Relations

It is noteworthy that the present authors have little to say about the traditional division between Indians and Ladinos. In part this has to do with the fact that in virtually all the Indian communities the Mayas have gained most critical leadership positions at the local level. This does not mean that the ethnic-racial split between Indians and Ladinos has disappeared, as is indicated by the strong Ladino opposition to bilingual schools in the highlands (Maxwell), Mayan versus Ladino religious revitalization in Coban (Adams), socioeconomic advances being made by Mayas but not Ladinos in Todos Santos (Barrera Nuñez), and the deep cultural distinctions the Mayan vendors in Antigua (Little) maintain between themselves and local Ladino authorities.

Much of the focus in the chapters has shifted to interrelations between the

Mayas themselves, suggesting that relations of class, religion, political ideology, and cultural identity within the Indian sectors have become increasingly important. This is particularly evident in the cases of Sololá (Smith) and Todos Santos (Burrell). In both communities political and ethnic ideologies have divided the Mayas there into factions that differ with respect to whether development should take place primarily through social (political, economic) means or through cultural (Mayan *costumbre* [custom or tradition]) means.

Internal and External Sociocultural Influences

Perhaps the clearest statement about the nature of both internal and external influences now operating in the communities under study is given in the chapter on Tecpán (Benson and Fischer). The authors describe a situation in which both local and international agencies have significant influence in the community. On the one hand, internal sociocultural inequalities, many of them with long histories in the community, create hostility that leads to local violence; on the other hand, national and global political and economic policies foment swirling conflicts in the community (such as the violent demonstration against governmental attempts to raise local property taxes). Goldín and Rosenbaum describe a similar situation in the neighborhood communities of Guatemala City, where municipal officials largely ignore the sociocultural problems of these poor *vecinos* (neighbors). Nevertheless, these authors insist that at a more general level global neoliberal policies are responsible for the economic hardships and inequalities found in such poverty-stricken communities.

The chapters in this volume suggest that some of the most dynamic and also conflictive forces operating in the communities are related to dramatic changes in the so-called civil society. For example, the NGOs—most of them involving both local and international patrons—are described as being active in all of the communities. The most notable case is Totonicapán (DeHart), where an ambitious banking and development NGO (CDRO, the Cooperation for Rural Development of the West) was created initially by Indians in the community but is now heavily financed and administered by European countries. The NGOs per se do not appear to elicit violent conflicts, but they do cause resentment between those benefiting from them and those who do not. This kind of resentment is well illustrated by the problems surrounding the CDRO organization in Totonicapán (DeHart) as well as an NGO in Todos Santos (Barrera Nuñez) dedicated to the teaching of Spanish along with exposing participants to the traditional features of Mayan culture (such as Mayan ritual).

Other civil society changes mentioned in the chapters have resulted in more serious forms of conflict. Particularly ominous is the emergence of *maras* (gangs) in most of the communities under study. A dramatic instance of gang activity is described for Todos Santos (Burrell). The conflict created by these gangs is based on a struggle between the older traditional authorities and the younger, more modern gang members. The conflict has resulted in violence, including the murder of a young gang leader. It is argued that many factors influence the emergence of gangs and the conflicts associated with them, including new ideas introduced by returning young Mayan immigrants from the United States, the legacy of civil war violence as the way to settle problems, and the overly militant practices of local police and civil patrollers. Gangs are mentioned in connection with other communities such as Tecpán (Benson and Fischer), Coban (Adams), and Guatemala City (Goldín and Rosenbaum); and they may very well be present in virtually all the communities of Guatemala at the present time.

Lynchings have been so common in the Mayan communities of Guatemala over the past few years that they should also be seen as another example of ominous changes in civil society, although they are not discussed in depth in this volume. Like the gangs of Todos Santos, the community crowds that carry out the lynchings appear to be rebelling against more traditional and ineffective local and national authority.

Religious groups constitute an additional dynamic element in the changing civil society of the Guatemalan communities. The chapter on Coban (Adams) provides the most dramatic case of religious changes influencing community life subsequent to the civil war period. In the rural areas of the Verapaz region, the Mayas have revitalized traditional Mayan religion by stressing the importance of "revelation" obtained through trances and other spiritist practices. The participants in this kind of revitalized religion have been strongly opposed by educated urban Mayas and Ladinos who subscribe to more formal Catholic theology as well as secular ideologies. The story of the murder in Coban of the Mayan leader Antonio Pop Caal is a dramatic reminder of the kinds of conflicts, often violent, that religious change within the civil society can lead to in the Mayan communities.

The Pentecostal evangelicals of Nebaj (Philpot-Munson), who now represent some 40 percent of the population in that community, dramatically illustrate the power that religion can generate. These evangelical Indians, for example, have created their own view of the civil war and its legacy, based on a special interpretation of the Bible. Most evangelicals there prefer not to dwell on the past violence (for example, they oppose exhuming the bodies of those killed during the civil war), nor to fix blame. Such issues, it is claimed, are best left to a forgiving God. This kind of religious view works against the policies of the NGOs (including the UN Mission for Verification of Human Rights in Guatemala [MINUGUA]), but it is widespread in the Nebaj community and appears to have significantly reduced violence while generating considerable internal solidarity.

Another potentially significant component of civil society mentioned by Richard Adams in the original *Harvest of Violence* was the returning refugees and migrants from the United States and other countries. However, while several of the chapters herein refer to Mayan refugees and migrants returning to their communities, little account of the impact they might be having on social life is presented. The notable exception is the chapter on Todos Santos (Burrell), which describes how returning young men from the United States have become important leaders of gangs and, hence, challengers of the local authority structure.

Interpreting the Violence through a Moral Paradigm

We turn now to the question of whether or not the authors of *Mayas in Postwar Guatemala* continue to interpret the civil war violence based on what Stoll (in chapter 12 of this volume) refers to as a particular moral paradigm that enshrines "the insurgency's redemptive claim to represent the Guatemalan people." Stoll asserts that such scholarly interpretations of civil war and postcivil war developments have generally failed to express the complex culpability behind the civil war violence. Specifically, most scholars have assumed that the guerrillas were liberators of the Mayan peoples, while the Guatemalan military state (aided by the United States) was the primary source of violence and oppression. According to Stoll, those who adopt this moral paradigm do so despite the fact that the Indians themselves tend to see the causes of violence in less black-and-white terms. The issue is important because the moral interpretation, largely made by foreigners, has tended to internationalize events in Guatemala, thus lending powerful legitimacy to the work of human rights groups, development-oriented NGOs, and international mediators of the Peace Accords.

A careful reading of the chapters herein suggests that, in general, this moral paradigm has probably influenced to some degree the thinking of all the authors. The interpretation of past and present violence is, for the most part, guided by other paradigms and issues. This is patently the case for the authors who do not specifically address in their chapters the issue of moral responsibility for the civil war violence. Judith Maxwell, for example, is primarily concerned with how well the dictates of the Peace Accords on bilingualism have been implemented in the diverse Mayan communities of Guatemala. Burrell describes the post–Peace Accord violence in Todos Santos primarily in terms of economic failures that have limited opportunities for the youth and led to rebellion against the local political structure. Monica DeHart is not primarily concerned with violence in Totonicapán but rather shows that it is possible for local NGO-assisted development to occur in Third World capitalist settings. And Timothy Smith attempts to demonstrate that in Sololá local politics has taken on a life of its own, which transcends and in many ways replaces the moral debates over the violent national and international politics of the past.

Some of the authors specifically address the issue of army versus guerrilla blame for the violence of the civil war and its aftermath. José Oscar Barrera Nuñez makes direct reference to Stoll's moral paradigm in his account of the impact that foreigners and humanitarian organizations are having on social life in Todos Santos. He argues that scholars and other outsiders have interpreted the Todos Santos view of the violence in a misleading way that is nevertheless difficult to challenge. J. Jailey Philpot-Munson, in her study of evangelicals in Nebaj, notes that even though the army was primarily responsible for the violence in the community during the civil war period, as previously shown by Stoll, the Indians there remain ambivalent about the actions of both the army and the guerrillas. Furthermore, she cites evidence that former guerrilla fighters in the area now support the presence of military security forces. And Barbara Bocek briefly describes the debate taking place within Tierra Blanca over which group is to blame for the violence of the civil war: the insurgency or the counterinsurgency. She suggests that before the Peace Accords the Mayas there tended to assign primary blame to Rigoberta Menchú and the guerrillas, but subsequently they have begun to favor the moral position adopted by Menchú and other human rights advocates.

For some of the authors, Stoll's moral paradigm has exercised significant influence on their interpretation of past and present violence in the Guatemalan communities, even though their concerns are more with post–civil war developments and the impact of neoliberal policies on them. Goldín and Rosenbaum do not discuss the civil war violence that afflicted the lower-class neighborhood communities of Guatemala City, but they do point to the failure of neoliberal policies to provide for the socioeconomic needs of the people residing there. Benson and Fischer generally accept the moral paradigm described by Stoll but clearly want to move beyond it. As "ethical anthropologists," they are concerned about neoliberal agendas that tend to facilitate the highly generalized violence afflicting Tecpán and other communities of Guatemala. Abigail Adams in a general way is guided by a paradigm that assigns moral blame to the army for the violence in Coban (for example, she thinks that, despite evidence to the contrary, the military *may* have been responsible for Pop Caal's death), but she is primarily interested in understanding the rise of religious revitalization rather than assigning blame for past and present violence. And Walter Little is not directly concerned with determining moral culpability for the ongoing violence against the vendors of Antigua, but rather points to the impact on violence from long-term "inequalities" in Guatemalan society caused by the corrupt capitalist form of political economy. Furthermore, from a strongly empirical perspective, he attempts to deny the "postmodern" nihilistic argument that the vendors cannot comprehend the violence afflicting them nor target their opposition to it.

Impact of the Civil War on the Pan-Maya Movement

Finally, let us briefly return to Richard Adams's prediction, in the conclusions to the first *Harvest* volume, that the civil war would cause the Guatemalan Indians to act with increased political awareness and to employ their Indian identity in the process of achieving that awareness. This issue receives relatively little attention in this present volume, particularly with respect to the possible impact that the revolutionary (civil) war might have had on the aggressive attempt by the Indians to create a Mayan cultural identity that spans the diverse communities and social sectors of Guatemala as a whole (the so-called Pan-Maya Movement).

Despite the widespread attention that the Pan-Maya Movement has received in the scholarly literature, the fundamental relationship between the civil war violence and the Mayan movement has not received the recognition by scholars that it deserves. This relative void is due, no doubt, to the fact that many Ladinos and Mayas in Guatemala fear that references to the war might endanger the peace agreements now being implemented. Nevertheless, any serious attempt to revisit the impact of the civil war on the Mayas of Guatemala should provide some evaluation of the role that the war has played in the Mayas' movement to create a national or even civilization (Pan-Mayan) supra-culture.

A useful starting point in this direction would be to note that in a profoundly important way the Guatemalan revolution was a Mayan revolution, despite the fact that at the highest levels insurgency leadership came from the Ladinos (although we should not underestimate the importance of Mayan leadership either, a topic that deserves more attention than it has received to date). Furthermore, in the long scope of Guatemalan history, the civil war can be seen as a continuation of past Mayan rebellions, some of which, like the civil war itself, were inspired by liberationist and nationalist goals. Furthermore, the recent civil war provided the Mayas with experiences that inevitably politicized and schooled them in radical thinking and tactics, including the use of violence for political purposes (as attested by numerous references in this volume to recent militancy on the part of the Mayas)!

Any discussion of the historical consequences of the Guatemalan civil war, then, should take into account the massive participation of the Mayas in that war: as guerrilla recruits, civilian supporters of the guerrillas, loyalists to the state in opposition to the guerrillas, and as victims of repression by the army (and, to a much lesser extent, violence by the guerrillas). Account should also be taken of the fact that Mayas were affected by, and in turn affected, the revolution in dramatically different ways. For example, the educated Mayan sector, with strong ties to the Guatemalan middle class, was decidedly divided over direct participation in the civil war. Some of them sympathized with the insurgent movement, but, in general, as professionals their political preference was for reform rather than revolution.

This sector has grown considerably since the end of the war; and, as has been frequently pointed out by scholars, its leaders have led the way in fomenting a powerful but nonviolent Pan-Maya Movement. It is likely that this sector alone has the vision and knowledge necessary to understand Mayan culture in its broadest historical and national parameters. In addition, these are the Mayas who best understand the complex social relationships that exist between the diverse Mayan sectors as well as the different cultural expressions that correspond with the multidimensional Mayan social divisions.

It is important to keep in mind that many Mayas are still reticent to discuss the involvement of Mayas on the side of the insurgency, much less proclaim the "revolution" as their own. Nevertheless, with the passage of time and continued improvement in personal safety in Guatemala, it is likely that most Mayas will come to see the revolution as an heroic undertaking and beneficial to the Mayan quest for political liberty and cultural solidarity (direct evidence for this claim can be found in *Mayas in Postwar Guatemala,* especially in the chapters by Smith, Bocek, and Benson and Fischer).

It would seem, then, that the Mayas' civil war experience, as terrible as it was, forced them to recognize their shared past and present and, in the process, to adopt more universal and transcendental cultural ideas. This unifying politico-cultural process has become so powerful that it may be virtually impossible to reverse in the years to come.

References

Acevedo, Joviel
  2003   Summary of speech on Guatemalan teachers' strike. Electronic docu-
         ment, http://www.bctf.bc.ca/Social/isp/steg/AcevedoSpeech.html, accessed
         March 8, 2008.
Adams, Abigail
  2003   Antonio Pop Caal: Obituary. Guatemala Scholars Network Newsletter, Fall.
  1999   The Word, Work and Worship: Engendering Evangelical Culture between a
         Highland Maya Town and the United States. Ph.D. Dissertation, University
         of Virginia.
Adams, Abigail, and James Brady
  2004   Ethnographic Notes in Q'eqchi' Cave Rites: Implications for Archaeological
         Interpretation. *In* In the Maw of the Earth Monster: Studies of Meso-
         american Cave Use. James A. Brady and Keith Prufer, eds. Pp. 301–327.
         Austin: University of Texas Press.
Adams, Richard, and Santiago Bastos
  2003   Las relaciones étnicas en Guatemala, 1944–2000. Antigua, Guatemala: CIRMA.
Amnesty International
  1989   Guatemala: Human Rights Violations under the Civilian Government.
         London: Amnesty International.
Annis, Sheldon
  1988   Story from a Peaceful Town: San Antonio Aguas Calientes. *In* Harvest of
         Violence: The Maya Indians and the Guatemalan Crisis. Robert M. Car-
         mack, ed. Pp. 155–173. Norman: University of Oklahoma Press.
  1987   God and Production in a Guatemalan Town. Austin: University of Texas Press.
Annis, Sheldon, and Peter Hakim
  1988   Direct to the Poor: Grassroots Development in Latin America. Boulder, CO:
         Lynne Rienner.
Appadurai, Arjun
  1998   Dead Certainty: Ethnic Violence in the Era of Globalization. Public Cul-
         ture 10(2):225–248.

Apreciación de asuntos civiles (G-5) para el area Ixil
1982   Revista Militar 27:25–72.

Arias, Arturo, ed.
2001   The Rigoberta Menchú Controversy. Minneapolis: University of Minnesota Press.

Arnson, Cynthia, ed.
1999   The Popular Referendum (Consulta Popular) and the Future of the Peace Process in Guatemala. Working Paper #241. Woodrow Wilson International Center for Scholars, Latin American Program.

AVANCSO
2000   Heridas en la Sombra. Texto Para Debate No. 16. Guatemala: AVANCSO.
1989   *Por Si Mismos: Un estudio preliminar de las maras en la Ciudad de Guatemala.* Guatemala: AVANCSO.

Azpuru de Cuestas, Dinorah, and Mitchell A. Seligson
2004   The Political Culture of Democracy in Guatemala. Nashville, TN: Latin American Public Opinion Project.

Ball, Patrick, Paul Kobrak, and Herbert F. Spirer, eds.
1999   State Violence in Guatemala, 1960–1996: A Quantitative Reflection. Washington, DC: American Association for the Advancement of Science. Electronic document, http://shr.aaas.org/guatemala/ciidh/qr/english, accessed March 7, 2008.

Barrera Nuñez, Oscar
2005   Imaginaries and Desires: Transcultural "Love Affairs" in Guatemala. Ph.D. Dissertation, Department of Anthropology, University of Washington.

Barrios, Lina
1998a   La alcadía indígena en Guatemala: De 1821 a lal Revolucion de 1944. Guatemala: Universidad Rafael Landívar, Instituto de Investigaciones Económicas y Sociales.
1998b   La alcadía indígena en Guatemala: De 1944 al presente. Guatemala: Universidad Rafael Landívar, Instituto de Investigaciones Económicas y Sociales.

Bastos, Santiago, and Manuela Camus
2003   Entre el mecapal y el cielo: Desarrollo del Movimiento Maya. Guatemala: FLACSO.
1993   Quebrando el silencio: Organizaciones del Pueblo Maya y sus demandas. Guatemala City: FLACSO.

Benson, Peter
2004   Nothing to See Hear. Anthropological Quarterly 77(3):435–467.

Benson, Peter, and Edward F. Fischer
2007   Broccoli and Desire. Antipode 39(5):800–820.

Bourdieu, Pierre, et al.
2000   The Weight of the World: Social Suffering in Contemporary Society. Stanford: Stanford University Press.

Brintnall, Douglas
1979   Revolt against the Dead: The Modernization of a Maya Community in the Highlands of Guatemala. New York: Gordon & Breach.

Brown, Robert McKenna
1996   Maya Language Loyalty Movement. In Maya Cultural Activism in Guatemala. Edward Fischer and Robert McKenna Brown, eds. Pp. 165–177. Austin: University of Texas Press.

Buck-Morss, Susan
2000   Dreamworld and Catastrophe: The Passing of Mass Utopia in East and West. Cambridge: MIT Press.

Burgerman, Susan
2005   Voices from the Parallel Table: Civil Sector Intervention in the Guatemalan Peace Process. In Dilemmas of NGO Peacebuilding with Former Enemies. Henry F. Carey and Oliver Richmond, eds. Pp. 85–92. London: Ashgate.
2001   Moral Victories: How Activists Provoke Multilateral Action. Ithaca, NY: Cornell University Press.

Burgos, Elisabeth
2001   Memoria, transmisión e imagen del cuerpo. In Stoll–Menchú: La Invención de la memoria. Mario Roberto Morales, coordinator. Pp. 19–86. Guatemala: Consucultura.
1984   Me llamo Rigoberta Mencha: Y asi me nacio la conciencia. Mexico City: Siglo Veintiuno Editores.

Burrell, Jennifer
2005   "Peace Processes": Power and Politics after War in Todos Santos Cuchumatán. Ph.D. dissertation, Department of Anthropology, New School for Social Research.

Buvinic, Ana, Andrew Morrison, and Michael Shifter
1999   Violence in Latin America and the Caribbean: A Framework for Action. Technical Study. Sustainable Development Department Inter-American Development Bank.

Calder, Bruce Johnson
1970   Crecimiento y cambio de la iglesia católica guatemalteca, 1944–1966. Guatemala: Estudios Centroamericanos #6.

Carey, David, Jr.
2006   Engendering Mayan History: Kaqchikel Women as Agents and Conduits of the Past, 1875–1970. New York: Routledge.
2004   Maya Perspectives on the 1999 Referendum in Guatemala: Ethnic Equality Rejected? Latin American Perspectives 31(6):69–95.
2001   Our Elders Teach Us: Maya-Kaqchikel Historical Perspectives Xkib'ij Kan Qate' Qatata'. Tuscaloosa: University of Alabama Press.

Carmack, Robert M.
1995   Rebels of Highland Guatemala: the Quiché-Mayas of Momostenango. Norman: University of Oklahoma Press.

Carmack, Robert M., ed.

1988   Harvest of Violence: The Maya Indians and the Guatemalan Crisis. Norman: University of Oklahoma Press.

CIIDH-GAM

1996   Quitar el Agua al Pez: Análisis del Terror den Tres Comunidades Rurales de Guatemala (1980–1984). International Center for the Investigation of Human Rights (CIIDH) and The Mutual Support Group (GAM). Guatemala City: Guatemala.

Cleary, Edward, and Hannah Stewart-Gambino, eds.

1997   Power, Politics, and Pentecostals in Latin America. Boulder, CO: Westview Press.

Cojtí Cuxil, Demetrio

1997   Ri Maya' Moloj Pa Iximulew, El Movimiento Maya (en Guatemala). Guatemala: Editorial Cholsamaj.

1989   El neocolonialismo del sistema educativo gualtemalteco. Lecture to Oxlajuj Aj. Antigua, Guatemala.

1987   Ensayo sobre las Variedades de Enseñanza Bilingüe: Desde el Bilingüismo Etnocida hasta el Bilingüismo Etnocida. Guatemala: Ministerio de Educación.

Comisión de Esclarecimiento Histórico (CEH)

1999   Conclusions and Recommendations. English-language summary of Guatemala: Memoria del Silencio. Guatemala. Electronic document, http://shr.aaas.org/guatemala/cehreport/english/toc.html, accessed July 8, 2008.

Cooperación para el Desarrollo Rural de Occidente (CDRO)

1998a   Propuesta de Regionalización. Carta de CDRO a los miembros del consorcio. October 28.

1998b   Uk'ux Wuj (rev. ed.). Internal document.

1997   Saq Tzij. Informational brochure. Totonicapán, Guatemala: CDRO.

1995   Saq Tzij. Informational brochure. Totonicapán, Guatemala: CDRO.

Das, Veena, Arthur Kleinman, Mamphela Ramphele, and Pamela Reynolds, eds.

2000   Violence and Subjectivity. Berkeley: University of California Press.

Dayan, Joan

1995   Haiti, History, and the Gods. Berkeley: University of California Press.

DeHart, Monica

2008   A Contemporary Micropolitics of Indigeneity. Latin American and Caribbean Ethnic Studies 3(3): forthcoming.

2003   Local Power in 3-D: Development, Democratization and Decentralization in Guatemala. Paper presented at the American Anthropological Association Annual Conference, Chicago, November.

2001   What's "Ethnic" about Ethnic Development? Constructing Community and Local Power in Totonicapán. Ph.D. dissertation, Stanford University.

Diamond, Sara
1989   Spiritual Warfare: The Politics of the Christian Right. Boston: South End
        Press.
Diener, Paul
1978   The Tears of St. Anthony: Ritual and Revolution in Eastern Guatemala.
        Latin American Perspectives 5(3):92–116.
Edelman, Lucila, Diana Kordon, and Dario Lagos
1998   Transmission of Trauma: The Argentine Case. *In* International Handbook
        of Multigenerational Legacies of Trauma. Yael Danieli, ed. Pp. 447–463.
        New York and London: Plenum Press.
Editorial
1999   Siglo Veintiuno, July 24, p. 14.
Evans, Timothy Edward
1991   Percentage of Non-Catholics in a Representative Sample of the Guatema-
        lan Population. Paper presented to the Latin American Studies Association,
        Crystal City, Virginia.
Falla, Ricardo
1994   Massacres in the Jungle: Ixcán, Guatemala, 1975–1982. Boulder, CO: West-
        view Press.
1978   Quiché rebelde: Estudio de un movimiento de conversión religiosa, rebelde a
        las creencias tradicionales, en San Antonio Ilotenango, Quiché (1948–1970).
        Guatemala City: Editorial Universitaria de Guatemala.
Farmer, Paul
2004   An Anthropology of Structural Violence. Current Anthropology
        45(3):303–325.
2003   Pathologies of Power: Health, Human Rights, and the New War on the
        Poor. Berkeley: University of California Press.
Ferguson, James
1999   Expectations of Modernity: Myths and Meanings of Urban Life on the
        Zambian Copperbelt. Berkeley: University of California Press.
Fischer, Edward F.
2004   The Janus Face of Globalization: Economic Production and Cultural
        Reproduction in Highland Guatemala. *In* Pluralizing Ethnography: Com-
        parison and Representation in Maya Cultures, Histories, and Identities.
        John M. Watanabe and Edward F. Fischer, eds. Pp. 257–290. Santa Fe, NM:
        SAR Press.
2001   Cultural Logics and Global Economies: Maya Identity in Thought and
        Practice. Austin: University of Texas Press.
Fischer, Edward F., and Peter Benson
2006   Something Better: Hegemony, Development, and Desire in Guatemalan Ex-
        port Agriculture. Social Analysis 49(1):3–20.
Fischer, Edward F., and Robert McKenna Brown, eds.
1996   Maya Cultural Activism in Guatemala. Austin: University of Texas Press.

Fischer, Edward F., and Carol Hendrickson
2002   Tecpán Guatemala: A Modern Maya Town in Local and Global Context. Boulder, CO: Westview Press.
Foxen, Patricia
2007   In Search of Providence: Transnational Mayan Identities. Nashville, TN: Vanderbilt University Press.
Freidel, David, Justin Kerr, and MacDuff Everton
1995   Maya Cosmos. New York: Perennial.
Freire, Paulo
1970   Pedagogy of the Oppressed. New York: Continuum.
FUNCEDE (Fundación Centroamericana de Desarrollo)
2000   Diagnostico del Municipio de Sololá. Guatemala: FUNCEDE.
García, Oscar
2004   Van 311 asesinadas. Sigue violencia en la ciudad y el interior contras las mujers. P. 5. Al Día, August 10.
Garrard-Burnett, Virginia
1998   Protestantism in Guatemala: Living in the New Jerusalem. Austin: University of Texas Press.
Garzon, Susan, Robert McKenna Brown, Julia B. Richards, and Wuqu' Ajpub'
1998   The Life of Our Language. Austin: University of Texas Press.
Geertz, Clifford
2000   Available Light: Anthropological Reflections on Philosophical Topics. Princeton: Princeton University Press.
Godoy, Angelina Snodgrass
2002   Lynchings and the Democratization of Terror in Postwar Guatemala: Implications for Human Rights. Human Rights Quarterly 24(3):640–661.
Goldín, Liliana R.
1996   Economic Mobility Strategies among Guatemalan Peasants: Prospects and Limits of Nontraditional Vegetable Cash Crops. Human Organization 55(1):99–107.
Goldín, Liliana R., and Linde Asturias de Barrios
2001   Perceptions of the Economy in the Context of Nontraditional Agricultural Exports in the Central Highlands of Guatemala. Culture and Agriculture 23(1):19–31.
Goldman, Francisco
2007   The Art of Political Murder: Who Killed the Bishop? New York: Grove Press.
González, David
2000   Rights in Guatemala: At Risk Still. New York Times, November 5: sec. 1, p. 12.
González de la Rocha, Mercedes
2001   From the Resources of Poverty to the Poverty of Resources? The Erosion of a Survival Model. Latin American Perspectives 28(4):72–100.
Grandin, Greg
2004   The Last Colonial Massacre: Latin America in the Cold War. Chicago: University of Chicago Press.

Green, Linda

2003   Notes on Mayan Youth and Rural Industrialization in Guatemala. Critique of Anthropology 23(1):51–73.

1999   Fear as a Way of Life: Mayan Widows in Rural Guatemala. New York: Columbia University Press.

Guatemala Human Rights Commission, USA (GHRC)

2004   Summary of the Department of State Human Rights Report on Guatemala. GHRC. Electronic document, www.ghrc-usa.com, accessed March 7, 2008.

2003   Guatemala Human Rights Report. September 15, vol. 15(17–18):4.

Haeserijn, Esteban, Padre

1979   Diccionario K'ekch'i'–Español. Guatemala City: Editorial Piedra Santa.

Hale, Charles R.

2006   Más Que un Indio: Racial Ambivalence and Neoliberal Multiculturalism in Guatemala. Santa Fe, NM: SAR Press.

1997   Forum on Anthropology in Public: Consciousness, Violence, and the Politics of Memory in Guatemala. Current Anthropology 38(5):817–838.

Handy, Jim

2004   Chicken Thieves, Witches, and Judges: Vigilante Justice and Customary Law in Guatemala. Journal of Latin American Studies 36:533–561.

Harding, Susan

2001   The Book of Jerry Falwell: Fundamentalist Language and Politics. Princeton: Princeton University Press.

Hendrickson, Carol

1995   Weaving Identities: Construction of Dress and Self in a Highland Guatemala Town. Austin: University of Texas Press.

Hertz, Robert

1960   Death and the Right Hand. Trans. Rodney Needham and Claudia Needham. London: Cohen & West.

Hinshaw, Robert

1988   Tourist Town amid the Violence: Panajachel. In Harvest of Violence: The Maya Indians and the Guatemalan Crisis. Robert M. Carmack, ed. Pp. 195–205. Norman: University of Oklahoma Press.

Hopenhayn, Martín

2001   No Apocalypse, No Integration: Modernism and Postmodernism in Latin America. Durham, NC: Duke University Press.

Human Rights Review

1999   Truth, Fact, and Fiction in the Human Rights Community: Essays in Response to David Stoll's *Rigoberta Menchú and the Story of All Poor Guatemalans*. Authors include Daphne Patai, Joan Bamberger, Brian D. Haley, Daniel Levine, and Luis Roniger. Human Rights Review 1(1):78–112.

Huntington, Deborah, and Enrique Domínguez

1984   The Salvation Brokers: Evangelicals in Central America. NACLA Report on the Americas 18(1):2–36.

IADB (Inter-American Development Bank)
1999   How Is Violence Measured? Technical Note 2. Pp. 1–7. Sustainable De-
        velopment Department. Washington, DC: Inter-American Development
        Bank.
INE (Instituto Nacional de Estadistica)
1996   Censos '94: X Censo nacional de población y V de habitación. Departemento
        de Sololá. Guatemala City: INE.
Jonas, Susanne
2000   Of Centaurs and Doves: Guatemala's Peace Process. Boulder, CO: Westview
        Press.
Jurado, Amalia Eraso
2000   La Violencia Intrafamiliar en Guatemala. *In* Suplemento Hablemos,
        UNICEF y el Periódico, p. 13.
Kleinman, Arthur
1999   Experience and Its Moral Modes: Culture, Human Conditions, and Dis-
        order. *In* The Tanner Lectures on Human Values, vol. 20. Grethe B. Peter-
        son, ed. Pp. 357–420. Salt Lake City: University of Utah Press.
Kleinman, Arthur, Veena Das, and Margaret Lock, eds.
1997   Social Suffering. Berkeley: University of California Press.
Klima, Alan
2002   The Funeral Casino: Meditation, Massacre, and Exchange with the Dead in
        Thailand. Princeton: Princeton University Press.
Kobrak, Paul
2003   Huehuetenango: Historia de una guerra. Huehuetenango: Centro de Estu-
        dios y Documentación de la Frontera Occidental de Guatemala (CEDFOG).
1999   Organizing and Repression in the University of San Carlos, Guatemala, 1944
        to 1996. Washington, DC: American Association for the Advancement of
        Science.
1997   Village Troubles: The Civil Patrols in Aguacatán, Guatemala. Ph.D. disser-
        tation, Department of Sociology, University of Michigan.
Kymlicka, Will
2001   Politics in the Vernacular: Nationalism, Multiculturalism, and Citizenship.
        Oxford: Oxford University Press.
Laclau, Ernesto, and Chantal Mouffe
1985   Hegemony & Socialist Strategy: Towards a Radical Democratic Politics.
        London: Verso.
Lancaster, Roger
1992   Life Is Hard: Machismo, Danger, and the Intimacy of Power in Nicaragua.
        Berkeley: University of California Press.
Lara, Julio
2004   Matan a 2 Mujeres. Prensa Libre, Agosto 17, 2004:12.
Latin American Perspectives
1999   If Truth Be Told: A Forum on Stoll and Menchú. Authors include Jan Rus,

Carol A. Smith, Norma Stoltz Chinchilla, Victoria Sanford, Georg M. Gugelberger, Elizabeth Burgos, Gary H. Gossen, and David Stoll. Special issue, Latin American Perspectives 26(6):5–88.

Le Bot, Yvon

1995　La Guerra en Tierras Mayas: Comunidad, Violencia y Modernidad en Guatemala (1970–1992). Mexico: Fondo de Cultura Económica.

Levenson-Estrada, Deborah

1994　Trade Unionists against Terror: Guatemala City, 1954–1985. Chapel Hill: University of North Carolina Press.

Little, Walter

2004a　In Between Social Movements: Dilemmas of Indigenous Handicrafts Vendors in Guatemala. American Ethnologist 31(1):43–59.

2004b　Mayas in the Marketplace: Tourism, Globalization, and Cultural Identity. Austin: University of Texas Press.

Littrell, Mary Ann, and Marsha Ann Dickson

1999　Social Responsibility in the Global Market: Fair Trade of Cultural Products. Thousand Oaks, London, New Delhi: Sage Publications.

López García, Julián

2001　Aqui es otro modo:'Los ch'orti' y la capacitaciónen derechos humanos. In Los derechos humanos en tierras mayas: Política, representaciones y moralidad. Pedro Pitarch and Julián López García, eds. Pp.127–160. Madrid: Sociedad Española de Estudios Mayas.

Lovell, George

2000　A Beauty That Hurts: Life and Death in Guatemala. Austin: University of Texas Press.

Lutz, Christopher

1994　Santiago de Guatemala, 1541–1773: City, Caste, and the Colonial Experience. Norman: University of Oklahoma Press.

MacCannell, Dean

1992　Empty Meeting Grounds: The Tourist Papers. London: Routledge.

Manz, Beatriz

2004　Paradise in Ashes: A Guatemalan Journey of Courage, Terror and Hope. Berkeley: University of California Press.

1988　Refugees of a Hidden War: The Aftermath of Counterinsurgency in Guatemala. Albany: State University of New York Press.

Manz, Beatriz, Elizabeth Oglesby, and José García Noval

1999　De La Memoria a la Reconstrucción Historica. Serie Autores Invitados No. 3. Guatemala: Asociacion para el Avance de las Ciencias Sociales.

Marsden, George M.

1980　Fundamentalism and American Culture. Oxford: Oxford University Press.

Martin, David

1990　Tongues of Fire: The Explosion of Protestantism in Latin America. London: Basil Blackwell.

Maxwell, Ixq'anil Judith, Gloria Enoe Son Chonay, Ixcha'im Marliny Son Chonay, and Ixim Nik'te' M. Carmela Rodríguez

2004   Maja'il Kaqchikel (Nab'ey): Kaqchikel Autoaprendido. Guatemala City: Ministerio de Educación. Book and audio CD.

Maxwell, Judith M., and Robert M. Hill

2006   The Kaqchikel Chronicles. Austin: University of Texas Press.

Mayén de Castellanos, Guisela

1986   Tzute y jerarquía en Sololá. Guatemala City: Museo Ixchel del Traje Indígena.

McAllister, Carlota

2003   Good People: Revolution, Community, and *Conciencia* in a Maya-K'iche' Village in Guatemala. Ph.D. dissertation, Department of Anthropology, Johns Hopkins University.

Mendoza, Carlos, and Edelberto Torres-Rivas, eds.

2003   Linchamientos: ¿Barbarie o "justicia popular"? Guatemala: Colección Cultura de Paz.

Miller, Daniel, ed.

1994   Coming of Age: Protestantism in Contemporary Latin America. Lanham, MD: University Press of America.

Mingat, Alain, and Carolyn Winter

2002   Education for All by 2015. Finance and Development 39(1). Electronic document, www.imf.org/external/pubs/ft/fandd/2002/03/mingat.htm, accessed July 8, 2008.

Misíon de Naciones Unidas de Verificacíon en Guatmala (MINUGUA)

2002   Year Report 2002. Electronic document, www.minugua.guate.net, accessed January 7, 2005.

Montejo, Victor

2005   Maya Intellectual Renaissance. Austin: University of Texas Press.

1999   Voices from Exile: Violence and Survival in Modern Maya History. Norman: University of Oklahoma Press.

1987   Testimony: Death of a Guatemalan Village. Willimantic, CT: Curbstone Press.

Moodie, Ellen

2006   Microbus Crashes and Coca-Cola Cash: The Value of Death in "Free Market" El Salvador. American Ethnologist 33(1):63–80.

Morales, Mario Roberto, ed.

2001   Stoll–Menchú: La Invención de la Memoria. Guatemala City: Consucultura.

Moser, Caroline

2001   The Gendered Continuum of Violence and Conflict: An Operational Framework. *In* Victims, Perpetrators or Actors? Gender, Armed Conflict and Political Violence. Caroline Moser and Fiona Clark, eds. Pp. 30–52. New Delhi: Kali for Women.

1998   The Asset Vulnerability Framework: Reassessing Urban Poverty Reduction Strategies. World Development 26(1):1–19.

1996   Confronting Crisis: A Comparative Study of Household Responses to Poverty and Vulnerability in Four Poor Urban Communities. Environmentally Sustainable Studies and Monograph Series 8, World Bank, Washington, DC.

Moser, Caroline, and Cathy McIlwaine
2001   La violencia en el contexto del posconflicto según la percepción de comunidades urbanas pobres de Guatemala. Washington, DC: Banco Mundial/ASDI.

Moser, Caroline, and Elizabeth Shrader
1999   A Conceptual Framework for Violence Reduction. LCR Sustainable Development Working Paper No. 2. Urban Peace Program Series. World Bank, Washington, DC.

Municipalidad Indígena de Sololá (MIS)
1998   Runuk'elen ri Q'atb'äl Tzij Kaqchikel Tz'oloj Ya'/Autoridad y Gobierno Kaqchikel de Sololá. Guatemala City: Cholsamaj.

Nader, Laura
1997   Controlling Processes: Tracing the Dynamic Components of Power. Current Anthropology 38(5):711–737.

Napier, David
2004   Public Anthropology and the Fall of the House of Ushers. Anthropology News 45(6):6–7.

Nash, June
2001   Mayan Visions: The Quest for Autonomy in an Age of Globalization. New York: Routledge.

Nelson, Diane M.
2001   Phantom Limbs and Invisible Hands: Bodies, Prosthetics, and Late Capitalist Identifications. Cultural Anthropology 16(1):303–312.
1999   A Finger in the Wound: Body Politics in Quincentennial Guatemala. Berkeley: University of California Press.

Oakes, Maud
1951   The Two Crosses of Todos Santos. New York: Pantheon Books.

Observatorio Centroamericano sobre Violencia (OCAVI)
2007   Número de Víctimas y Tasas de Homicidios Dolosos en Guatemala (1999–2006). Electronic document, www.ocavi.com/doc_files/file_390.pdf, accessed July 8, 2008.

Oficina de Derechos Humanos del Arzobispado de Guatemala (ODHAG)
1998   Guatemala Nunca Más. Guatemala: Informe Proyecto Interdiocesano de Recuperación de la Memoria Histórica (REMHI). Available from http://www.odhag.org.gt.

Painter, James
2007   Crime dominates Guatemala campaign. BBC News. Electronic document, http://news.bbc.co.uk/2/hi/americas/6643935.stm, accessed July 8, 2009.

Paley, Julia
2001   Marketing Democracy: Power and Social Movements in Post-Dictatorship Chile. Berkeley: University of California Press.

Peacock, Susan C., and Adriana Beltrán
2003   Hidden Powers: Illegal Armed Groups in Post-Conflict Guatemala and the Forces behind Them. Washington DC: Washington Office on Latin America.

Polos de desarrollo
1984   Revista Militar 31:75–88.

Pop, Alvaro
2003   Antonio Pop Caal. Biography. Manuscript, property of Abigail Adams.

Prensa Libre
2003a   Acciones ilegales: Medidas de seguridad en Todos Santos están al margen de la ley. February 20. Electronic document, www.prensalibre.com, accessed July 8, 2008.

2003b   Amedrentados como en el conflicto armado: Todos Santos Cuchumatán se halla bajo medidas ilegales de resguardo. February 20. Electronic document, www.prensalibre.com, accessed July 8, 2008.

2003c   Pandillas asuelan en Todos Santos. Medida: Alcaldes de Huehuetenango denuncian inseguridad. March 4. Electronic document, www.prensalibre. com, accessed July 8, 2008.

2003d   Sugieren a comité no abusar de funciones: Agrupaciones buscan solución al problema suscitado en Todos Santos. February 22. Electronic document, www.prensalibre.com, accessed July 8, 2008.

Preti, Alessandro
2002   Guatemala: Violence in Peacetime—A Critical Analysis of the Armed Conflict and the Peace Process. Disasters 26(2):99–119.

Rahnema, Majid
1992   Participation. *In* The Development Dictionary: A Guide to Knowledge as Power. W. Sachs, ed. Pp. 158–176. London: Zed Books.

Rancière, Jacques
1994   Names of History. Minneapolis: University of Minnesota Press.

Reilly, Charles
1997   Speech at the International Conference of Mayors. Maimi, FL.

1995   New Paths to Democratic Development in Latin America. Boulder, CO: Lynne Rienner Publishers.

REMHI (Proyecto Interdiocesano de Recuperación de la Memoria Históca)
1998   Guatemala: Nunca más. Guatemala City: Oficina de Derechos Humanos del Arzobispado de Guatemala (ODHA). Also accessible on-line at http://www.odhag.org.gt/03publicns.htm, accessed July 8, 2008.

Restall, Matthew
2001   The Janus Face of Maya Identity in Post-Conquest Guatemala. *In* Maya Survivalism. Ueli Hostettler and Matthew Restall, eds. Pp. 15–23. Markt Schwaben, Germany: Verlag Anton Saurwein.

Rico, Maite, and Bertrand de la Grange
2003   Quien mato al obispo? Autopsia de un crimen político. Mexico: Editorial Planeta Mexicana.

Robicsek, Francis
1983   Maya Book of the Dead: The Ceramic Codex. Norman: University of Okla-
        homa Press.
Rodgers, Dennis
2006   Living in the Shadow of Death: Gangs, Violence and Social Order in Urban
        Nicaragua, 1996–2002. Journal of Latin American Studies 38(2):267–292.
Rosaldo, Renato
1988   Culture and Truth: The Remaking of Social Analysis. Boston: Beacon
        Press.
Rosenbaum, Brenda
2000   Of Women, Hope and Angels: Fair Trade and Artisan Production in a
        Squatter Settlement in Guatemala City. In Artisans and Cooperatives.
        Kimberly Grimes and B. Lynne Milgram, eds. Pp 85–106. Tucson: Univer-
        sity of Arizona Press.
Salvesen, Hilde
2002   Guatemala: Five Years after the Peace Accords: The Challenges of Imple-
        menting Peace. A Report for the Norwegian Ministry of Foreign Affairs.
        International Peace Research Institute, Oslo (PRIO).
Sampson, Steven
2003   "Trouble Spots": Projects, Bandits and State Fragmentation. In Globaliza-
        tion, the State and Violence. Jonathan Friedman, ed. Pp.309–342. Walnut
        Creek, CA: AltaMira Press.
Sanford, Victoria
2003   Buried Secrets: Truth and Human Rights in Guatemala. New York: Palgrave
        Macmillan.
Saqb'ichil/COPMAGUA (Coordinación de Organizaciones del Pueblo Maya de
Guatemala)
1996   Acuerdo sobre Identidad y Derechos de los Pueblos Indígenas. Versión Maya
        Ilustrada. Guatemala City: Editorial Saqb'e.
Schirmer, Jennifer
1998   The Guatemalan Military Project: A Violence Called Democracy. Philadel-
        phia: University of Pennsylvania Press.
1997   Universal and Sustainable Human Rights? Special Tribunals in Guatemala.
        In Human Rights, Culture, and Context: Anthropological Perspectives.
        Richard A. Wilson, ed. Pp. 161–186. London: Pluto Press.
Schröder, Ingo W.
2003   The Political Economy of Tribalism in North America: Neotribal Capi-
        talism? Anthropological Theory 3(4):435–456.
Sherman, Amy
1997   The Soul of Development: Biblical Christianity and Economic Transforma-
        tion in Guatemala. Oxford: Oxford University Press.
Sieder, Rachel, ed.
1998   Guatemala after the Peace Accords. London: Institute of Latin American
        Studies, University of London.

Smith, Bryan
1998   Religious Politics in Latin America: Pentecostal vs. Catholic. Notre Dame,
        IN: University of Notre Dame Press.
Smith, Carol
1990a   Class Position and Class Consciousness in an Indian Community:
        Totonicapán in the 1970s. *In* Guatemalan Indians and the State, 1540
        to 1988. Carol Smith, ed. Pp. 205–229. Austin: University of Texas Press.
1990b   The Militarization of Civil Society in Guatemala: Economic Reorganization
        as a Continuation of War. Latin American Perspectives 17(4):8–41.
1988   Destruction of the Material Bases for Indian Culture: Economic Changes in
        Totonicapán. *In* Harvest of Violence: The Maya Indians and the Guatema-
        lan Crisis. Robert Carmack, ed. Pp. 206–231. Norman: University of Okla-
        homa Press.
Smith, Carol, ed.
1990c   Guatemalan Indians and the State, 1540 to 1988. Austin: University of Texas
        Press.
Smith, Timothy J.
2004   A Tale of Two Governments: Rural Mayan Politics and Competing De-
        mocracies in Sololá, Guatemala. Ph.D. dissertation, State University of
        New York at Albany.
Smith, Timothy L.
1962   Called unto Holiness: The History of the Nazarenes. Kansas City: Nazarene
        Publishing House.
Stephens, John Lloyd
1993   Incidents of Travel in Central America, Chiapas, and Yucatan. Karl Acker-
        man, ed. Washington: Smithsonian Institution Press.
Stern, Steve
2006a   Battling for Hearts and Minds: Memory Struggles in Pinochet's Chile, 1973–
        1988. Durham: Duke University Press.
2006b   Remembering Pinochet's Chile: On the Eve of London 1998. Durham:
        Duke University Press.
Stølen, Kristi Anne
2007   Guatemalans in the Aftermath of Violence: The Refugees' Return. Philadel-
        phia: University of Pennsylvania Press.
Stoll, David
1999   Rigoberta Menchú and the Story of All Poor Guatemalans. Boulder, CO:
        Westview Press.
1998   Human Rights, Land Conflict, and Memories of the Violence in the Ixil
        Country of Northern Quiché. *In* Guatemala after the Peace Accords. Rachel
        Sieder, ed. Pp. 42–56. London: Institute for Latin American Studies.
1997   To Whom Should We Listen? Human Rights Activism in Two Guatemalan
        Land Disputes. *In* Human Rights, Culture, and Context: Anthropological
        Perspectives. Richard A. Wilson, ed. Pp. 187–215. London: Pluto Press.

1994   "Jesus is Lord of Guatemala": Evangelical Reform in a Death-Squad State. *In* Accounting for Fundamentalisms: The Dynamic Character of Movements. Martin Marty and Scott Appleby, eds. Pp. 99–123. Chicago: University of Chicago Press.

1993   Between Two Armies in the Ixil Towns of Guatemala. New York: Columbia University.

1990   Is Latin America Turning Protestant? The Politics of Evangelical Growth. Berkeley: University of California Press.

1988   Evangelicals, Guerrillas, and the Army: The Ixil Triangle under Ríos Montt. *In* Harvest of Violence: The Maya Indians and the Guatemala Crisis. Robert M. Carmack, ed. Pp. 90–116. Norman: University of Oklahoma Press.

1983   Fishers of Men or Founders of Empire? The Wycliffe Bible Translators in Latin America. Cambridge: Cultural Survival.

Stone, Michael

1990   Paper presented to FLACSO Guatemala.

Taussig, Michael

1992   The Nervous System. London: Routledge.

Tedlock, Barbara

1983   Time and the Highland Maya. Albuquerque: University of New Mexico Press.

Tedlock, Dennis

1985   Popol Vuh: The Definitive Edition of the Mayan Book of the Dawn of Life and the Glories of Gods and Kings. New York: Simon & Schuster.

Thomas, Kedron

2006   Maya Entrepreneurs and the Global Textile Trade. Anthropology News 47(8):13–14.

Thomas, Kedron, and Peter Benson

2008   Dangers of Insecurity in Postwar Guatemala Revista. Harvard Review of Latin America 7(2):38–41.

Thompson, Ginger

2004   Tattooed Warriors: The Next Generation; Shuttling between Nations, Latino Gangs Confound the Law. New York Times, September 26, query.nytimes.com.

Tiney, Juan

2000   Lucha por la Tierra. *In* Tierra y Espiritualidad Maya. Coban/Guatemala: Centro Ak Kutan/Voces del Tiempo.

Tzaquitzal, Efrain, Pedro Ixhíu, and Romeo Tíu

1999   Alcades comunales de Totonicapán. Guatemala: Editorial Serviprensa C.A.

United Nations Human Development Report (UNHDR)

2000   La Fuerza Incluyente de Desarrollo Humano. New York: United Nations.

1998   Guatemala: Los Contrastes del Desarrollo Humano. New York: United Nations.

United States Department of State
2001   U.S. Department of State: International Religious Freedom Report. Released by the Bureau of Democracy, Human Rights, and Labor. Electronic document, http://www.state.gov/g/drl/rls/irf/2001/5656.htm, accessed July 8, 2008.

Warren, Kay
2003   Voting against Indigenous Rights in Guatemala: Lessons from the 1999 Referendum. *In* Indigenous Movements, Self-Representation, and the State in Latin America. Kay B. Warren and Jean S. Jackson, eds. Pp. 149–176. Austin: University of Texas Press.
1998   Indigenous Movements and Their Critics: Pan-Maya Activism in Guatemala. Princeton: Princeton University Press.
1989   Symbolism of Subordination: Indian Identity in a Guatemalan Town. Austin: University of Texas Press.

Washington Office on Latin America
2007   Transnational Youth Gangs in Central America, Mexico and the US. Washington Office on Latin America, March.
2006   Youth Groups in Central America: Issues in Human Rights, Effective Policing and Prevention. Washington Office on Latin America, November.

Watanabe, John
1992   Mayan Saints and Souls in a Changing World. Austin: University of Texas Press.

Weisbrot, Mark, Dean Baker, Egor Kraev, and Judy Chen
2001   The Scorecard on Globalization, 1980–2000: Twenty Years of Diminished Progress. Center for Economic and Policy Research. Electronic document, www.cepr.net, accessed February 22, 2008.

Westropp, Mary
1983   Christian Counterinsurgency. Cultural Survival Quarterly 7(3):28–31.

Wilkinson, Daniel
2002   Silence on the Mountain: Stories of Terror, Betrayal and Forgetting in Guatemala. New York: Houghton Mifflin.

Wilson, Everett
1997   Guatemalan Pentecostals: Something of Their Own. *In* Power, Politics, and Pentecostals in Latin America. Edward Cleary and Hannah Stewart-Gambino, eds. Pp. 139–163. Boulder, CO: Westview Press.

Wilson, Richard
1998   The Politics of Remembering and Forgetting in Guatemala. *In* Guatemala after the Peace Accords. Rachel Sieder, ed. Pp. 181–196. London: Institute of Latin American Studies, University of London.
1997   Human Rights, Culture, and Context: An Introduction. *In* Human Rights, Culture, and Context: Anthropological Perspectives. Richard Wilson, ed. Pp. 1–27. London: Pluto Press.
1995   Maya Resurgence in Guatemala: Q'eqchi' Experiences. Norman: University of Oklahoma Press.

Wolf, Eric

1982   Europe and the People without a History. Berkeley: University of California Press.

World Bank

2005   Decentralizing Education in Guatemala: School Management by Local Communities. Education Notes. Washington, DC: World Bank. Electronic document, http://www1.worldbank.org/education/pdf/EduNotes_Guatemala.pdf, accessed September 17, 2006.

Yashar, Deborah J.

2005   Contesting Citizenship in Latin America: The Rise of Indigenous Movements and the Postliberal Challenge. Cambridge: Cambridge University Press.

Contributors

Abigail E. Adams, professor of anthropology at Central Connecticut State University, is a sociocultural anthropologist. She has published on Mayan cultural revitalization (including spirit possession), U.S.–Central American relations, and post-violence political culture, including Guatemala's 1944–54 decade of progressive democracy and the 1954 CIA-sponsored coup d'état.

José Oscar Barrera Nuñez is based in Mexico, where he is an independent consultant offering applied research to local and foreign governments, NGOs, and socially and environmentally responsible firms. He has conducted extensive research on the relations between indigenous peoples and Westerners.

Peter Benson, assistant professor of anthropology at Washington University in St. Louis, is author of the forthcoming *Good Clean Tobacco: Citizenship, Moral Life, and Biocapitalism in North Carolina* and coauthor of *Broccoli and Desire: Global Connections and Maya Struggles in Postwar Guatemala* (Stanford University Press, 2006).

Barbara Bocek is a Guatemalan specialist for Amnesty International–USA. She wrote the original version of her chapter while serving as a K'iche'-speaking Peace Corps volunteer and worked in Peru throughout the 1980s before moving to Guatemala in 1992.

Jennifer L. Burrell is an assistant professor of Anthropology at University at Albany, SUNY, and is a board member of the Institute of Mesoamerican Studies at Albany. She has published numerous articles and chapters on Todos Santos Cuchumatán in the postwar period.

Robert M. Carmack is Professor Emeritus of Anthropology at the University at Albany, SUNY. He is also the editor of *Harvest of Violence: The Maya Indians and the Guatemalan Crisis* (University of Oklahoma Press, 1988) and author of *Rebels of Highland Guatemala: The Quiche-Mayas of Momostenango* (University of Oklahoma Press, 1995). Much of his research has been conducted among the K'iche' Mayas of highland Guatemala.

Monica DeHart is an assistant professor of anthropology at the University of Puget Sound in Washington State, where she teaches in the Comparative Sociology Department and the Latin American Studies Program. She is completing a book, to be entitled "Ethnic Entrepreneurs: Identity and Development Politics in Latin America." Her research focuses mainly on the relationship between identity politics and development.

Edward F. Fischer is a professor of anthropology and the director of the Center for Latin American and Iberian Studies at Vanderbilt University. He is author of *Cultural Logics and Global Economies: Maya Identity in Thought and Practice* (University of Texas Press, 2001), coauthor of *Tecpán Guatemala: A Modern Maya Town in Local and Global Context* (Westview, 2002) and *Broccoli and Desire: Global Connections and Maya Struggles in Postwar Guatemala* (Stanford University Press, 2006), and coeditor of *Maya Cultural Activism in Guatemala* (University of Texas Press, 1996).

Liliana Goldín is a professor of anthropology at Florida International University in Miami. In addition to writing numerous articles, she is the author of *Procesos Globales en el Campo de Guatemala* (FLACSO, 2003) and *Global Maya: Work and Ideology in Rural Guatemala* (University of Arizona Press, 2008). She is conducting a longitudinal study of households involved in wage labor in international (*maquila*) factories located in Guatemala's central highlands.

Walter E. Little is an associate professor of anthropology at the University at Albany, SUNY, and codirector of Tulane University's Oxlajuj Aj Kaqchikel Maya Language and Culture course. He is the author of *Mayas in the Marketplace: Tourism, Globalization, and Cultural Identity* (University of Texas Press, 2004) and co-author of *¿La ütz awäch? Introduction to Kaqchikel Maya Language* (University of Texas Press, 2006). In 2005, he and other U.S. and Mayan academics and activists formed the Guatemalan Emergency Relief Fund.

Judith M. Maxwell is a professor of anthropology at Tulane University. She has coauthored *The Kaqchikel Chronicles* (University of Texas Press, 2006) and *¿La ütz awäch? Introduction to Kaqchikel Maya Language* (University of Texas Press, 2006). Co-construction of knowledge in the academic endeavor is a key theme in her research and teaching. She has collaborated with UNICEF, the Academia de las Lenguas Mayas de Guatemala, and the Guatemalan Ministry of Education in training Mayan linguists and developing pedagogical neologisms.

J. Jailey Philpot-Munson is in anthropology at the University of Chicago, where she is finishing her Ph.D. She is currently working in the nonprofit sector in Detroit, Michigan. She has conducted research in Nebaj, Quetzaltenango, Cabricán, and Guatemala City, Guatemala. She has also studied cross-cultural communication and discipline techniques within the Oakland, California, school district.

Brenda Rosenbaum is a member of the Institute for Mesoamerican Studies. She is the author of *With our Heads Bowed: The Dynamics of Gender in a Maya Community* (Institute for Mesoamerican Studies, 1993). She is the founder of Mayan Hands, a fair trade project that markets the textiles of women's cooperative groups, and she works with Oxlajuj B'atz, an educational project that organizes workshops on self-esteem, democracy, leadership, and the development of new skills.

Timothy J. Smith is an assistant professor of anthropology at Appalachian State University. He is completing a book on the cultural legacy, history, and leadership of the Kaqchikel Maya of Sololá, Guatemala, from 1490 through 2003, which focuses on intra-communal struggles over representation and identity formation under colonial rule and in the post-colonial and post-war eras.

David Stoll is a professor of anthropology at Middlebury College. His books include *Is Latin America Turning Protestant?* (University of California Press, 1990), *Between Two Armies in the Ixil Towns of Guatemala* (Columbia University Press, 1993), and *Rigoberta Menchú and the Story of All Poor Guatemalans* (Westview, 1999). He conducted his first research in Guatemala in 1978 and he is currently talking to Nebajenses about illegal immigration to the United States.

Index